The Parliament Choir

The Parliament Choir

Twenty Years of Political Harmony

First published 2021 by

www.wordsbydesign.co.uk

ISBN: 978-1-914002-14-4

Further copies of this book, as well as details of other publications and services, are available from

www.wordsbydesign.co.uk

Typeset in Optima

www.parliamentchoir.org.uk

Cover photograph by Edward Webb

Contents

CLARENCE HOUSE

As The Parliament Choir celebrates its twentieth anniversary, I just wanted to convey my warmest congratulations to all those who have been involved with this remarkable enterprise.

The Choir brings together Members of Parliament, Members of the House of Lords, staff and others associated with the Houses of Parliament to sing together. It also provides an opportunity for its members to work in harmony, as well as adding musical accompaniment to such occasions as the Golden Jubilee of Her Majesty The Queen and the commemoration of the end of the First World War.

The fact that this choir is under the direct auspices of the Speaker of the Commons and the Lord Speaker makes it a unique institution. It is not only a vital part of Parliamentary life, but it also fosters essential international friendships by means of splendid concerts over recent years with choirs such as those of the German Bundestag, the National Assembly of Korea and the Parliament of the Czech Republic.

Harmony, of course, can only be achieved by different voices. Since its inauguration at the beginning of the Millennium, the Choir has shown how those from varied backgrounds and different views can unite in a common love of music and with the shared ideal of friendship and understanding. As you mark this significant anniversary, I send my kindest wishes for your continued success in the future.

The Speaker

There is nothing more inclusive than the Parliament Choir – so it is my pleasure to congratulate its members on bringing harmony to the Palace of Westminster for 20 years.

It's the lack of hierarchy that makes it so wonderful and so unique, in that anyone who holds a pass, be it MP, peer, or member of staff can join.

There are no auditions – the only demand made on new members is that they are passionate about singing and happy to attend rehearsals.

It is also one of the few places in Parliament where political opponents can put aside their ideological differences to instead enjoy the fun of singing in harmony.

As we all know, singing together – be it at a football match, or in a church – is a great way of relieving stress. It's that feeling of togetherness, being focused as one that brings so much happiness to participants and listeners alike.

The Choir is part of the life of Parliament, singing at special occasions, such as the commemorations of the beginning and the end of the First World War and the Golden Jubilee of Her Majesty the Queen.

Furthermore, it fosters cross-country links as singers from the Bundestag Choir, the Choir of the Korean Parliament and the Slovenian Choir have sung with it over the years.

It goes without saying that we all wish the Parliament Choir a very happy 20th birthday – and will continue to enjoy its endeavours for many years to come.

Sir Lindsay Hoyle MP, Speaker of the House of Commons

Lord Speaker

This book is a celebration of the Parliament Choir and its success over the last 20 years. As Lord Speaker, I am the Co-President of the Parliament Choir – something I consider to be a great honour. The Choir has always been an exceptional body, but it was not until 2019 that it was established as a unique entity under the direct patronage of the two Speakers. It remains the only group in Parliament to be granted this status, something which says a great deal about how much the Choir is valued.

While the House of Commons and the House of Lords co-habit the Palace of Westminster, they work and function rather separately. They have their own facilities and libraries, even the colour of the carpet reflects which 'side' of the building you are about to enter. However, the Choir crosses the divide. It is common ground, neutral territory. MPs and Peers, staff and other parliamentary passholders all gather for the same purpose and enjoyment.

As I know from personal experience, politicians are often guilty of talking across each other – passionately debating from across the despatch boxes. However, the marvellous thing about Westminster is that those same politicians can leave the Chamber, walk into the Chapel of St Mary Undercroft and stand shoulder to shoulder, singing in harmony. It is a testament to the dedicated work of those who support the Choir that individuals can come together as friends, to reflect, sing and cement relationships in such a visible – and vocal – way.

I have had the pleasure of seeing the Choir perform in the past, and I hope to be able to see them again in the not too distant future. It is without a doubt, a jewel in the crown of Parliament. I have only heard positive experiences from both its members and those who have listened to their performances. I could hardly imagine the Choir not existing, and I am confident they will continue to be a thriving part of Parliament long into the future.

Lord Fowler, Lord Speaker of the House of Lords until 2021

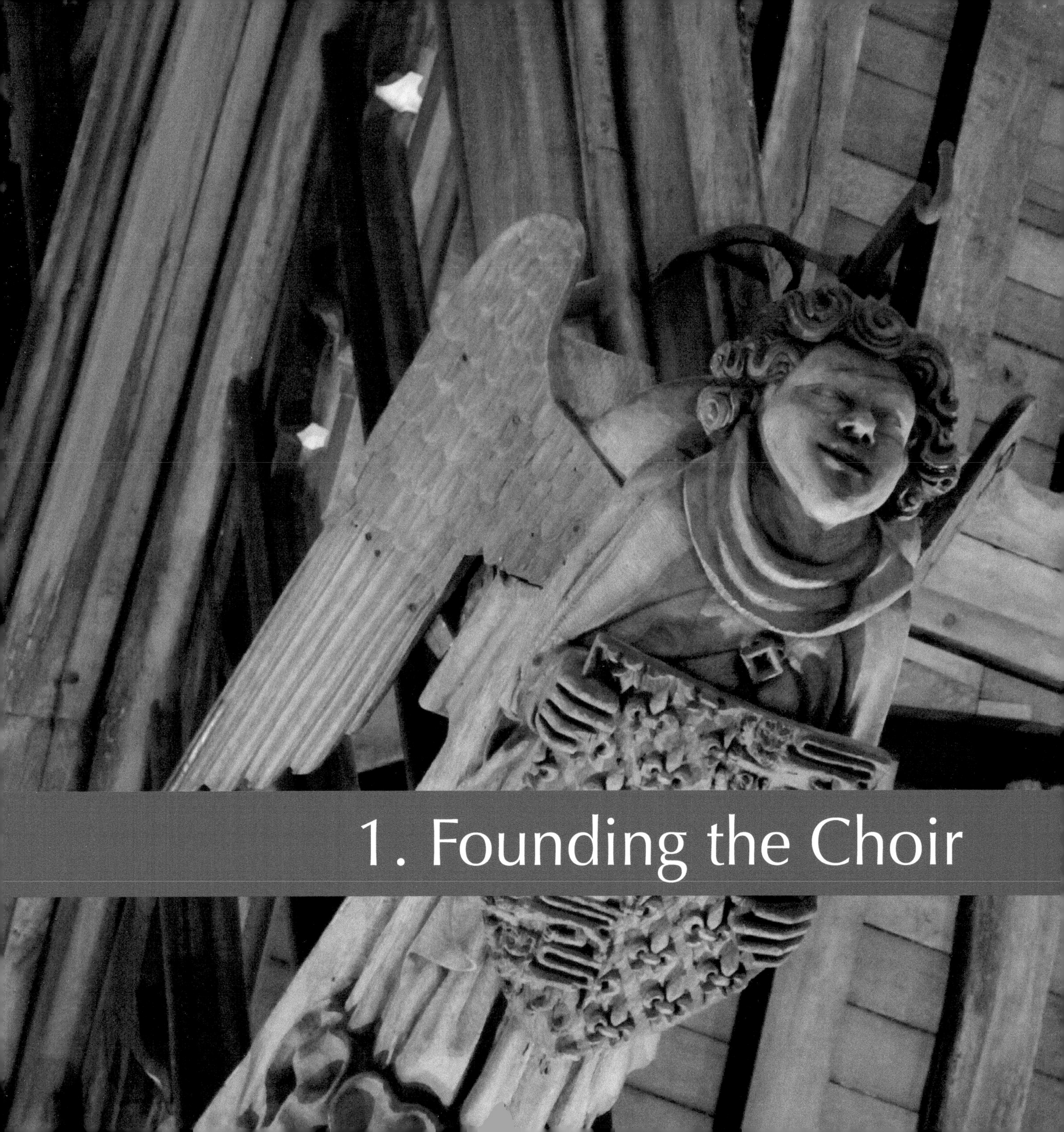

1. Founding the Choir

Introducing the Parliament Choir

The Parliament Choir is a choral society, usually numbering between 120-150 members, most of whom work within the Palace of Westminster, as Members of the House of Commons or House of Lords, their researchers and office staff; and as officers and officials employed in every aspect of the work and life of Parliament. The Choir meets weekly within the Palace when Parliament is in session, to rehearse in the Chapel of St Mary Undercroft just off Westminster Hall.

It presents three or four concerts a year and, as part of its mission to encourage young musicians, engages brilliant young soloists, sometimes working alongside renowned artists of the concert and opera stage. Southbank Sinfonia, the orchestra of young professional instrumentalists, is the Choir's regular orchestral partner.

The Choir is a registered charity and its charitable aims include the promotion of singing by public performance and giving assistance to young singers and musicians. Over the last few years the Choir has taken on an increasingly ambassadorial role for the United Kingdom Parliament with successful concerts abroad and has sung alongside other parliament choirs, both in their countries and in London. Originally set up as an All-Party Parliamentary Group, in recognition of its widening reputation, in 2019 – approaching its twentieth anniversary – it was awarded unique status as a Special Entity within Parliament under the patronage of the Speaker of the House of Commons and the Lord Speaker.

This book offers a celebration of the life and history of the Choir. Written by the Choir's members and friends, it benefits from the Choir's ethos of inclusivity and collaboration. Historical accounts, personal reminiscences and special memories come together to tell the story of the first 20 years of the Parliament Choir.

Beginnings

Lord Filkin, Founder-Chair, and Simon Over, Founder-Conductor and Music Director describe the genesis of the Parliament Choir.

We still do not remember which of us first suggested it, but we do know we discussed the idea on a walk from Fulham to Pimlico in 2000 and agreed to explore founding a choir in Parliament. (It was a joint foundation in every way, but Simon says he recalls Geoff saying 'Well, let's form a choir in Parliament then.') We consulted others, held a meeting with Baroness Hollis, Lord Jenkin and Baroness McIntosh who were all supportive. The late Baroness Hollis said, 'Good idea, please make it happen!'

Then the hard work started. We thought that the Choir should be open to anyone who worked in Parliament whether MPs, Peers or staff. This was unusual as MPs, Peers and staff tend to inhabit separate worlds, but it has been one of the great strengths of the Choir that it is open to all, with little party-political animosity and a more equal spirit. Status in the Choir comes from singing ability, not role within the Palace of Westminster.

We had to form the Choir as an All-Party Parliamentary Group or it would have had no position nor access to facilities. We had to apply for charitable status, and we set one of its charitable objectives to support young

First concert on 6 December 2000, Messiah *at St Margaret's Church, Westminster Abbey. Emma Kirkby (on left) the soprano soloist.*

musicians, whether as players or singers. We had to find somewhere to rehearse, a piano or organ, an administrator and funding. Simon gained agreement to use the Chapel and the organ and between us we appointed Jane Jacomb-Hood as Choir Secretary. Over ten years she became an institution herself and contributed greatly to the Choir's friendly atmosphere.

Significantly, we agreed it should be a non-auditioning choir, open to all, so that anyone working in Parliament who wanted to sing great works could do so. For some this has been life-enhancing, giving a new opportunity to sing, learn, form friendships and share in making glorious music. But it also meant more rehearsals and so higher costs. Since its inception, the Choir has benefited hugely from support from BT and we had a great 15-year relationship with John Anderson, Director of BT Government who caught the vision. BT supported our ambitions, enabling us to stage large and challenging works in iconic venues in the UK and abroad.

We had to recruit MPs, Peers and staff for the rehearsals for our first concert, *Messiah*, to be performed in St Margaret's, Westminster. Many were interested, some sceptical, some thought that as there had never been a choir in Parliament there could not be one now.

This first *Messiah*, after a year or so setting it up, might not have been our best concert ever (although the soloists, including Dame Emma Kirkby, now one of our Patrons, were excellent), but we had started, and thus began the warm relationship the Choir was to develop with Commons, Lords and the administration becoming, in time, a parliamentary institution itself. This was greatly confirmed in 2019 when the Lord Speaker and Speaker of the House of Commons jointly conferred the status of a special entity within Parliament on the Choir. We are now a formal part of Parliament.

The Choir has been a source of learning and of friendship, a place where people of many different backgrounds connected to Parliament, whether spouses, PAs, research assistants, telephonists, police, and even the Clerk of the Parliaments and Black Rod, are united in song. People have described it as the only truly egalitarian institution in the Palace of Westminster.

We have worked together over 20 years in differing ways to help the Choir develop artistically and in reputation. As for many people in the Choir, our own friendship has deepened through the love of choral music and preparing to perform it. We are delighted to celebrate all that so many people have done to make this idea a reality – on to the next 20 years!

Dame Cheryl Gillan, who died in 2021, was one of the MPs who joined the Choir at the beginning, and became a valued Trustee and Treasurer.

What a wonderful and unique team the Parliament Choir has proved to be. As a founder member and, like many of our singers, with a complex parliamentary life, I missed the exhilaration of making music with others that I had experienced predominantly in my youth. An active member of the 'music wing' at school, when I first came to London in my twenties, I had auditioned for the London Symphony Orchestra Chorus under the late lamented Richard Hickox and enjoyed, in my spare time, indulging my love of music, including a memorable Queen's Coronation Jubilee concert. I was particularly delighted to meet him again with the Parliament Choir and he was so encouraging about the ethos and capability of the Choir, as well as the clear pleasure it was bringing in an egalitarian fashion across all areas and amongst a wide selection of people associated with parliamentary life. That was praise indeed for the Choir which has been one of the most joyful things to come out of Westminster. There is no doubt that the skilled hand of Simon Over moulded a silk purse from a sow's ear as, with no auditions to join, he has worked with – in my case (and, dare I say it, a few others) – a voice of little talent with a dedication that has yielded some wonderful results.

But it was not just the energy, drive, patience and fantastic musicianship of Simon, but also the inventive and soul-reaching composing from Nicholas O'Neill. Nick, our resident composer, brought international harmony. When we sang with the Bundestag Choir, his *Of All Persons and Estates* sent shivers not just down British spines but European ones too.

Aside from the music, choirs have to be managed and the business of running a choir is so very complicated when a Parliament is involved. As one of the officers of the group, I often held meetings of the business managers of the Choir who were members volunteering to do that extra job or people who preferred not to sing but to lend support with the administration. My office in the 'gods' of Portcullis House saw many a meeting where we wrestled over membership fees, venues, timetables, sponsorship, soloists, permits and promotion, often over a glass or two (as meetings usually took place long after normal working hours were finished). Parliamentary life has so much pressure and stress associated with a functioning democracy, but even in these business meetings you could see the enjoyment and devotion to a gentler side of our democratic institution that has proved itself to be capable of producing great beauty and harmony. The Parliament Choir is a 'workplace choir' from the toughest of workplaces, but it shows you what pleasure for performers and audience alike can emanate from great teamwork.

Patricia, Baroness Hollis of Heigham, was a Labour Peer who played an important part in setting up the Parliament Choir. She died in 2018. Here, her partner, Lord Howarth of Newport, pays tribute to her devotion to the Choir.

Baroness Hollis of Heigham

Patricia was proud to have worked with Geoff Filkin, Simon Over and BT in establishing the Parliament Choir. Why had no one thought of doing so over the previous centuries? Apart from the marvellous music-making at Westminster, right at the heart of our national life, the Choir brought people together – all parties, both Houses, politicians and staff.

She loved singing and made it a priority, whatever else she had to do, to attend rehearsals and performances. It was only when her illness meant she no longer had the breath control to sing nor the stamina to stand for any length of time, that, to her great sadness, she had to give up.

Patrons

At the beginning, the Choir's two Patrons were Sir Thomas Allen and Richard Hickox. Hickox had been Organist and Master of Music at St Margaret's from 1972 to 1982, and was therefore a predecessor of Simon Over. He honed his skills as a choral conductor in those years and took part in various local festivals. 'He was brilliant with singers and incredibly skilful at getting the best out of them, both the amateurs and the professionals,' said Sir Clive Gillinson, a former Managing Director of the London Symphony Orchestra. Beloved by musicians for his warmth, enthusiasm and extraordinary energy, he was renowned as a champion of twentieth-century British music. Amongst many other roles, he was President of the Elgar Society. When the Parliament Choir sang Elgar's *The Apostles* in Westminster Cathedral in the year of his death, Simon was able to dedicate the performance to his memory in tribute.

I found myself, for the first time, giving the ebullient Rossini Figaro's aria in one of the most important sites of Christian worship in the Western world.

Sir Thomas Allen

Sir Thomas Allen, a founding Patron of the Choir, has been for 50 years one of the most renowned lyric baritones worldwide, and one of the most versatile, distinguished in oratorio, recital and above all in opera. He has sung with the Choir in the 2003 Coronation Jubilee concert, in Mendelssohn's *Elijah* and Elgar's *The Apostles* and in 2019, his final London appearance, in *The Dream of Gerontius*. He describes below the enduring importance of choral singing to the country's cultural tradition.

It's nothing if not amazing to consider briefly the assortment of moments that accrue when you live day by day in the unusual circumstances of lockdown. Thankfully, the current situation is without parallel for the vast majority of us unless, of course, you've experienced long periods of time on a battlefield, or its musical equivalent, inundated by the works of Richard Wagner.

Such a moment came to me a few weeks ago when, somewhere on the internet, I found myself staring at an old photograph of Church Street in my old hometown of Seaham Harbour. There, an effort is being made to maintain and even restore some of the original frontages of its buildings. Alas, many of them are long gone, the most prominent of which was the tall dark central structure of the Methodist Chapel. My mind raced back to a very different world, sometime in the early 1950s when, along with family and the rest of a capacity audience, we took our places for a performance of Haydn's *Creation*.

Before the war, and for quite some years afterwards, it wasn't uncommon for such a place as that modest chapel in a small town in the middle of the Durham coalfield to host such singers as Isobel Baillie, Robert Easton, Heddle Nash and, of course, Kathleen Ferrier. It was the singers' lot then to travel the length and breadth of the country for their livelihood – at one moment in one of our great cathedrals, the Albert Hall, or Hallé in Manchester, and the next in just such a chapel as this in Church Street. One day with Sir Malcolm or Sir Adrian, or Sir John, or Sir Thomas, the next under the baton of a devoted amateur who might well have just finished drying off after a bath in front of the fire, following a hard shift at one of the three collieries for which the town was renowned.

How did this come about? Choral singing, the simple answer. Wherever you looked there were choirs. Choirs of schoolchildren, of boys in great and small places of worship. Massed ranks in Glasgow, Huddersfield, Newcastle and Sunderland. Choir singing isn't an invention of the past five years. They were there alongside the communities that spawned them and they sang wonderfully well, full-throatedly giving magnificent performances. Hardly a surprise, then, that the old picture brought back memories.

Many years later, I was to be involved in a concert with a relatively new choir consisting of some familiar faces, a commendable mix of Red and Blue. The excitement of singing in the ancient hall of Westminster with those massed ranks in front of a future King! The excitement builds only to be dashed. Where the Prince would sit on that occasion became the target of an original piece of roofbeam which, thank heaven, chose a few days before the concert rather than the concert itself to come tumbling down.

Now, the beauty of working with an assembly of somewhat influential people is that they have influence, and where for everyone else the concert would have to be shelved, we were able to reassign the event to a venue not too far away – namely Westminster Abbey. Now, I've no doubt discussions went on at every level as to how to gain the necessary permissions for such a thing, at a lower level than mine: the switch took place with apparent seamlessness.

We gathered together for a programme designed for a very different kind of arena and I found myself, for the first time, giving the ebullient Rossini Figaro's aria in one of the most important sites of Christian worship in the Western world. Not only that, the venom and evil of Puccini's police chief Scarpia was next on my schedule. His entry into the 'Te Deum' with all the force I could muster, was the very thing that might bring a response from above, not only from the Almighty but also some earlier stonemason who would now see one of his ashlars drop onto the head of a less than princely subject.

I'm happy to report it was not to be, as a result of which I'm able to write of the next decade and more, of my continuing history with the Choir and what they sing: Mendelssohn and his *Elijah*; Elgar and his beautiful *The Apostles*. Then Elgar and *Gerontius* in celebration of Cardinal Newman's canonisation and, as it happens, my last London concert. All of this I would not change. Singing is a memorable and very special experience and I thank you all for realising that those 20 years ago.

4 December 2019 The Dream of Gerontius *in Westminster Cathedral: Sir Thomas Allen sings the role of the Priest from the pulpit*

Dame Emma Kirkby has been a Patron of the Choir since 2008. Despite insisting that her professional career was down to luck, she has been at the forefront of the early music movement since the 1970s and her distinctive soprano voice, remarkable for its clarity of tone and diction, has made her one of the best-loved and recognisable singers of our time. Although she has made more than 100 recordings, she is a passionate advocate for live performance. She was the soprano soloist in *Messiah*, the Choir's first concert in 2000, and she returned to sing in Mozart's *Coronation Mass* in 2011.

How amazing that 20 years have passed since I had the honour of singing in the Parliament Choir's first *Messiah*! I remember a heartfelt and joyous performance from everyone involved, and my delight then that our politicians and the parliamentary community were dedicating some of their precious time to choral singing.

My most important musical moment as a teenager was meeting William Byrd's *Mass for Four Voices*. Falling in love there and then with Renaissance polyphony, I also sensed the truth of Byrd's preface to his book, *Psalmes Sonnets and Songs 1588*. I cannot resist quoting the first five of those eight points again:

> *Reasons briefly set down by the Author, to persuade everyone to learn to sing.*
>
> First, *it is a knowledge easily taught, and quickly learned, where there is a good master, and an apt scholar.*
>
> Second, *the exercise of singing is delightful to Nature, and good to preserve the health of Man.*
>
> Third, *it doth strengthen all parts of the breast, and doth open the pipes.*
>
> Fourth, *it is a singularly good remedy for stuttering and stammering in the speech.*
>
> Fifth, *it is the best means to procure perfect pronunciation, and to make a good Orator.*

So by now with the Parliament Choir there have been 20 years of such a fine process! I hope that someday a researcher will investigate the effect of this on the vital business of both Houses…

Choral music caught me then and held on to me throughout my time at university and during my career, since I have always unconsciously looked and listened for singing partners, whether they are voices or instruments. Though Britain has a long and rich choral tradition, until recently perhaps it was thought of as a rather niche activity; now, thanks to the likes of Gareth Malone, I am thrilled to say that many more of us generally respect, love and even engage in choral singing. In my other favourite field, vocal consorts, we have something like a Golden Age now, and dedicated professional ensembles. Earlier in my career these had numbered four or five per country, but are now to be heard in their dozens. Some of these have also worked tirelessly in our schools to pass on their joy and their skill to hundreds of children, so I am optimistic about the future.

Even in the coronavirus emergency, with its dire warnings about massed voices, it is so good to know that the Parliament Choir, like other groups, has stubbornly continued to meet online for serious work on repertoire and technique – so once everyone can gather again for live performances, what terrific sounds there will be! Congratulations, then, to Simon and his team, and to all Choir members, for these two decades of hard work and happy inspiration.

'Second, the exercise of singing is delightful to Nature, and good to preserve the health of Man.'

Musical Direction

Simon Over, Music Director and Principal Conductor, describes his multi-tasking life as Music Director.

'What does Simon do between our Monday rehearsals?' a former member of the Choir once asked Nick. Perhaps people believe that I turn up on a Monday, talk, wave my arms about, and then disappear for a week – but of course there are many things that happen between rehearsals.

For every concert there are months, sometimes years of planning: choosing the music, fitting it to particular occasions and buildings, accommodating particular requests; then choosing where is best for that concert, considering how it suits the music and forces involved. In consultation with Nick, we choose which edition of the music to use and source the scores. Then there's the selection and booking of performers; first the soloists, considering how their voices will blend and complement each other, whether they're available and willing, what their fees might be, all within the budget we have for that concert; then there's the orchestra (if it's Southbank Sinfonia, is it the current players or alumni, how many extras do we need and for which rehearsals?), or for smaller concerts, it might be booking individual players. Rehearsal schedules need to be produced and communicated to all relevant parties. For bigger concerts when we need larger forces, I discuss collaborations with other choirs: Coventry Cathedral Chorus, St Alban's Bach Choir and Mosaic (the chamber choir in *Gerontius* which I prepared and rehearsed for the performance in St Alban's, where they're based). Rehearsal schedules for the General Rehearsal on performance days are usually worked out to within a minute (4.00 – Kyrie, 4.07 Gloria, 4.11 Et in terra pax). Professional musicians work in three-hour sessions and if you go over by a minute, you need their permission; much more and additional fees are payable. You never know when something unforeseen might hold up a rehearsal (I've experienced power cuts, crucial soloists or players delayed, lighting problems, performers being ill or having the wrong music) and it's my responsibility to deal with the problem and still to have rehearsed everything within the scheduled rehearsal time. I keenly feel the responsibility for bringing the constituent parts together and making it all work.

Before we embark on rehearsing any piece of music there is much preliminary work to be done. Marking up a full score on average takes around 15 minutes per page, analysing who plays and sings what and when. The score of *War Requiem* is 238 pages long and at one point has 44 staves on one page (orchestra, chamber orchestra, chorus, soloists, all performing at once, as in the illustration), so that's many hours of desk work. I must research the work's history and the background against which it was written, to set it in context, to know the whole work thoroughly.

Then I have to ensure that costs for the concert are covered: working out a budget and, if it involves large resources, trying to identify those who might support the extra costs. For *Gerontius* for instance, I spoke to both the Elgar and Newman Societies and to a number of individuals who have a particular love of the work and might, for personal

War Requiem *score: this page showing 44 staves*

Simon Over, Music Director

reasons, have wished to support the performance. I meet potential supporters and promoters. For example, Katherine Bennett, who now sings in the Choir, was Senior Vice President for Airbus in the UK when we met and came up with the idea of the RAF100 concert at the Central Church of the RAF.

There are site visits to concert halls to oversee arrangements: to make sure everything will fit, to plan the staging, order the delivery of instruments and to confirm that the staff of the hall and the Choir and orchestra staff, for example, are in touch with each other.

Projects and relationships with other choirs have to be carefully followed through, especially with those abroad. Before we worked with the Bundestag choir, I went to Berlin for meetings, returned to add flesh to the bones of the concept, then went back a couple of times to take rehearsals. It was important to assure the Germans that the choirs would work well together and that their smaller choir would not be swamped by our greater numbers.

Every year for 'A Westminster Christmas' we try to take up themes of the preceding year – so, in 2014, because of the German connection, I suggested to Nick the *Stille Nacht/Silent Night* sequence which he took and brought into being with his inimitable genius. In 2016, wanting to acknowledge Jo Cox's tragic death, we discussed how that might be marked. At the beginning of a relationship with the Choir of the National Assembly of Slovenia, we considered how the London Slovenian choir might be introduced, and invited their Ambassador to attend the concert. We like to think about other ways of representing the year just ending, and select readers and readings and instrumentalists to balance the familiar and unfamiliar, the jolly and the thoughtful, the easy and the challenging.

I have various meetings with people in Parliament who have general ideas and suggestions. The structure of the Choir means that for 20 years there has been a new Chairman every two years, so it has been important to identify Members of Parliament in the Choir who have appropriate skills as well as the time to devote to the Choir. I also seek to ensure an even number from Commons and Lords, and a balance of Left and Right. I attend Trustee Board meetings, asking the Board to consider ambitious projects and answering questions about how they can work – for example *Belshazzar's Feast* in the Festival Hall, the Armistice centenary concert in Westminster Hall, and taking the Choir abroad.

When a concert is broadcast, as many have been for Classic FM, that has to be negotiated, and arrangements made for promotional articles, interviews for the BBC and others (for example 2019's *New Yorker* feature on the Choir, linking Brexit and *Gerontius*), and most recently speaking on Times Radio.

General administration is also part of my remit: acceptance of new members, contributing to newsletters and the website, organising any music in Parliament which involves the Choir. I was engaged in the business of the Choir's change of status from All Party Parliamentary Group to the unique Special Entity within Parliament.

Above all, I have to listen, convince, inspire, and carry the vision forward. This is more testing when people make quick judgements about works and share them readily with others. To convert the response, 'This is boring and too difficult; I don't like it so I'll sit it out,' to 'That was a truly memorable project; I'm so glad I was able to be part of it,' is quite a challenge.

Of course, by no means am I on my own; I have (and have had) the most remarkable colleagues who work (mostly for no reward) on many of these tasks and relationships. I am extremely indebted to them for their time, wisdom, passion and sheer hard work for the Choir.

'I think we did rather well, don't you?' I'm often asked at post-concert receptions, and as I reply in the affirmative, I have the image of a swan gliding on the surface with all of the background work paddling away below the surface.

'I think we did rather well, don't you?' I'm often asked at post-concert receptions, and as I reply in the affirmative, I have the image of a swan gliding on the surface with all of the background work paddling away below the surface.

Simon Over

Nicholas O'Neill, Chorus Master, Composer-in-Residence, traces the path of a remarkable collaboration.

The story of how I ended up accompanying the Parliament Choir is one of my favourites, a single decision made over 20 years ago that has led to one of the most fruitful collaborations of my musical life and a long-standing artistic partnership. I was in Guildford in the late 1990s when I received a phone call to deputise for a choir rehearsal, playing the organ. The fee was paltry and I would need to catch a train within the next half hour in order to make it, and pay more for the ticket than I would earn for the rehearsal, but against the wishes of my then girlfriend, standing next to me as I took the call, I accepted the engagement with the words, 'You never know where this might lead.' As it turned out, the rehearsal was with a choir by the name of the Antioch Singers and the session was directed by a certain Simon Over.

I had bumped into Simon previously in London, in the way musicians do, but now I quickly found myself working with him more or less every week, not least because the fee offered by the choir was so small that it proved well-nigh impossible to find a deputy. Thus, fleetingly, we began our partnership, for the choir folded soon thereafter and we went our separate ways. Through one of the singers of that choir, though, I ended up accompanying at Trinity College of Music and, following another of those musical threads, as accompanist for the brand-new University of Greenwich Choir. It was at this point, probably over a year since I had last heard from him, that I received a call from Simon. He was involved in setting up a new choir for Parliament and would like me to consider taking on the role of accompanist. I agreed with enthusiasm, but needed to finish that term's work at Greenwich, after which I switched organ benches and began to spend my Monday evenings at Westminster instead.

I often describe the Choir in those early days as have-a-go heroes, and I know that the standard was not as high as it is now, but even from the start there was something special about this group of singers. I can still remember the nerves I felt when I started, turning up with long hair, leather jacket and T-shirt (there is less hair now and the leather jacket is long gone, but the T-shirts remain) in this pillar of the establishment, and I am sure that a couple of quizzical glances were cast in my direction. However, eventually I settled in, although at that stage my role was very much that of accompanist and accompanist only. We would regularly have other directors come

Nicholas O'Neill in self-reflective mood

in and deputise for Simon, until one week he found himself unable to find somebody… so I stepped up to the podium for the first time. Again, nerves. How to establish one's authority over a group of people who are certainly used to voicing their own opinions?

I decided to impose myself upon the Choir immediately with my favourite combination of hard work, always with the music as its central focus, and humour, sometimes – maybe too often? – expressed in the form of slightly acerbic barbs, although my hope was always that they would be taken in the affectionate manner in which they were delivered. I have never forgotten and never forget that non-professional singers turn up because they want to, and pay for the privilege, so the director's task is not only to improve standards but to ensure that enjoyment is derived from the process.

From those early days the Choir grew, and with it my role gradually expanded to take on the title of Chorus Master (definitely not Choir Master!), but I was also asked to perform other tasks behind the scenes, such as arranging parts for concerts, running vocal sessions for groups of singers, and providing programme notes, talks and articles. I cannot quite remember how I came to write *Sweet Was the Song*, but it was a brave move on Simon's part to ask me to provide something for that particular year's carols. According to my catalogue we first performed this in Portcullis House on 13 December 2005. It may seem a cliché, but I genuinely had no inkling of where that little piece would lead in terms of my role with the Choir.

Compositionally, the next few years were spent arranging (behind the scenes work, one might say), but an opportunity came my way in 2010 which truly opened the gates. *Of All Persons and Estates*, a setting of the daily prayers given in both Houses, was performed alongside Mozart's *Requiem* in Westminster Hall, and was truly a piece that belonged to the Choir. It was in 2011 that my role with the Choir was further expanded to include the position of Composer-in-Residence. Of all the things that I have managed to achieve through the years, I think that this particular role with this particular choir is my favourite, a position that allows me to provide music that, ideally, excites and pushes the Choir while playing to its strengths. I am not generally a proud person, but I do take great pride and pleasure in this position, not least because I am the first composer to be associated officially with Parliament for nearly 500 years.

The last was another Nicholas, Nicholas Ludford, a figure who dwelled in the shadows until his music emerged from obscurity in the 1990s thanks to a set of discs by The Cardinall's Musick. Here was a composer who wrote in the florid and mellifluous style of that Catholic generation just before the split from Rome brought with it the adoption of English rather than Latin in worship, and the idea that music should be simple, syllabic and communicative rather than reflecting the glories of heaven. Compare Tallis's *Sancte Deus* with *If Ye Love Me* and you will hear the difference immediately, but while Tallis survived and even thrived, it seems that Ludford laid down his pen and wrote no more. He was associated with St Margaret's (and is buried there) but his daily work was done in what was the royal palace, in

I can still remember the nerves I felt when I started, turning up with long hair, leather jacket and T-shirt in this pillar of the establishment, and I am sure that a couple of quizzical glances were cast in my direction.

Nicholas O'Neill

St Stephen's Hall where the king and his court worshipped, and in the Undercroft, where the music filtered down to the less privileged.

At an event in 2016 we were fortunate enough to hear music by Ludford performed in the locations for which it was written – smaller simpler Mass settings for daily use (in which he likely sang) in the Undercroft, and then the 'Agnus Dei' from his *Missa Lapidaverunt Stephanum* in the Hall for which it was presumably written. In a brief talk at the event I spoke of Ludford's music finally being freed 'from the frozen calligraphy of the page', but I was taken aback to realise just how well he understood the space in which his music would be performed. To have two of my own pieces performed at the same event was both thrilling and humbling.

From the time of my appointment as Composer-in-Residence, the pieces began to flow in more regular fashion (*O God of Earth and Altar, Te Deum Laudamus, The Human Seasons, High Flight, A Certain Everlasting Polyphony*) and the Christmas pieces and arrangements became more of a fixture (*Awhile A'wandering, We Three Kings, Through the Fair, Ar Hyd y Nos, The Angel Gabriel, Gabriel that Angel Bright, The Oxen*) while other commissions began to arrive as well from members of the Choir, such as *Why Should We Not Sing?* commissioned by Lord Thomas of Gresford to celebrate the 150th anniversary of the birth of David Lloyd George and performed at the National Liberal Club, and *1215: Foundation of Liberty* for the 800th anniversary of the sealing of Magna Carta.

One of the aspects of the Choir that thrills me the most is our sense of togetherness and the way that we bring harmony, both literally and metaphorically, to a place where people are often staunchly opposed to each other ideologically.

Nicholas O'Neill

There are three pieces that stand out above the others, though, and which have an importance in terms of the Choir that lifts them a little in my memory. First is *Tu es Petrus*, which was part of a thrilling concert in Notre-Dame de Paris and which, thanks to Edward Webb's camera, has produced one of my favourite photos, taken as I thank the Choir. We had premiered this work in the very dry acoustic of Cadogan Hall, but it was conceived for Notre-Dame and, of course, it used material written by Pérotin who lived and worked in the building centuries ago. I could swear that I saw his ghost in the shadows of the choir stalls at certain points, that I could feel his presence. This was an unforgettable experience, not least because the Cathedral tends not to allow music by living composers.

One of the aspects of the Choir that thrills me the most is our sense of togetherness and the way that we bring harmony, both literally and metaphorically, to a place where people are often staunchly opposed to each other ideologically. Nobody, however, was unaffected by the murder of Jo Cox MP in 2016, and I was approached soon thereafter by a member of the Choir to write something in her memory, initially an elegy. I suspected that this would send the wrong message so, instead, we turned the piece into a Christmas work, with a message about holding onto light and standing fast for good things. The piece was *This Light of Reason*, setting a luminous (what else?) text by John Donne, and I am glad that it continues to be performed by various groups, spreading its message like the candle flame to which it refers.

Possibly the most personal of all was *Carol for Jane*, in memory of Jane Slowey, and setting a text written by Kate, Simon's wife. Jane was a vibrant member of the Choir, and I often had the pleasure of teaching her on a one-to-one basis – I remember one particularly enthusiastic discussion about Dangermouse when I spotted her wearing a badge – so this was a work composed from a highly personal point of view, not least because Kate's text was written following a conversation with Jane herself that summer.

I have mentioned that the standard of the Choir has improved over the years, but the truth of the matter is that Simon and I are on a never-ending mission to refine the way the Choir sings and approaches music. The first true turning point was, I believe, the performance of the Verdi *Requiem* in 2004, since when we have gone from strength to strength, performing works which previously we would have regarded as beyond our means, such as *The Dream of Gerontius*. In exploring these pieces, we have expanded our knowledge and technique to the extent that I believe many people would find it hard to credit that we are, at heart, a non-audition choir.

I hope that at least part of that improvement is due not solely to the notes but to a knowledge of the musical matters behind them, and I hope also that my perspective as a composer allows the Choir to understand in greater detail not just the 'how' of composition but also the 'why', although often we need to find our own answers to these questions. Understanding these concerns, the decision-making processes that the composer faces when putting pen to paper in the act of creation, is crucial in being able to appreciate the music as opposed to just the notes.

In conclusion, I also need to mention one of the qualities that makes the Choir unique. In many regards there is no other choir like the Parliament Choir, but the quality I need to highlight is the Choir's social aspect, which I find so strong. The monthly choir suppers have certainly contributed to this (although I am often heading in the opposite direction down the A303 by then), but there are many other times when this shines through, especially in the visits to Anghiari. Whether for the weekend of the Maratona or for the festival itself, these trips form one of the highlights of the musical year for us, and the opportunity to sit at Bar Baldaccio or attend a chamber concert in one of those beautiful streets is a perfect antidote to the daily stresses and strains of Westminster. Anghiari has provided some of our most memorable choral experiences as well, from the out-in-out-in Mendelssohn *Lobgesang* to the Mozart *Requiem* in a packed Sansepolcro Cathedral and, most memorably of all, the Verdi *Requiem* in Piazza Baldaccio.

Being a part of the development of the Parliament Choir from its inception has been one of the greatest joys of my musical life, and my association with the Choir is something that I never take for granted and which I continue to enjoy. Mondays come and Mondays go, but each one represents, I hope, a small improvement on the one before as we continue our journey towards ever greater musical excellence. May we long continue to work hard and with good humour and companionship, and bring harmony to Westminster.

> On the subject of voices, I cannot let slip the opportunity to remind your Lordships of that excellent cross-party initiative, the Parliament Choir, of which I am proud to be a member although I was unable to sing last night, I am very sorry to say. It is a magnificent example of political harmony and the best fun that I have yet discovered to be had in the Palace of Westminster on a Monday night.

Baroness McIntosh of Hudnall, as quoted in Hansard, 26 November 2003, Debate on the Address

2. People

Lord Filkin

Chairmen

Lord Filkin CBE (2000–02)

The Founding Chairman takes pleasure in the development of the Choir over 20 years.

Simon and I were delighted when the Choir had performed its inaugural concert in St Margaret's Westminster. But the real hard work started then, making it a success. After twenty years, the Choir has vastly exceeded our expectations, thanks to the hard work and generosity of so many in the Choir and its many friends. It is now a well-loved Parliamentary institution, has performed wonderful concerts and is an ambassador for Parliament at home and abroad.

Looking back, some of the founding principles of the Choir created its potential and its challenges. A key decision was to form it as a non-audition choir. But that was testing, we were amateur when we started. Simon and Nick had to work hard to turn us into a choir that could hold its own with most in the UK and abroad, which over two decades they have done. The second fundamental principle was that the Choir should be open to anyone who worked in Parliament. These principles and the fact that the Chair changed every two years, increased the demands on Simon. He has had to do much more than provide musical leadership. Everyone knows he is a gifted musician and a warm human being who inspires people to give of their best musically, socially, and financially.

Some know that he has been a great musical entrepreneur bringing about amazing works performed in iconic buildings. Concerts in Notre-Dame, the Bundestag, York Minster, St Vitus Cathedral Prague, Coventry Cathedral and Westminster Abbey, have been for many of us highlights of our lives. But securing such venues, and organising works like *The Dream of Gerontius* and Verdi's *Requiem* with large orchestral forces and raising the money to do so, has been extraordinary. It requires entrepreneurship, ambition, hard work and persistence. Simon has led this process; without him, we would have stayed as a workplace choir. Last, largely unseen, Simon has done an enormous amount to support the governance, management, and finances of the Choir, through challenging times.

Jonathan Sayeed (2002–04).

As Chairman Jonathan Sayeed put forward the case for a lot more sponsorship, more concerts and generally setting a template for future activity, recognising that he would be building on a sound musical foundation. The high watermark of his chairmanship was the Coronation Jubilee concert in 2003, and thereafter he set ambitious targets for the Choir, for example, pushing for the performance of the Verdi Requiem *in 2004, a huge undertaking for the Choir at the time. He warmly embraced the idea of the 'house orchestra', Southbank Sinfonia, which was set up during his chairmanship. And he showed another side when, the morning after the Jubilee concert, he took bacon sandwiches round to the team who were dismantling at top speed the staging in the Abbey! Jonathan writes:*

Of the time I spent in the Parliament Choir, the 2003 concert scheduled for Westminster Hall but moved to the Abbey at short notice was the great spectacular. But, for me, the 2004 Verdi *Requiem* concert in Westminster Cathedral was equally memorable for it was when I felt the Choir came of age. This most operatic of requiems requires subtle singing and intonation and the fact that the Parliament Choir achieved this before a discriminating audience clearly demonstrated how far the Choir had progressed since its inception.

The Parliament Choir was always likely to be of public interest, given the nature of its membership. This was fortunate in many ways. Grand venues were made available, renowned soloists recruited, large audiences came and generous sponsorship was given. Most importantly, it secured the services of Simon Over, an inspirational Director of Music, who took a disparate group from the Palace of Westminster and through dedication, good humour, frequently required tact and outstanding skill melded them into a body worthy of being listened to. The hurdles he faced were sometimes unusual. During votes in the Lord's or the Commons whole sections of the Choir would decamp only to reappear a quarter of an hour later providing there was not another immediate vote, and they could only rehearse when Parliament was sitting. Many of the Choir could not sight-read, some did not even read music, but we were a Choir that was for everyone who worked in the Palace and we were determined that we would continue as a 'non-audition' choir open and welcoming to all.

Baroness Walmsley (2004–06).

Joan Walmsley was responsible for introducing the monthly choir suppers which used to be held in the Atrium of Portcullis House until it was closed in the evenings, and which now take place in the House of Lords cafeteria. They are such a good way of getting to know fellow choir members. She describes the highlights of her membership of the Choir.

Of course, my most personal memory is my wedding to Martin, Lord Thomas of Gresford, who joined the Choir soon after I did. When we married on 21 October 2005, in the Chapel where we rehearse, I was the Chairman of the Choir and some choir members kindly agreed to sing for the service from the back of the Chapel around the organ. Instead of the usual organ wedding march for my entry to the Chapel, I chose the sung version (mostly by the ladies of the Choir) of the wedding march from *Lohengrin*. I will never forget the lovely sound they made as I

Wedding of Baroness Walmsley to Lord Thomas of Gresford, 2005, in the Chapel

descended the steps of the Chapel on my son's arm. We chose to have the piece sung in German since we felt that the reference to 'see the young bride' might have brought forth some rather unseemly snorts of laughter from our guests, as I was 62 at the time and my husband was 68. Hardly young! Only my German sister-in-law got the joke, and she was too polite to laugh. The Choir was also invited to our pre-wedding concert at St John's, Waterloo, the night before the wedding and several members joined us to hear our 'Desert Island Discs' played by Southbank Sinfonia and sung by the London Welsh Chorale, of which we were also members at the time.

Of course, the Choir has always been a family affair with several married couples, parents and daughters as members. I well remember, on the night we sang the *Nelson Mass* in the Chapel at Greenwich, we were having drinks in the evening sun before going into the Painted Hall for a memorable candlelit dinner, when a young choir member confessed that she was pregnant with her first baby. She now has two! I'm not sure who was the most thrilled, she or her father who sings with the basses.

Other memorable moments have been our trips abroad. Prague was so cold but so beautiful and we had a wonderful time, extended for a couple of days because, although the snowploughs kept Prague Airport open, they could not do as well at Heathrow and we all scrambled to get any flight we could find to get home. I was most impressed by Lord German who had one of those new-fangled iPad thingumajigs and he found a flight home quicker than any of us.

Notre-Dame had the longest echo I have ever heard and I loved Nick O'Neill's *Tu es Petrus* written specially for that concert. Little did we know the destruction that would happen to that wonderful building a few years later.

I was a founder member of the Choir, joining soon after I came into the House of Lords in May 2000. I was a Millennium Pier… er Peer. Somebody in our Whips' Office said, 'Does anyone here sing? They want to set up a choir and are having a meeting about it.' I went along to the meeting and came out as a Vice-Chair – you know how it is! So, the Choir has been part of my whole career in the Lords and through it I have met many wonderful people who I would not have come across in my normal working day. I have had the privilege of singing some wonderful music in

A post-rehearsal choir supper in the Lords cafeteria. Lady Walmsley and Lord Thomas are fifth and sixth down on the right

wonderful places and, most of all, being trained and conducted by the lovely Simon Over and Nick O'Neill. We have been so lucky to be able to work with musicians of such high calibre who always challenge us… but not too much. I love all the pieces Nick has composed for us, even though at first glance I wasn't so sure about a few of them. They have always grown on me. Christmas would not be the same without our concerts in the Atrium or St John's Smith Square but then, I am a mug for carols, especially those written or arranged by Nick.

For many years I have been encouraging Simon to let us sing *The Dream of Gerontius* and in 2019 we finally got the chance. It is one of my favourite pieces of music and I found our performance particularly moving. I do so look forward to having the chance to sing it again in the Vatican.

Baroness Cohen of Pimlico (2006–08).
Baroness Cohen's tenure as Chair was distinguished by her organisation of the Choir's administrative and financial structure.
I became Chairman in 2006. It was by then clear that we needed more administrative help, particularly with accounting, but it was not clear how to finance it. BT, already so generous, were reluctant to increase their sponsorship, so rather than look elsewhere for increased sponsorship to service, which would have been beyond the capacity of the Choir, we decided that we would go on with BT's tactful and undemanding provision and rely on getting subscriptions from the Choir to make up the gap. I agreed to take this on and cope with the resultant accounting. Jane, our Choir Secretary, agreed to increase her hours and do the accounts as well.

In the 2005 election, our former Chairman, Jonathan Sayeed, lost his seat (as happens to MPs). My long-standing friend from our undergraduate days, Anne Campbell, MP for Cambridge and a fellow alto, also lost her seat but we gained Sarah Teather MP in 2003, who held hers with an increased majority in 2005, a soloist-class soprano, who added greatly to our ranks.

The period of my chairmanship was a bit like the curate's egg – good in parts. The Choir increased its numbers – both Members and staff – and its prestige, and we successfully introduced a subscription system. Doing the accounts on top of being Choir Secretary proved a bit too much for Jane, and I was only able to give her limited help. We were, however, bailed out by generous and qualified help from a hereditary Peer who was not even a member of the Choir, accountant Lord Lyell.

Even with subscriptions from the Choir we were forced to conclude that our plans might be too ambitious. My diary for March 2006 records that Jane and I presented a budget to the Committee which indicated that putting on four concerts in prestigious surroundings in the next year could not be financed. I also thought it would somewhat exceed my administrative capacities. Both Simon and our loyal sponsor BT were able to agree that three concerts, two at Cadogan Hall and one at somewhere of historic interest, could combine the modest requirements of our sponsor, Simon's artistic wishes, my administrative capacities and the available budget. Cadogan Hall was a particularly useful venue – it was

Anyone at Westminster, from Peers to kitchen porters, can join; but there's nothing ragtag about the sound they produce: joyful and disciplined, lifting every spirit.
Matthew Parris

close enough to get to in a hurry, and came complete with vital services such as ticket selling and refreshments, which eased the strain on the Committee and choir members who were otherwise charged with the job of taking and selling rather more tickets than they necessarily wanted. Both of the Cadogan Hall concerts were a great success, but the star venue of that year was the Tower of London, secured for us by General Sir Sam Cowan, lately Chief of the Defence Logistics Organisation, for whom I had been a first non-executive director until 2005. The Tower is a deeply romantic place, for all its sinister history, and watching the Ceremony of the Keys under a late evening sky, champagne glasses in hand after the concert, was a privileged treat.

...being a member of the Choir was one of the greatest privileges of my 25 years in Parliament and the thing I missed most when I resigned.
Alun Michael

I enjoyed it all hugely and carry good memories – the Choir singing 'Happy Birthday' in four parts for my birthday on 4 July 2005 and all the seven concerts we managed to perform in the two years. I remember with particular pleasure rehearsals with the perfectionist Chorus Master, Nick O'Neill, which put us all into much better shape to respond to Simon's conducting, as well as educating us in the history of music.

Alun Michael

Alun Michael (2008–10)

Alun Michael presided when the Choir presented concerts with a different sort of repertoire: opera choruses and songs from musicals; when we took our supporters into the very centre of the Palace: 'Hatched, Matched and Dispatched', and also the first broadcast with Classic FM: Messiah *in York Minster.*

What's the connection between the Parliament Choir and COVID-19? They are polar opposites – the first brings joy, the second brings misery – so can anything positive come from COVID-19 and the disruption of lockdown? Well, for me COVID-19 brought two challenges. First, take more exercise and avoid becoming a slug. Second, listen to music at the same time.

So for a couple of hours each day I've walked the streets, fields and coastline near my home in South Wales, concentrating in a way I've never done before on the music, and it took me back in time to the Parliament Choir, the oasis of calm and harmony in the chaos of parliamentary life.

First was a historic Proms performance of Mendelssohn's *Elijah* – bringing back to life the memory of a stunning evening in Westminster Cathedral with Tom Allen, a great friend of the Choir, and unforgettable music.

Next night, as I walked, came an Elgar concert – bringing back the intensity of when we performed *The Apostles* in the same venue. That evening, nobody was allowed to move in the interval because of renovation work in the Cathedral – so we asked former Secretary of State for Northern Ireland, Paul Murphy, to explain his lifelong devotion to Elgar's music.

A classic Proms recording of Handel then provided a reminder of our Invitation *Messiah* in York Minster – the culmination of a week in which Simon and the stars of Southbank Sinfonia worked in schools across York to create a stunning concert in the Transport Museum as we prepared for our own concert in the Minster.

I didn't join the Choir by accident but as the result of an accident – running from

DEFRA for a vote when I was a Minister, I sustained a leg injury in mid-flight down the stairs and ended up in St Thomas' Hospital. Friends in the Choir, including Betty Williams MP, said that if I couldn't run I'd have to join the Choir for some London exercise. They promoted the myth that all Welshman can sing, something I've spent a lifetime disproving. But it opened up a new world for me – truly an unintended but wonderful consequence of those musical leaders who established the Choir because it was the only way they could get to sing in the crazy environment of the Commons and the Lords.

Apart from the revelation of enjoying great music, it was exciting to join one of the most democratic institutions in the land, with fellow choristers from every background and rank on the Parliamentary Estate – from Clerk or PA or Badge Messenger to Black Rod or Cabinet Minister. The MP or Peer is only special in getting away with walking (or running) out in mid-rehearsal for a vote. That in itself is a crazy arrangement, but being a member of the Choir was one of the greatest privileges of my 25 years in Parliament and the thing I missed most when I resigned to stand for election as Police and Crime Commissioner for South Wales.

Without that crazy institution I would never have got under the surface to feel the magic of Haydn and Mozart or Britten and Elgar and Mendelssohn – and 15 years later, in the desert era of COVID-19, I wouldn't have found myself stretching legs and brain and thinking back to the days when Simon and Nick opened my eyes and my ears to the wonders of choral music.

The most bizarre memory of all is of our expedition to Prague to join the Czech Parliament Choir in the freezing nave of the Cathedral to sing together Jan Jakub Ryba's compelling *Christmas Mass*; then, afterwards, warming up in the Archbishop's Palace to discover that snow had closed Heathrow and we were threatened with remaining abroad for Christmas and the New Year. Inventiveness triumphed and most of us made it back over land or on airlines that sounded like something out of a Harry Potter novel, leaving us with yet another unique experience with the Parliament Choir to celebrate and enjoy.

We must also celebrate our 'house band' (Southbank Sinfonia) which has brought young musicians from across the world to make music, to learn and to grow together. Can that

The critical eye: Prague December 2010 Nicholas O'Neill and Simon Over for once are members of the audience

survive the increasingly introverted nature of today's Britain?

I can't imagine how frustrating it must be for fine musicians such as Simon and Nick to see MPs one minute and Peers the next jumping up in the middle of rehearsal and disappearing – wandering back later in dribs and drabs having been corralled in the inevitable and endless machinations of the daily job. Their tolerance – combined with consummate professionalism and expertise – is what has kept us entranced and engaged with the music we make and share. We struggle to explain the Parliament Choir, because it shouldn't work and it shouldn't make sense – but it works, as a triumph of music and hope over the normal laws of discipline in harmony.

That's what makes it a typically British institution, driven by optimism and two wonderful talents, and long may it continue.

Lord Filkin (2010–11)

Lord Filkin returned to chair the Choir for a second term from 2010-11.

Lord German (2011–13)

Lord German was behind the Choir's first international ventures abroad. Having taken part in the Christmas concert in Prague it was he who first approached the German Bundestag to suggest the two parliament choirs sing together to commemorate the centenary of 1914. Before that happened, he linked up with the Korean Parliament Choir resulting in the concert in Cadogan Hall.

Prague in December 2010 was an opening highlight for me – having just joined the

Sir Bernard Jenkin MP, Anna Yallop, Eilidh Whitehead (then MP), Nicholas O'Neill, Baroness Corston and Denise Westbury in New Palace Yard, with Big Ben and the Elizabeth Tower behind

House of Lords in June 2010. It was the first time I have performed a concert in coat, hat and gloves, and where the internal temperature in St Vitus Cathedral was a balmy -8ºC. In gaps in rehearsal we sheltered by the massive TV lights for warmth. The Cardinal who sat in the front row of the performance had a glorious thick red cape which gave him a great deal of comforting warmth, unlike the shiveringly cold Nick O'Neill who sat nearby, and my wife with Bill Grose who had a small hip flask for comfort. But the effect of snow and Christmas 'all around' was just magical. The Czech text was incredibly difficult, since it appeared to have no vowels, but with a knowledge of Welsh you quickly learn that some letters are vowels, even if they don't appear to be at first glance.

The link with the Bundestag was an eye-opener for me – to discover the size and scale of the operation of the German Parliament. As Choir Chairman at the time, I spotted a video of their choir on the Bundestag website. I followed it through with a number of emails, and eventually – after several months – I secured a series of appointments with the President of the Bundestag's team as well as their choir. The British Ambassador was very helpful and his deputy – a choral singer himself – helped with the protocol and meetings. Simon and I turned up for our first 'official meeting' to be faced by a group of about 20 officials – all with a role to play in testing out whether joining together our two choirs was possible. The rest is history – two concerts to remember the beginning and end of the First World War – but you can imagine my disappointment at missing the joint event in the Bundestag. I turned up at London City airport to find the flight had been cancelled, and the only alternative was a flight from Heathrow which would have arrived after the concert had finished.

Over the years, we have had many broadcasts of our concerts by Classic FM. Their sound engineer was Iestyn from Neath. I discovered that, apart from the huge array of microphones and recording equipment used to capture the sound of the Choir and Southbank Sinfonia, he did all of the editing at home. His great skills came into their own at the Central Hall Westminster Christmas concert – a monster of an event – featuring their huge, newly-refurbished organ with its 32-foot pedal pipes. All well and good until one of them 'cyphered' – remained open – during the course of the concert. The music continued until the end of the piece accompanied now by this penetrating low note. We then had a break whilst the Central Hall organist located the offending pipe and stopped the note. Fearful of what this would sound like in the broadcast I asked Iestyn what he would do in editing it. The Welsh wizard managed to all but eliminate it from the broadcast, sparing the blushes of the Choir and the Central Hall.

John Rutter taking the study day in St Peter's Vere Street

Mr Christmas – John Rutter – came to a choir study day to take a rehearsal with us. It was a memorable occasion. He chatted freely with choir members beforehand, and I had the chance for lunch with him as well. An absolutely charming and self-effacing gentleman, John opened his rehearsal with a claim that he was only seven handshakes from Beethoven – tracing back from a handshake he had to that person with an earlier composer and so on. My daughter, son-in-law and grandchildren were in London that day on a shopping expedition, and they popped in to watch the beginning of our rehearsal. My grandson was enthralled until the moment in the rehearsal which involved singing and then sitting on your chair at appropriate words in the music. Thankfully, my grandson spoke in a whisper – but I still heard him – 'that Rutter is a nutter!' Most uncalled for – but it was the most physical performance I can remember the Choir ever giving.

At one point everybody in my office was singing in the Choir and we joked that a job interview to work for me might involve an audition.
Dame Caroline Spelman

Dame Caroline Spelman (2013–15)

Dame Caroline Spelman took on the Chair for the first collaboration with the Bundestag Choir in 2014. Her background as a linguist and her links with European business were especially valuable in helping to bring about this ambitious concert.

One of the best things about our Parliament is its choir. That simple statement belies the fact that few Parliaments have their own choir and the recognition of our own has been well worth all the struggles along the way. It is testament to the vison of our Music Director, Simon Over, and the parliamentarians who first shared it, that their perseverance has brought the Choir to its present standing. They realised that those who work in the long-hours culture of Parliament stood no chance of making choir practice outside Westminster and so created a choir open to all who work on the Estate. I was not quite a founder member as I missed the very first concert, but the enthusiasm of my secretary, Katy, who assured me, 'You will really enjoy this if you join,' got me involved. Workplace choirs have now become very popular, although 20 years ago our Parliament Choir was something of a trailblazer. At one point everybody in my office was singing in the Choir and we joked that a job interview to work for me might involve an audition. We allowed ourselves the treat of playing the music we were about to rehearse just before choir practice to get us tuned in. This led to the MP next door, Sir Nicholas Soames, calling round to ask what was the glorious music I was playing and thus he discovered Rachmaninov's *Ave Maria*. Whether or not they sang, those who have worked for me through the two decades of my parliamentary career have become great supporters of all our concerts and some of them support the Choir financially as Friends.

I remember the first concert I sang in as if it was yesterday. That was Fauré's *Requiem* and I was spellbound in one of the rehearsals to hear the voice of my colleague, Sir Bernard Jenkin, soaring upwards into the roof of St Margaret's Church opposite Parliament, as he sang the solo part. Although we hear MPs speak, we rarely hear each other sing. There have been so many concerts that it's hard to pick out those which had the greatest impact but, without a doubt, those where we have sung abroad at the invitation of other Parliaments leave the kind of memory which make one pinch oneself and say, 'Did we really do that?'

After the bombing of the Bataclan concert hall in Paris we suggested showing our solidarity with the French Parliament by offering to sing for them, and Simon Over asked his friend and colleague Pierre Brouchoud, Directeur, Musique Sacrée à Notre-Dame, whether we might do a concert there. He agreed; they were delighted to support the event (before the fire, of course). It's a building resonant with history but also full of resonance, being so tall and long. There are several seconds of delay between the choristers emitting a note and the audience hearing it, so our very skilful Chorus Master and Composer-in-Residence, Nick O'Neill, brilliantly factored this into his stunning work, *Tu es Petrus*, commissioned for the occasion and based on the music of medieval Notre-Dame composers. Music speaks louder than words and our French hosts applauded enthusiastically to demonstrate how our gift of music touched them in dark times. What happened in Paris could so easily happen here and, indeed, similar horrors have, so the solidarity was poignant.

My time as Chairman of the Choir coincided with the centenary of the outbreak of World War One and the idea of singing together with the choir of the German Parliament was conceived. The Germans were nervous about commemorating the Great War, but we assured them that our acts of Remembrance do not glorify war but remember with respect all the lives lost and the sacrifices made. Lord German, Paul Farrelly MP, Simon and I visited the Bundestag and we were able to reassure them of this. In 2014, the Bundestag Choir with their charismatic Serbian conductor, Žarko Bulajić, came over to sing with us Mendelssohn's *Hymn of Praise*, chosen to set an appropriate tone of remembrance. The President of the Bundestag, Dr Norbert Lammert, gave a deeply moving speech in English, without notes, to a packed audience of 1,200 in Westminster Hall.

It was a logistical challenge to bring so many people together to sing in a building of such antiquity but Black Rod, who was also a member of the Choir, brought about a triumph in getting everyone in on time and Dr Lammert away on time to catch a flight from Biggin Hill. Our choir members put the German choir members up in their own homes and this hospitality helped to form firm

Caroline Spelman MP before the 1914 centenary concert in Westminster Hall

Richard Stokes, who coaches the Choir on how to sing in German, with Lord German before the 1914 centenary concert with the Bundestag Choir in Westminster Hall

friendships between them. Our German guests were adamant we should go and sing in their brand-new Parliament building in Berlin. So in 2016 we travelled to Berlin to perform a Christmas concert together, as both nations share a tradition of carol singing. I remember rehearsing while looking out over the River Spree and seeing white crosses on the opposite bank. These mark the places where those trying to scale the Berlin Wall had lost their lives. The exquisite sound of Lauridsen's *O Magnum Mysterium* seemed to float out across the river to touch the bank and reflect the tragic history of this place.

Shortly after our visit, one of Berlin's Christmas markets was a terrorist target and we felt all the more deeply for our friends in the Bundestag. Our firm friendship led to another concert together, in Westminster Hall, this time to mark the centenary of the 1918 Armistice. I worried that repeating the success of 2014 might not have been possible, but the strong bonds we created carried us through all the challenges that such a great event poses. I must also mention Anna Yallop, the Choir's Chief Executive. She is a great positive life force behind our efforts, always believing we can do it.

The international musical collaborations are just one of the most remarkable things about the Choir. This was recognised by the Foreign and Commonwealth Office in the most generous way when they hosted our visitors at a reception in the Locarno Suite, and their permanent secretary spoke so warmly of the benefit that the Choir brings to bilateral relations between Britain and its allies. Long may this continue.

Mark Prisk (2015–17)

Mark Prisk continued to establish and reinforce international links. During his tenure as Chair the Choir performed in Paris and Berlin.

The Choir was one constant in my parliamentary career. I was first elected in 2001 and joined later that year. I stayed a member right up until I stepped down, 18 years later. Throughout that time, even when a Minister, I managed to keep practising and to perform in the majority of our concerts. It was and remains a wonderful family within Parliament, reaching across both Houses and bringing friendship and occasional solace to my time at Westminster.

In 2002, we were due to mark the Queen's Jubilee by singing in Westminster Hall.

Mark Prisk MP, when Chairman of the Choir, with his wife Lesley Titcomb before the concert in the Bundestag, Berlin

Sir Robert Worcester and Mark Prisk in Westminster Hall

I remember our Patron Thomas Allen striding through Westminster Hall rehearsing, his glorious voice filling the cavernous space and attracting every policeman and security guard to see what was going on. They stayed and clapped.

In 2016, when I was Chairman, we made two overseas trips, one to Paris, the second to Berlin. Our trip to Paris was in response to the dreadful terrorist attacks on many musical venues in the city the previous year. We were honoured to sing in Notre-Dame and I shall never forget the extraordinary acoustic of that magnificent Cathedral. A whole eight seconds I believe, so even those at the back of the 900-strong audience heard every note. Considering what has happened since to Notre-Dame, those memories are particularly poignant.

Later that year we sang at the German Bundestag in Berlin. Given that the UK had only recently voted to leave the EU, this was an extraordinary moment, and not without challenges. Ironically, the rehearsals highlighted one major difference between us and them. As we finished the singing, it was announced that our colleagues would like to practise coming on and off stage. Once, you might think, but no. For over 20 minutes we practised. We came on, we went off, and we learnt when to step backwards, forwards and even sideways with military precision. Some of our basses were none too pleased, not least at the loss of drinking time.

Our Chorus Master, Nick O'Neill, found the layout of the Bundestag buildings even more challenging. We had started the day ready to rehearse in a specially allocated room. Where was Nick? No one knew. Then we looked out of the window across the river and there, walking purposefully, was the man himself. We shouted but he couldn't hear us. Then someone rang his mobile and we watched him – almost in slow motion – gradually turn and look across at all of us waving at him. He looked at the water and looked at us. He shook his head and then finally found his way to us. To mark the occasion, on our return to Westminster, I presented him with a pair of water wings, for future emergencies.

My last major concert whilst still an MP was *The Dream of Gerontius*, in Westminster Cathedral. I was not keen on it at first. However, I learnt to love it, so it's a reminder that to grow, we need to step outside our comfort zone.

Simon Over understands this and has always struck the right balance between seeking musical excellence and nurturing an enjoyable, welcoming environment when we come together to sing. In any place of work that would be tricky, but at Westminster it's a remarkable feat.

Baroness Hayman of Ullock (2017–19)

Baroness Hayman (as Sue Hayman MP) chaired the Choir until the 2019 General Election. Highlights of her term were the New Zealand collaboration Gallipoli to the Somme *and the 1918 Armistice centenary concert.*

I was so excited when I found out that there was a Parliament Choir. I had been disappointed that I'd had to give up singing in my local choir when elected as an MP, as I could no longer make the rehearsals. Singing has always been an important part of my life and the Parliament Choir became a particularly important part of my Westminster life – not just for the joy of singing, but also for the friendships and for keeping me sane during some tough political years!

There are two concerts that I will always remember, both from 2018. The first was when we performed the European premiere of Anthony Ritchie's *Gallipoli to the Somme* at the Sheldonian Theatre in Oxford. It is an extraordinary piece of music and incredibly moving. Members of the audience came over

Sue (now Baroness) Hayman welcomes the audience to the 1918 centenary concert in Westminster Hall

to me in tears afterwards as it is such a powerful piece.

The other occasion was the concert in Westminster Hall with the German Bundestag Choir to commemorate the 1918 Armistice. I was always proud to say that I was the Chair of the Parliament Choir, but never more so than when welcoming our audience that evening. To be able to sing the Mozart *Mass in C minor* to honour our forebears and to demonstrate the great friendship and respect between our two nations today was a moment I will always treasure.

Parliamentarians Who Sing

Alan, Lord Beith

I remarked that with the cocktail buzz you wouldn't have known it was a House of God. His reply, 'While you were singing you would have, believe me!'
Viscount Bridgeman

In the dark days when the Commons regularly sat until one or two in the morning, and we were hanging around waiting to vote, I used to talk about forming a Glee Club to enjoy music while we waited. I totally failed to carry this through, so imagine my delight when enterprising colleagues, particularly from the Lords, established a Parliament Choir! I think I was in it from the beginning, and my memory goes back to the excitement of performing *Messiah* with Emma Kirkby as soloist. I was grateful to the Choir for singing at the reopening by the Historic Chapels Trust of the German Lutheran Church in East London, and glad to facilitate a major concert we gave in Methodist Central Hall. It was wonderful to have such a high standard of professional direction from Simon and Nick. Apart from the pleasure of singing, what made life in the Choir so special was the friendship and fellowship across party lines and with staff from every part of Parliament and at every level. In the Choir we really were all equal in status, even if not in vocal quality!

Long may the Choir continue – it is now an essential part of the life of Parliament, and not just for those who sing in it.

Viscount Bridgeman

I am an Old Contemptible, the Mons Star, as an original member. I remember the 'shakedown cruise' we did with *Messiah*, I think our first and only concert we did at St Margaret's, where Simon was the Director of Music. Looking back at our early concerts, I am embarrassed we had the face to make a charge at all.

It has been a thrill to sing with the Choir for the whole of its existence and looking back, one is amazed at the improvement in quality of singing which we have achieved under Simon and Nick. They are very different in style but totally complementary. In addition, Nick is an accomplished musical scholar, with a deep love of Bach.

Simon reminds us that we are now well towards the upper end of the amateur non-audition choirs in London (all holders of a parliamentary pass are automatically welcomed – a shrewd judgement by our Two Wise Men who know that with our growing reputation only serious singers will apply). Guest members are subject to a vigorous voice test from Nick.

In musical terms I suppose our greatest achievement to date was *The Dream of Gerontius* in Westminster Cathedral. After the concert I met a Labour colleague, Lord Griffiths, who is a Methodist Minister. I remarked that with the cocktail buzz you wouldn't have known it was a House of God. His reply, 'While you were singing you would have, believe me!'

Among other memorable experiences was the Britten *War Requiem* in Coventry Cathedral on the 70th anniversary of the bombing where we were hosted by the Saint Michael's Singers from Coventry and joined by the German Choir of London. The silence at the end of the performance was an experience I shall never forget.

Baroness Corston

When I was a member of the Choir, and as the Vice Chair and Trustee, I had enormous respect for the dedication shown by so many in making the Choir an effective ambassador for our Parliament. Our concerts in the UK and abroad played a great part in showing another face of Parliament.

Sir Bernard Jenkin MP

A Lifeline of Sanity in a Pretty Mad World

I attended the Choir's first concert, a *Messiah* in St Margaret's Westminster conducted by Simon Over, and encouraged everyone associated with it to continue. Why had Parliament not had a choir before now? My father, Lord Jenkin of Roding, who sang in that concert, became one of its first Trustees. I was a very busy member of the Shadow Cabinet at the time, but I joined to sing in my first ever Bach *Christmas Oratorio*, soon after the Choir was formed. The Bach is an exacting piece, particularly as we sang it in original German text. German is a wonderful language to sing, because the rhythm and inflection of words make sense of the music.

Every rehearsal felt like being released from the crabbed drudgery of daily work into a different world of emotion, colour and light. And when you get immersed in a piece, it lives with you all the time, whatever you are doing. It lifts you out of yourself and puts a spring in your step. With great music ringing in your head, you can suddenly be transported and the world around you seems so trivial. This is why music becomes such an important part of some people's lives and why, in particular, a workplace choir (which is what the Parliament Choir is) can make such an important contribution to wellbeing in the workplace. You may not have much direct contact with the Parliament Choir, but we have become woven into the fabric of life in and around the Palace of Westminster.

'A Westminster Christmas' 2020: two of the three kings, David Lammy MP and Sir Bernard Jenkin MP, socially distanced

Two founder members of the Choir, Lord Jenkin of Roding and his son, Sir Bernard Jenkin MP

I am not always a good attender of rehearsals and have, on occasion, had to drop out of a performance at the last minute. I missed singing a performance of *Messiah* because, as Shadow Defence Secretary, I had to speak in a defence debate. On the other hand, having had some professional training before choosing a different career, Simon has, on occasion, allowed me a certain licence to join a performance without much rehearsing (something I do not take for granted). For many performances, there is, however, nothing like letting the Chorus Master teach us the notes! The Choir often chooses difficult repertoire. Singing in Czech was particularly taxing, and getting the right note and timing for entries in Britten's *War Requiem* tests the most expert singers.

The high points for me include the great music we have made under Simon's sensitive and inspirational direction – his quiet modesty, so unlike many of the big egos in conducting, undersells his quality as an amazing leader of people and a great musician, well deserving of wide recognition; Verdi's *Requiem*, Britten's *War Requiem*, Elgar's *The Apostles*, and then the *Gerontius*, as well as the requiems by Mozart and Brahms; and the brilliant young musicians of Southbank Sinfonia, our partner orchestra, formed and directed by Simon, add immeasurably to the quality of our performances.

We have watched Simon and our Composer-in-Residence, Nick O'Neill, grow in stature and artistic confidence over the years. Simon has become formidable: more insistent that we watch him and get our heads out of our scores, and more demanding that we deliver a quality performance. Halfway through a final rehearsal of *The Apostles* in Westminster Cathedral, there was a sense that the Choir was all over the place, missing entries, not concentrating, heads down and getting out of time, and taking the thing too casually. In the break, I sensed Simon's anxiety about the evening's performance and suggested to him it would do no harm if he lost his rag with the Choir, to give us a bit of a shock. Later he did that, and we delivered a great performance that evening.

The Parliament Choir does not just happen on its own. It involves an immense amount of hard work and commitment from Simon, the Trustees and a core group of volunteers. At times, our existence seems to hang by a slender financial thread. We have no endowments or capital, but live a hand-to-mouth existence. As a member of the Board of Trustees, I can vouch we keep in mind our charitable purpose, the responsibility we have for making sure we are viable, and how to manage the risks of every concert. We get free rehearsal space (in the Crypt) but must raise every penny to cover the costs of our Director, our Composer-in-Residence (who is also our repetiteur at rehearsal), hiring music, musicians, venues, lighting, sound systems, printing and staff. We owe an immense amount to a very few stalwarts who actually run the Choir. For someone like me, who grew up expecting music always to fill my life, the Choir has been a lifeline of sanity in a pretty mad world, and I expect it is the same for many others too, and perhaps that also explains why the Choir has built up such a strong, regular audience as well.

Introducing our concert of *The Dream of Gerontius* last year, Simon dedicated the performance to the memory of my father, who had served as a Trustee for much of the Choir's existence. *Gerontius* was my father's favourite work, which he had first sung as a Cambridge undergraduate, and then at Alexandra Palace in about 1960. All my family and many friends came to our 2019 performance to remember my father. The evening captured so much of the essence of my life. Music, the Choir, Westminster, politics and my family were all fused into one unforgettable experience.

David Lammy MP

It would not be an overstatement to say that my life was fundamentally altered after my primary school teacher, my local priest, and my mother conspired to send me for voice trials. Aged 11, in September 1983, success at those trials took me, with a boarding scholarship, to King's Cathedral School, Peterborough.

I look back on singing in Peterborough Cathedral with deep fondness and nostalgia. Singing nearly every day was my training ground in dedication, and the vehicle that brought me to an unexpected life. I learned the importance of repetition in the service of excellence that would serve me well throughout my career. As Culture Minister decades after, I joked with my wife that I only had the discipline to go through my Red Box each day because of the strict routine I followed as a chorister. In fact, I doubt I would have become the MP for Tottenham if I had not spent my formative years in Peterborough. Singing also literally trained my voice; I would not be as amplified as I am in the Commons Chamber were it not for these years.

Though I sang until the end of my schooldays, I did not sing again as an adult until I joined the Parliament Choir in 2010. I have not been able to take part in the Choir's many activities as much as I would like; I don't like to perform unless I can get the practice in, and the London riots, Windrush and Brexit certainly haven't made finding the time easy. The Choir has nonetheless been the source of many memories for me. Singing a duet with Bernard Jenkin with the possibility of interruption by the division bell was a uniquely parliamentary happening. More poignantly, not long before she died, it brought me great joy to have my mother-in-law arrive unexpectedly at a concert.

Overall, I have found catharsis, joy and relaxation when singing with the Choir. I simply love singing the classics and the Christmas concerts. Even the warm-up exercises delight me. As with any choir, it is certainly a kind of therapy.

Parliamentary life can, at times, feel like the work of a lone trader, while a choir, especially one comprised of Members and staff alike, cannot be anything other than collaborative. It is necessary and excellent that the Choir is still going 20 years after it was founded, and I look forward to continuing to be a part of it.

Parliamentary life can, at times, feel like the work of a lone trader, while a choir, especially one comprised of Members and staff alike, cannot be anything other than collaborative.

David Lammy MP

Sir David Lidington

Looking back after 20 years, I wonder why on earth it took so long to get a parliamentary choir started. I had been in the Commons for eight years. Like most MPs, I'd worked for a

David Lidington MP responding to Dr Norbert Lammert's welcome, before the concert in the Bundestag 2016

...for some years Alan Beith, Alun Michael and I (Liberal, Labour, Conservative) rehearsed side by side, like some downmarket parliamentary version of the Three Tenors.
Sir David Lidington

long time to get selected and elected. It was the job I had wanted. But it's true that whenever I was asked whether there was anything that I regretted, I would reply that it was that the demands of sitting hours had meant that, for the first time since my early years at school, I had been unable to continue choral singing.

So many of us owe a huge debt of gratitude to Geoff Filkin, Tricia Hollis and the others who took the initiative. Over the last two decades the Choir has overcome party divisions – for some years Alan Beith, Alun Michael and I (Liberal, Labour, Conservative) rehearsed side by side, like some downmarket parliamentary version of the Three Tenors. It has enabled Leavers and Remainers to find common cause, and it has also brought together the disparate tribes at Westminster: not just MPs and Peers but secretaries, parliamentary management, clerks, police officers – even the occasional journalist.

Mary Macleod

Where there is discord, may we bring harmony. And where there is despair, may we bring hope.

The Parliament Choir is at the heart of the Palace of Westminster. On a Monday evening, when debates are at full flow in the Chambers of the House of Commons and the House of Lords, below in the Crypt, some beautiful music reverberates around the glorious gold surrounds of the Chapel of St Mary Undercroft, right next to Westminster Hall. A group of parliamentarians and staff of all political backgrounds and some of none, join together and collaborate with each other in their love of music as part of the Parliament Choir. The music transcends partisan politics and depressing disagreements, and instead shows harmony, unity and hope.

Harmony: The Choir brings politicians together with differing views and visions, but they sing in harmony, as if with one voice. This is a symbol of the reality of Parliament, where there may be discord in the Chambers at times when parliamentarians debate issues that matter to them, but there is also harmony in so many areas behind the scenes as MPs and Peers work together in Committees, on campaigns and within all-party groups, to create solutions and deliver change that is much needed for the country. Creating harmony is also seen through the work of the Choir internationally, when we have collaborated with other parliamentarians, with one of the most memorable and poignant concerts being the commemoration of the 1918 Armistice, singing Mozart's *Mass in C minor* with the German Bundestag Choir in the UK Houses of Parliament. An evening to remember.

Unity: What is special about the Parliament Choir is not only the hard work, creativity, time and energy that goes into each concert, but that the Choir works in a united partnership – parliamentarians, staff, others connected to Parliament and with the corporate sector, getting brilliant backing from organisations such as BT and Airbus. And for concerts such as the moving RAF 100 celebration, Airbus gave superb support throughout. Having some members of the Choir who are not parliamentarians strengthens who we are, and is a symbol of how each part of the economy and community cannot achieve much by working in isolation. It is a wonderful example of what politicians do daily, working with Government, the public and private sectors, collaborating with community and civil society to create something stronger and better for the future.

Hope: At a time in our history where much in life is uncertain, where there is constant change and with many challenges ahead, the Parliament Choir shows what is best about Parliament – people who are committed to community and country, full of purpose and service, wanting to be the change they want to see in the world and trying to create a better life for all across society. Just as music can be uplifting, inspiring and healing, so politicians have an important role to play in giving people something to believe in and allowing them to hope for the future.

From concerts in London, Paris, Germany and Tuscany, my love for the Choir increased as we were encouraged to grow as singers and become even better as the years progressed. We are blessed by having a great team organising the Choir, showing the best of human endeavour and teamwork, with the brilliant Simon Over leading the Choir and wonderfully supported by our talented resident composer, Nick O'Neill.

The Parliament Choir, therefore, is an image of what the country wants from their parliamentarians – innovating and creating change, building a stronger society and world, working together to deliver good, creating harmony where there is discord, finding truth and a way forward where there is error, and when there is despair, we help to inspire, bring people together and give them hope of a better tomorrow.

At a time in our history where much in life is uncertain, where there is constant change and with many challenges ahead, the Parliament Choir shows what is best about Parliament – people who are committed to community and country, full of purpose and service, wanting to be the change they want to see in the world and trying to create a better life for all across society.

Mary Macleod

Genista, Baroness McIntosh of Hudnall

This is how I recall the story. One day, many years ago when the world was young, an idea was born in the minds of a small group of far-seeing people. One of them was Simon Over, then on the music staff of Westminster Abbey. The others were Lord (Geoffrey) Filkin and the late and much-lamented Baroness (Patricia) Hollis, who had both been in a choir run by Simon but found it difficult to make time for rehearsals in their busy political lives. It occurred to them that Parliament, in all its strangeness and diversity, would be an excellent place to find, form and rehearse

Baroness Walmsley (left) and Baroness McIntosh: front-row altos

another one. So they sought out like-minded members of the parliamentary community, MPs, Peers and staff, who might be interested. I was one of those early recruits.

I had sung in choirs before, and music had always been a big part of my life, but my sight-reading skills were modest, and I no longer had any idea what sort of noise would come out of my mouth if I started to sing again. Nevertheless, the vision of a choir in Parliament (that I didn't have to audition for) was irresistible. I signed up, quickly finding myself drawn into discussions about how the Choir might be constituted and eventually becoming one of its first Trustees. In those early conversations we talked about the possibility that the Choir might have as one of its key objectives the support of young musicians. This became, and remains, one of its defining characteristics. Many brilliant young artists have performed with us, sometimes alongside the greatest singers of our day such as Sir Thomas Allen and Dame Felicity Lott. Most still mention the Parliament Choir in their biographies years after the event, recognising the importance of the early opportunity they were given. Full disclosure: my own daughter, now an established professional singer, was among the first to benefit from this decision. Being in the Choir when your child is a soloist is a uniquely uncomfortable experience – equal parts intense pride and intense anxiety.

In the past 20 years I have sung in most of our concerts. Each one has been a joy in its own way, but some stay in the memory more vividly than others. For me, these include twice singing the Verdi *Requiem* in Westminster Cathedral; the extraordinary privilege of performing Britten's *War Requiem* in 2010 in Coventry Cathedral, the place for which it was written; the angry solemnity of *Gallipoli to the Somme* in 2018; and the 2017 performance of *Belshazzar's Feast*, a great roller-coaster of a piece, at the Royal Festival Hall. My youngest grandchild was born as we sang.

Everything our brilliant Chorus Master, Nicholas O'Neill, has written for us over the years has been a joy to sing. He knows the Choir inside out and writes for what we do well, whilst always pushing us a little further than we think we can go. He's also a scholar, a great teacher and one of the funniest people I know. And he's very nice to altos.

A choir, especially an amateur choir, is a complex social organism. Our membership ranges across all ages and musical ability. It includes people who attend every rehearsal, week in week out, and sing in every concert no matter how far afield. Others participate less regularly, usually because of the demands of the parliamentary timetable. Some are trained musicians; others (like me) have slowly improved our modest musical skills under Simon's keen eye and can now mark up a score and read it reasonably competently whilst remembering to watch the conductor – mostly. Some are brilliant volunteer organisers of everything from choir seating to choir suppers. Some are party animals – Anghiari is the high spot of their year – some are not. What we all have in common is a love of making music together. There's nothing to beat the adrenaline rush at the start of a concert as Simon raises his baton and the orchestra plays the opening bars. The wet Monday evening

There's nothing to beat the adrenaline rush at the start of a concert as Simon raises his baton and the orchestra plays the opening bars.
Baroness McIntosh

rehearsals you didn't want to go to, the despair of thinking you'll never learn the notes, all forgotten in the pure joy of singing. Simply the best.

Robert Rogers, Lord Lisvane

In our kitchen at home in Herefordshire there is a giant clip frame with all the posters from the early days of the Choir, together with (a moment of immodesty) a poster for a performance of Stainer's *Crucifixion* with me as the bass soloist. My solo career declined rapidly thereafter, but the Choir embarked upon two decades of ever-increasing achievement and success, in terms of performance standards, public profile, wider involvement and even – given our international links – benign political influence. The Choir has also 'caught the moment' with concerts to commemorate the Queen's Coronation Golden Jubilee as well as the year in which Her Majesty became our longest-reigning monarch, the bicentenary of the death of Nelson, the centenary of the Royal Air Force, and the commemoration of the 1918 Armistice and the sacrifices of the First World War.

The fortunes and finances of the Choir have been guided by the skills and commitment of many parliamentarians, both Members and staff, but we have been extraordinarily lucky to have had a musical director and conductor, and an accompanist /répetiteur/conductor/composer, both of huge musical talent and enthusiasm. Not only that, but they have both had a cheerful and philosophical attitude to dealing with a large amateur choir of varying abilities and experience, not always of 100% attendance nor of 100% timeliness as they balance their parliamentary commitments with the much more delightful exploration of a wide range of choral music.

Simon and Nick have shown great faith in us, but every now and again they have stiffened the ranks with some ringers. During a break in rehearsals, I once turned to the charming chap next to me who said that he was a bit tired because he had flown in overnight from New York. 'Oh, yes,' I said, 'and what were you doing there?' 'Er, accompanying Bryn at Carnegie Hall.' And, of course, it was the delightful Malcolm Martineau. On another occasion I suggested to the contralto next to me that we should go for a drink. She demurred, saying that she needed to study the score. I expressed astonishment; she had seemed to be doing pretty well to me. 'No,' she said, 'I have to bone up on the choruses. I only know the arias in this work.'

We, the foot soldiers of the Choir, have been greatly privileged to sing alongside some of the greatest performers of the day: Dame Emma Kirkby (I remember the thrill of singing in the very first concert, *Messiah* in St Margaret's, with Emma as soprano soloist), Sir Thomas Allen, Dame Felicity Lott, Catherine Wyn Rogers, James Gilchrist, Michael George and so many others. And can any amateur choir have been so privileged as to sing in such wonderful surroundings? The Tower of London, the Royal Naval Chapel at Greenwich, Westminster Abbey, Westminster Cathedral, St John's Smith Square, York Minster, Coventry Cathedral, the Royal Festival Hall, the Banqueting House and many others.

As we complete our first two decades, Simon and Nick deserve special praise. Simon can put a tiger in the tank of any choir, and his special brand of fervour when necessary and calm when needed are both memorable and reassuring. I shall never forget his wonderful gesture to set us off in *Zadok* in Westminster Abbey – nor his equanimity in then keeping the State Trumpeters of the Household Cavalry on side when they were a hundred yards and half a beat away. And we have all benefited from Nick's extraordinary skills. There was a rumour that he once played a wrong note (in 2001, I think it was) – but the rumour was proved to be unfounded.

What a wonderful two decades. Here's to the next two!

Fiona Mactaggart

When I was first elected, I remember saying to Paul (now Lord) Boateng, 'How come I used to see you at the opera? I can never get there now because of having to be here to vote.' He replied, 'I missed the last act.' Well I am not prepared to part-enjoy opera, so being elected to Parliament crushed my participation in the cultural life of London. I was thrilled when the Choir was formed, and enthusiastically joined despite not being able to read music (I can decode it, rather like some of the children I had previously taught who could sound out written text without being confident of its meaning).

At the start, as I drove to and from my Slough constituency, I played Choraline discs, which use an oboe as the alto part, to learn the music and to supplement Simon's excellent rehearsals. Going into the beautiful St Mary Undercroft on Tuesday evenings to start with, but then on Mondays, naughtily missing the meeting of the Parliamentary Labour Party, was a welcome break in the routine of the week. Artistically, hearing music – some of which I knew well, others, such as the Ryba or Nick's compositions were completely new to me – and physically, making music uses muscles which don't get a proper workout in the largely sedentary life of Parliament.

At the second *Messiah* we were asked to invite a bass, tenor, alto and soprano from our constituencies, but I was not confident that I would find those from Slough, so I asked a good friend and bass, Tony Burch. However, then I could not make the concert, so I handed him over to colleague Helen Jackson to join her group. It's great that he is still an active member of the Choir.

While I was a Minister, between 2003 and 2006, I rarely attended rehearsals or concerts, but then I became an active member once again. One of the most challenging was the *Ryba Mass* – not only did I have to struggle to decode the music, but also to pronounce a language which sometimes includes words with four consecutive consonants.

I didn't make it to Prague for the repeat of that concert, but was thrilled to participate in the Paris concert. After a performance at the British Embassy, singing Nick O Neill's composition *Tu es Petrus* at Notre-Dame is a vivid memory, as we filled that glorious space with massive noise before the tragic fire.

My sister lives in Oxford, so I was able to stay with her and walk to the Sheldonian for our

I have left Parliament, but not the Choir. When I return for rehearsals, former colleagues tend to look askance, wondering what I am doing. It's not hard. I wanted to leave Parliament, but I do not want to leave one of the most stimulating and powerful musical experiences of my life – the Choir.

Fiona Mactaggart

wonderful and moving performance of *Gallipoli to the Somme*, I think that this, and the Britten *War Requiem* performance at Coventry Cathedral with local singers from Coventry, were real examples of how music can convey the horror of war and the value of peace.

I have left Parliament, but not the Choir. When I return for rehearsals, former colleagues tend to look askance, wondering what I am doing. It's not hard. I wanted to leave Parliament, but I do not want to leave one of the most stimulating and powerful musical experiences of my life – the Choir.

Sarah Teather

I joined the Parliament Choir the night before I was sworn in to Parliament after the Brent East by-election in 2003. The Choir was something of a sanity saver during my twelve years in Parliament. Music is a hugely important part of my life, but the nature of elected politics, with its madly long and unpredictable hours, makes singing with others pretty much impossible. Rehearsing on the Parliamentary Estate, with freedom to run for the division bell when required, made it possible for me to go on making music with others, and for that I am incredibly grateful.

We did some fun gigs in my time too. I particularly enjoyed singing *Elijah* in Westminster Cathedral, which is a grand location. And I recall having to perform a small solo as part of a trio in that.

The Choir was also an important source of unlikely friendships. You get to sing alongside people of all parties, in the Commons and the Lords. I came to know and hugely like Caroline Spelman through the Choir, as I recall slightly disrupting my willingness to be confrontational when we were shadowing one another on the Front Bench! It even laid the ground for a duet we performed for another charity event.

The most important friendships for me, ultimately, were with a number of the officers who work in the House, who I would simply never have come to know in any other setting. One of these friendships outlasted my time (and theirs) in Parliament, and is one I suspect I will keep for life. New friends are a precious gift and something I shall always thank the Parliament Choir for.

Parliamentary Staff Past and Present and Members' Spouses

Lady Horam

Group singing is cheaper than therapy, healthier than drinking, and certainly more fun than working out. It is the one thing in life where feeling better is pretty much guaranteed.

Group singing is cheaper than therapy, healthier than drinking, and certainly more fun than working out. It is the one thing in life where feeling better is pretty much guaranteed.
Lady Horam

Lieutenant-General David Leakey

The origins of Black Rod date back nearly 600 years to the 1350s – some would say a recent and minor development in the great span of British history! Certainly, there is no record of previous Black Rods having sung in the Parliament Choir. However, during my first week in office, I discovered the Choir rehearsing in the Chapel of St Mary Undercroft and I seldom missed a rehearsal thereafter.

Very few Members of either House, let alone members of the public, have more than

The Chapel of St Mary Undercroft looking East

Suffice to say that, during my seven years' tenure as Black Rod, the two-hour weekly choir rehearsal on a Monday evening in the Chapel provided a blissful, stimulating and refreshing retreat from the immediate and often pressing demands of 'Black Roddery' in Parliament.

David Leakey

the slightest notion of Black Rod's job. Most have a vision of a bemedalled, retired military officer making his (and now her) annual appearance at the State Opening of Parliament, banging on the door of the House of Commons Chamber armed with a Black Rod and wearing breeches, a Victorian court coat, stockings and diamante-buckled black patent leather slippers – no one would imagine that Black Rod would or even could sing bass in the Parliament Choir!

The truth is that Black Rod has a miscellany of operational responsibilities which are constantly changing when new appointees take over or as the structures of the Houses' administration are reshaped. During my tenure, responsibilities centred around 'security' – a 24/7 cause of major disruption to my family, social and sometimes choral life – contingency planning and preparations for the unthinkable disasters which could befall Parliament, including its no-notice relocation and continuity of full operating capacity at some other venue in London or elsewhere in the country, handling the emergency responses to daily incidents, orchestrating the ceremonial and other major 'events' on the Estate, co-ordinating access, discipline, public order and so on. Suffice to say that, during my seven years' tenure as Black Rod, the two-hour weekly choir rehearsal on a Monday evening in the Chapel provided a blissful, stimulating and refreshing retreat from the immediate and often pressing demands of 'Black Roddery' in Parliament.

One of the lesser-known facts about the Palace of Westminster is that in 1964 the Queen decided to hand over 'ownership' of the Royal Palace of Westminster respectively to the House of Lords and the House of Commons. A well-defined architectural map was drawn up to show which House was to own and control which parts of the Palace. However, in making these arrangements with Parliament, Her Majesty decided that certain parts of the Palace should, nonetheless, remain under the Sovereign's 'ownership'. These included the Sovereign's Entrance, the Robing Room and the Royal Gallery (all at the Lords' end of the Palace) and Westminster Hall and the Chapel of St Mary Undercroft (at the Commons' end of the Palace). The day-to-day management of these areas was delegated to Black Rod – sometimes referred to as the Queen's representative in Parliament. In reality, the Sovereign's 'agent'.

Perish the thought that Black Rod was ever party to the occasionally disruptive, albeit good humoured, 'back bench' behaviour by the basses in the Choir. However, admonishment or punishment was minimal because Black Rod's membership of the basses and the Choir, as the Sovereign's agent, was seen as advantageous with regard to potential challenges to the Parliament Choir's use of the Chapel (and its beautiful organ) for its rehearsals. For the seven years of my tenure as Black Rod and controller of the Royal Chapel, there was certainly no challenge or doubt about the Choir's priority for use of the Chapel; that precedent or tradition continues rock solid today.

But it was Black Rod's influence over the use of Westminster Hall and responsibility for organising and conducting major events in Westminster Hall that was most advantageous to the Choir, securing its use and setting the arrangements as a venue for some prestigious – even historic – concerts by the Choir, as reported elsewhere.

The most memorable of my personal Black Rod experiences in the Parliament Choir was on a day in May 2017 at the end of the final rehearsal in the Royal Festival Hall with three other choirs and the joint forces of the Southbank Sinfonia, two brass bands and the RFH organ, for our performance of Walton's *Belshazzar's Feast*. Simon Over completed the rehearsal with the usual reminders and announcements. The last of these was that it was Black Rod's birthday! Spontaneously, the massed voices of choral singers, orchestra, bands and the huge organ belted out 'Happy Birthday' to Black Rod – a huge sound in the Royal Festival Hall, which still rings embarrassingly in my ears. For that and for seven very happy years of singing in the Parliament Choir – thank you.

Delyth Jewell MS

Singing with the Parliament Choir was one of the greatest pleasures I had during my time working in Westminster. During the course of my time with the Choir, there were many funny incidents, a number of which seemed to revolve around the then Black Rod, David Leakey. After one concert, when I was relatively new to the Choir, I was standing waiting for a tube train and noticed that a man was standing at the other end of the platform and was carrying a red Parliament Choir folder. I went up to speak to him, introducing myself, and heard him say that he was with 'ACKROD'. I thought, 'Ah, I'm not sure what that acronym stands for,' so continued to talk about my work as a researcher. It was only when we stepped onto the tube a few minutes later that I realised that the man had told me that he was Black Rod. I was mortified, and explained that I hadn't recognised him without his tights.

A few months later, ahead of one of our concerts, my friends in the sopranos and I were lost in the corridors under the concert venue. David Leakey was somehow with us (he's in all of my best stories it seems!). We came upon a door that was locked and my soprano friends and I were trying desperately to push the door open. Quick as a flash, from behind us, Black Rod said, 'I tend to knock.'

The Parliament Choir was also one of the first times I encountered someone else called Delyth. Somehow, I'd been the only Delyth in my school in Wales, and I went to university in England so there weren't any Delyths there either. In my first rehearsal with the Choir, a kind lady had let me share her music, and at the end of the rehearsal I turned to thank her for doing so. I said 'my name's Delyth.' And she looked at me with astonishment, and said 'but that's my name.' No one around us could quite understand how novel it was for both me and Baroness Delyth Morgan to meet someone who shared our name!

Finally, I had bittersweet news in January 2019 when I learned that I would take a seat in the Welsh Parliament when my friend, Steffan Lewis, passed away. One of my soprano friends, Michaela, announced to the Choir at the end of rehearsal that that would be my last rehearsal. So many kind friends I'd made over the years of singing were incredibly supportive. I miss singing with the Choir very much. I hope that you'll be able to visit Wales soon.

Philippa Carling

A few of us current members of the Parliament Choir, including six or seven of the altos, have been members since the first concert in St Margaret's. An unusual feature is how far some of us travel to sing in the Choir. The ones I know about are David Orton from Nottingham, Virginia Hawkins from Gloucestershire and I come down from North Norfolk.

I was working in the Commons Library and after the 1992 election, Library Management conducted a staff survey asking for suggestions about the Library. Top of the list of suggestions was the desire for a choir. This showed the appetite for a workplace choir and the House of Commons Library Choir was born, predating the Parliament Choir by around seven years. We were lucky to have a couple of able choir leaders and pianists among the staff and we sang in Derby Gate in the lunch hour. So I was delighted when the Parliament Choir was formed in 2000. Now I have been singing for longer in the Parliament Choir after I retired from the Library than before it.

Singing is important to me primarily because I love music, particularly sacred music. It challenges the brain but also the body, because it is, after all, a physical exercise. But no matter how tired I might feel going into a choir practice, I forget that as soon as the practice begins and I always feel good afterwards. There is recent scientific research showing why this should be so. Choral singing is also, of course, a social activity and I have friends in the Choir, several of whom I knew from working in the House of Commons.

The only reason I got a job in Parliament was so I could join the Parliament Choir.
Maggy Dean

Maggy Dean

The only reason I got a job in Parliament was so I could join the Parliament Choir. Maggie Ronald is a founder member of the Choir and for years she kept telling me how wonderful the Choir was. Maggie and I go back a long way. As second altos we sang together in Goldsmiths Choral Union from the 1980s all the way through until she joined the Parliament Choir. In 2014, she told me Simon was looking for some additional 'confident' altos and was prepared to audition me one Monday lunchtime. So along I went. It's quite terrifying, singing alone in the Chapel. But I passed and was allowed to join as an extra. I was thrilled! Someone suggested I look for a job in Parliament, so a few months later I filled in an application form to be a Project Manager in the Parliamentary Digital Service. I got the job and the rest is history. I spent four of the best years of my life working in the Palace of Westminster on a cyber security programme, making Parliament a safer place for everyone working there. And every Monday I was privileged to sing glorious music in the Chapel with Simon and Nick. I'm immensely grateful to Simon for opening the door to me!

Libby Dewdney-Herbert

I was in the school choir but knew very little about the sheer joy of choral music until I was introduced to the Parliament Choir by a friend in 2000. Little did I know back then how much I was going to enjoy the next 20 years of singing and, in particular, the privilege of singing in some of the most historic and iconic venues in London.

Singing in a choir means so many things – I love the discipline of gathering together once a week and tackling a previously unknown work together. It has always been a big part of my week's structure, and on those rare occasions when I've had to miss rehearsals something is lacking. However tired I feel at the end of a working day, singing is such a positive and energy-giving thing and there's always a sense of achievement when a small section or bar falls into place, particularly if it's been a bit of a struggle!

Christine, Lady Judd

I have always loved music, especially early music, and sing in our small church choir in Cumbria. Frank (Lord Judd) and I welcomed the establishment of the Parliament Choir and attended many of the early concerts. Jean Corston, who used to sing first soprano, shared an office with Frank in the Lords and persuaded me to join, promising that I would not have to undergo an audition! I joined in 2008, sang in *The Apostles* that autumn, and have loved every minute!

When you are very busy and multi-tasking it is wonderfully relaxing to be able to concentrate on one thing for a couple of hours. I find it challenging, uplifting and refreshing. I love the joy of singing, the challenge of learning difficult things, the pleasure of deepening understanding of the music and, of course, the friendships made.

We played a recording of the Choir singing a section of the Mozart *C Minor Mass* at Frank's funeral, so important was the Choir to him.

Nicholas O'Neill and Simon Over leading a study day at St Clement Danes in 2019

Susan Madel

Coming into the Palace of Westminster to sing on Monday evenings is like coming home.

Both my first and second husbands entered Parliament in June 1970. My second husband, David, retired in 2001 and joined us in 2013; we were married soon after that.

I have always enjoyed singing in choirs apart from the busy years when I was a Conservative MP's wife with little children; my generation were very much part of constituency life.

Coming into the Palace of Westminster to sing on Monday evenings is like coming home.
Susan Madel

Then there was a career in public affairs. My last project, with Sir Stephen O'Brien, was creating the All-Party Parliamentary Group on Malaria and Neglected Tropical Diseases which he chaired, and which I co-ordinated from 2003 to 2017.

I joined the Choir in 2010 for therapeutic reasons after the death of my son Jonathan. (Although a successful lawyer, all he really wanted to do was go into Parliament.) Singing was a complete escape from reality for me.

Simon and Nick are such an inspiration: their brilliant musicality, painstaking attention to detail, their humour and patience have taught me so much. There is nothing more thrilling than singing those dizzy high octane runs in so many iconic venues.

Maggie Ronald

The thread running through these 20 years is the real pleasure of belonging to a group of like-minded people – many now good friends – and seeing our musical abilities flourish under the patient, thorough care of Simon and Nick. Long live the Parliament Choir!

The thing I always notice about singing is that I may arrive at the practice quite weary and flat but have much more energy and lightness by the end.
Maggie Ronald

My Dad was a music teacher, writing music and running various choirs, so singing regularly was part of family life. I started work in *The Times* office at Westminster in November 2000 and joined the Parliament Choir the following January, just missing the inaugural *Messiah*. (I have only missed about three concerts since then.)

Pre-retirement, it would be a full-on day in Westminster, mostly as senior caseworker for MPs. Now, Mondays start with a local exercise class and often an afternoon jaunt into town to catch an exhibition before the rehearsal.

The thing I always notice about singing is that I may arrive at the practice quite weary and flat but have much more energy and lightness by the end. Concentrating on learning a piece and getting out of your comfort zone gives you a real sense of achievement.

Daniella Fetuga-Joensuu

First and foremost, I believe that the Parliament Choir is one of the most reputable choirs of the world. I could be accused of being biased, of which I am utterly guilty, but that is why I became a member. I first got to know about the Choir through my colleagues and my boss at the House of Lords at the time. My former boss is still a member. I was already a member of my church choir, but the Parliament Choir is special, and not just because we rehearse in St Mary Undercroft, but due to the wonderful music we produce and the exquisite concerts. Prayer at Parliament for me is vital, and to be able to sing some of the best prayers is just magnificent. It is partly justice in action. I pray that music will never cease at Parliament. May the Choir continue to grow from strength to strength.

John Dawson

What I really like about the Choir is (as I have worked for Conservative MPs including Bob Blackman, Sir Oliver Letwin and Nickie Aiken for more than 10 years), that it is 'the staff choir.' Of course, I enjoy the singing very much, but also the social life and how the Choir breaks down barriers. No matter which political party a member belongs to we all get on well together, irrespective of title, income, race, ethnicity and sexual orientation. The Parliament Choir not only shows that it cares for its members but also that we care for others in the community, as was demonstrated in December 2019 when members of the Choir sang with members of a group of disabled singers from Colchester in the Speaker's State Apartments.

These are things that warm me to the Choir and I know have greatly contributed to its success over the last 20 years.

Annalise Pask

What I love most about the Choir are, without doubt, the friendships I have made through a shared love of singing: for fun, but at an ambitious standard we can be truly proud of. We are all amateurs but have had the privilege of singing in some extraordinarily special places. I have learned so much from Simon and Nick – their commitment, incredible musical talents, remarkable patience and good humour have made the Choir what it is.

Andrew Tuggey

Having been working in Parliament since January 2004, running the Commonwealth Parliamentary Association (CPA UK) in Westminster Hall opposite St Mary Undercroft, I eventually plucked up courage and joined the Parliament Choir as a second tenor in 2010. My previous singing had been as a choirboy and at school in Reading. It was a great decision and one of the best I have made. I was so glad I joined, but pretty cross with myself for not doing so earlier. Singing in the Parliament Choir is a great experience in so very many ways: jolly nice people from within and without Parliament, marvellous music sung in tremendous cathedrals, churches and concert halls, huge musical learning – and, of course, Simon and Nick! What a privileged experience it was being led, cajoled, taught, 'persuaded' by them both and conducted in such fantastic places by Simon, plus singing with our 'own' wonderful Southbank Sinfonia. The high spots? There were many. One has to be singing in Notre-Dame in May 2016 and feeling the music, especially Nick's *Tu es Petrus* being absorbed through that great Cathedral, up to the roof and floating all the way down the nave to the high altar. That experience, of course, has been made even more nostalgic because of the awful fire, but another was May 2017's performance of *Belshazzar's Feast* at the Royal Festival Hall. That was hugely exciting and so much fun. I also shall not forget the concerts at St John's Smith Square and the great camaraderie in the restaurant. Thank you, the Parliament Choir. I hugely miss singing with you all, but

Rehearsing in Notre-Dame

no longer working in Parliament and living in Monmouth makes it a little challenging, so I have exchanged my Red Leather folder for the Black Leather folder of the lovely Hereford Choral Society where we sing in the wonderful Hereford Cathedral and where one of our Patrons is the good Robert Rogers, the Lord Lisvane. That my first concert with my new choir was *The Creation* and the next planned is *Belshazzar's Feast* has been happily reassuring! I'm delighted, too, that my successor and members of the CPA UK team continue to sing in the Parliament Choir.

Lesley Titcomb

The Parliament Choir has been a real source of relaxation and support to me for nearly 20 years, since my husband (Mark Prisk) became an MP. I've found rehearsing and performing with the Choir to be a great way of switching off from the stresses of my own job. I've learnt a huge amount, my sight-singing has been transformed and my vocal range extended.

Christine Heald

I had wanted to join the Choir since its beginning, but children and pets kept me in Hertfordshire. Finally, in 2010, I decided I had to make time for myself and, with my great friend in the House, Diana Thompson, we turned up at the Chapel on a Tuesday evening (as it then was) and took the plunge. Our timing was good, as rehearsals of the Brahms *German Requiem* had just begun; perhaps not the easiest piece to start with but we were spurred on by the lovely Head of German from Westminster School, Richard Stokes, who came each week to help us with the pronunciation, and who regularly assured us that 'German is the language of love.'

Diana and I both knew several choir members and immediately felt at home. Our only confusion came at the end of each rehearsal when Simon started talking about those going to an unpronounceable place for an unpronounceable weekend (of course, it was the Anghiari Maratona!).

When Fiona, Choir Secretary for several years, announced that she was retiring, the Trustees faced a dilemma. They had been informed that BT was no longer able to give the generous support it had offered since the beginning of the Choir and finances had to be reviewed. Appointing another paid Secretary would stretch the budget, so I proposed to Caroline Spelman, then Chairman, and Mark Prisk, then Treasurer, that I would be willing to take over the admin until the situation became clearer. I became the Voluntary Secretary – how hard could it be? Of course, I had quite underestimated the amount of work Fiona had had to do and I turned to Diana for help, which she gave willingly. Gift Aid submissions to HMRC haunt us to this day. But the Choir team – Simon, Nick, the Trustees and above all, Anna as Choir Manager – kept us afloat during an exciting period. My proudest moments were being involved in bringing together our concerts in Notre-Dame and the Bundestag. I can still recreate in my mind the magic of those performances.

We have been extremely fortunate to have Aileen, an existing choir member, as Secretary. She has run the Choir with superb efficiency and good humour. During lockdown I missed everyone so much. It is wonderful to be back together.

Helen Wilkins

Being invited to join the Parliament Choir was an honour yet it filled me with conflicting feelings of ambivalence – it took me straight back to a memory of one assembly morning, sitting cross legged on mats aged five, in our school hall at Nakasero Prep School, Kampala, Uganda, when we were told auditions for the choir would take place the following week.

I was so excited as I loved singing and couldn't wait to tell my mother at school pick-up time. The following week I counted the days to the Friday audition thinking I would be able to impress them with my high notes. As luck would have it, I woke up with a sore throat the day before the audition and being a timid, yet proud, child told the teacher I had a sore throat and she accepted it. I was gutted. I held it together until I got home but when my mother asked me how it went, I burst into tears – so disappointed was I.

Why the sob story? Well as it happens, I did join the choirs in my next school and we won many competitions. When I became Verger of the Chapel of St Mary Undercroft and was involved in helping arrange the

Helen Wilkins, Verger, Chapel of St Mary Undercroft

Chapel for the Monday rehearsals, I used to have a quiet longing, wishing that I was singing with them. Alas, like the sore throat, my sight-reading ranges from non-existent to pitiful so did not dare. Imagine my joy, therefore, when Simon Over and others asked if I would like to join and the disappointment that I felt all those many years before was swept away by the wave of kindness, warmth and banter of the Choir members. To mention but a few, Anna Yallop, Aileen Walker, Sally Martin-Brown and Lady Heald have been supportive of all the Choir members, which enables us to just enjoy the rehearsals. I will always remember how thrilled, honoured and humbled I felt to be asked to read at the Christmas concert. Another memorable occasion was when the Bundestag Choir and the UK Parliament Choir sang in Westminster Hall. It was a privilege to be on the right side of history.

Another memorable occasion was when the Bundestag Choir and the UK Parliament Choir sang in Westminster Hall. It was a privilege to be on the right side of history.

Helen Wilkins

Guest Members

Although it is often assumed that the Parliament Choir consists exclusively of Members of Parliament, most members of the Choir are or have been employed on the Parliamentary Estate, whether as former Black Rod or archivist, as HR executive or one who works the telephones, as Hansard editor or as researcher. There are also several Members' spouses and some guest members, those who do not possess a parliamentary pass, but who have the pleasure and privilege of belonging, too. The only distinction is that these latter must audition to Simon and Nick, whereas all MPs, Peers and staff are free to join without qualification. As Mary Macleod writes, 'Having some members of the Choir who are not parliamentarians strengthens who we are, and is a symbol of how each part of the economy and community cannot achieve much by working in isolation.'

Solomon Abraham

Growing up in India, I had heard of the most iconic places in London such as Westminster Abbey, St Paul's Cathedral, the Royal Albert Hall and of course, the Houses of Parliament. After moving to the UK in the late nineties, while I had the privilege of singing in all these places with the London Philharmonia Chorus, never did I imagine I would be entering the Palace of Westminster one day to sing with the

Solomon Abraham

Parliament Choir! It was my friend Roger Woodward from the Imperial Male Voice Choir who arranged for an audition. Although I was not new to auditions, it never gets any easier. But Nick in his quiet but humorous way made me feel at ease and I soon enjoyed the feeling of singing in the beautiful empty chapel. And, to my pleasant surprise, I was invited to join the Choir!

Apart from the Parliament Choir, I am also a member of the Imperial Male Voice Choir and the Civil Service Choir. I also sing for a male voice quartet based in India with the sole purpose of promoting Gospel music in that part of the world. Thanks to technology, we have been able to produce a number of music videos both in English and in Tamil and promote them via YouTube.

The Parliament Choir has given me the opportunity to perform some exciting music in great venues and helped me to improve my musical knowledge and vocal production. I have also improved my musicianship under the direction of both Nick and Simon and it has given me the chance to make some wonderful new friends. David Orton's ever-present smile and Lord Wallace's friendly greetings make it feel good to be part of the bass section.

At the October 2018 concert to commemorate the 1918 Armistice, I was given the great privilege of representing the Commonwealth and read a poem in remembrance of the fallen soldiers from India who fought alongside the British troops in the First World War. It was one of the most humbling and cherished moments of my singing career. I hope the Choir continues to be a source of inspiration to many singers and grows from strength to strength.

Sally Cantello

I joined the Parliament Choir in 2007 in a year of great personal sadness and can genuinely say that it changed my life.

All choirs offer the chance to experience the joy of singing and the sense of community and harmony that comes from making music together. But the Parliament Choir, with the calibre of its directors, its naturally collaborative nature and the international links it has built over the years, offers its members so much more.

Firstly, it has access to some of the most prestigious venues, not only in the UK but across Europe. How many other non-auditioning amateur choirs get to sing in Westminster Hall, York Minster, Lancaster House, Cadogan Hall, Westminster Cathedral,

I recall from one of our early concerts, when we performed the Messiah in the Central Hall, and Simon thought it wise to add some 'reinforcements' to ensure that we sounded good enough (I assume that was his underlying aim...) Janet Cohen – Baroness Cohen, a stalwart alto in our first few years – turned to the young lady who came to sit next to her in our final rehearsal, and asked her in order to be sociable 'Have you sung this many times before?' To which the young lady replied 'Not the chorus parts.' Janet thought it was the most wonderful put-down.

William Wallace

One of the funniest moments for me in the Choir was when Nick told the basses that we were sounding far too posh in the Verdi Requiem. *I looked either side of me and there was a Viscount, two Lords and a Conservative MP.*
Edward Webb

Coventry Cathedral et al – not to mention Notre-Dame, St Vitus Cathedral in Prague and the German Bundestag?

The international relationships that have resulted in invitations to sing in these European venues have been a result of the Choir's gift for developing friendly collaborations, helped possibly by the prestige of being the choir of the UK's Parliament. So much pleasure has been had from performing alongside Czech, German, Italian, South Korean and New Zealand singers, particularly when joining with them in pieces integral to their culture.

The Choir's 'house band', Southbank Sinfonia (SbS), has offered the Choir the opportunity of working with gifted young players at the start of their careers. Many choir members have become supporters of the orchestra, financially and otherwise, and watch with avuncular pleasure as each year's cohort grows in skill and confidence and as the institution itself builds international prestige and renown. In addition, the Choir's performances with SbS have offered talented young singers a platform in top class venues as soloists, helping them with their nascent careers in this most difficult of professions.

And finally, the SbS link to the annual Anghiari Festival in Tuscany has led to many choir members collaborating with a local amateur choir to form the Anghiari Festival Chorus and sing together in stunning locations in and around this beautiful medieval fortified hilltop town. It was directly after my first visit to Anghiari that I met my husband, Bill, whilst sailing at Cowes. I'm sure the 'happy place' I was in after experiencing the joys of the festival helped the mutual attraction. As I said, the Parliament Choir changed my life!

Caroline Pereira

In the wake of losing my father back in the early spring of 2009, Lady (Rose) Luce, a dear family friend, asked if I would like to join the Parliament Choir as a temporary member in order to bump up numbers for *Messiah* to be performed in York Minster that autumn. I was flattered and delighted and without hesitation I jumped on board! A moment that I thought was to be short but sweet became and continues to be the greatest and the most pleasurable of journeys I could have wished for. To be part of a community of people that share the joy of singing but, equally, have many personal life stories to tell has been both humbling and touching. In equal measure it is the greatest honour and pleasure to be taught and guided by both Simon and Nick. It is their absolute dedication and energy that inspires us all. I personally cannot thank them enough. During the Covid-19 lockdowns the absence of our Monday evening rehearsals brought home how important the Choir is to me.

Tessa Murdoch

I joined the Parliament Choir in October 2019 at the suggestion of Hugh Merrill, a friend from the Silver Society. My late father, Sir Anthony Meyer (1920–2004), was Member of Parliament from 1964 to 1966 for Eton and Slough and then from 1970 to 1992 for West Flintshire which was renamed Clwyd, North-West in 1983. My mother, Barbadee Meyer, was a very active parliamentary wife so I was able to attend debates in my teens and often

Rehearsing Mendelssohn's Lobgesang

met my parents in the Palace of Westminster. Our two elder daughters, Iona and Frances, were baptised in the Chapel of St Mary Undercroft in June 1984 and March 1986 with a celebratory family tea for friends and godparents afterwards in the House of Commons. The opportunity to rehearse regularly in that sacred space and to sing as a soprano in Elgar's *The Dream of Gerontius* in Westminster Cathedral a month after the canonisation of John Henry Newman was irresistible. When the Choir Secretary asked for recommendations for readings for the 2020 Christmas concert at St John's Smith Square, I suggested the 'Christmas Poem' written by Alice Elgar in Rome in 1907 and first performed by the choristers of Hereford Cathedral in Hereford City Hall on New Year's Day 1908, a fact which I discovered when undertaking research for the V&A's Hereford Screen in 2016 in my capacity as V&A Head of Metalwork Collections.

Alan Walker gives an outsider's view from the Tenor section

My introduction to the Parliament Choir is relatively recent. After a rehearsal for a performance of Handel's *Messiah* with the St Paul's Cathedral Chorus in December 2015, I was approached on the southbound platform at City Thameslink station by Edward Webb, who confided that in addition to singing as

I feel immensely fortunate to have had the chance to take part in such a wide variety of music, in a range of extraordinary venues and among good friends.

Alan Walker

bass with the Chorus he was also singing with the Parliament Choir. He asked if I might like to try out for the tenor section.

Sight-reading some Poulenc was a challenging induction task, but the welcome was extremely friendly and both Simon and Nick are experts at coaxing the best from us. After a couple more rehearsals I was able to set an audition with Nick – terrifyingly, my first formal music assessment since the age of 17 (some years previously!). He skilfully guided me past any inadvertent errors and confirmed I would be allowed to join the Choir.

Thus began not only the immense privilege of rehearsing regularly in St Mary Undercroft but also a highly memorable series of concerts in splendid locations, with a fine group of singers and a range of very talented musicians. I feel immensely fortunate to have had the chance to take part in such a wide variety of music, in a range of extraordinary venues and among good friends. Thank you very much for having me, and here's to the next 20 years.

Roger Woodward

I came to the Parliament Choir from the St Paul's Cathedral Chorus in what was a series of extraordinary coincidences and I have the former England cricket captain, Alastair Cook, to thank. His father and I were school friends and, having been out of touch for 40 years, through Alastair, we got back together. Only then did I discover that Alastair, in his time, had been a chorister at St Paul's and his parents had joined the SPCC. They were still singing there, so I went along to the *St John Passion* in the Cathedral and that was it: a wonderful experience. I just had to join and have been singing *Messiah* in the Cathedral at Christmas ever since. After one *Messiah* rehearsal, recognising one of the basses, Edward Webb, on the City Thameslink platform I started a conversation which led to my discovery of the Parliament Choir. The opportunity to take part in the Choir's fascinating programme sounded really interesting and soon led to not only myself but another St Paul's tenor, Alan Walker, joining on the same night. What a thrill it was to assemble in Westminster Hall before the rehearsal (I still make a point of arriving early so that I can sit and absorb something from those historic stones) and after a week or two, to sing my chorus audition in the Chapel of St Mary Undercroft (possibly less of a thrill for Nick!). It has been a privilege to meet so many interesting people in the PC and to perform in such wonderful venues. I have been singing in groups of one sort or another for many years but I think that Nick and Simon's rehearsals have brought more improvement in my singing than I thought possible, particularly to my sight-reading. My first concert was in the Cadogan Hall, with Notre-Dame de Paris following shortly afterwards, with some very longstanding French friends in the audience, and I have taken part in practically every concert both at home and in three European countries since. I was really looking forward to my first maratona weekend and singing at the Vatican. The only reason for not having 'the full set' is because, unfortunately, the Westminster Christmas concerts have clashed with, for me, the unmissable performances of *Messiah* at St Paul's.

On a personal note: the Choir was a terrific personal help to me in May 2018. While at the final rehearsal for *Gallipoli to the Somme* I received a call from the hospital telling me that my mother had taken a turn for the worse. I left at once of course, but not in time, alas. Two days later, I decided that I would sing in the concert at the Sheldonian Theatre which was a very good decision. People were extremely kind and singing in the concert and seeing friendly faces really helped me focus and come to terms with a dreadful few days and right through to the performance in the QEH.

Alex Ellis, the new British High Commissioner to India, describes the experience of singing in the Choir as 'clearing the day's swirl'

The Choir has been a great enjoyment for me during our time in London. I had only started singing during my last posting in Brazil, in a pick-up choir of diplomats; I was told aged seven that I couldn't sing, and I thought that meant I could never sing – so it was a delight that I took the plunge in Brazil, nearer 50 than 40, and loved it. The Parliament Choir felt like a daunting step when I joined, at the start of 2018, but the basses are a friendly lot and I loved the performance – belting out Maori in the Sheldonian was a great start.

As I grew in confidence, so I enjoyed the rehearsals, and the need to concentrate cleared my mind of all the day's swirl; every Monday night at 8.15pm I would walk to the Tube with a bounce in my step, singing the tune we had been rehearsing, my telomeres repaired by the act of communal singing. No wonder the research shows it to be one of the healthiest of acts.

And what a treat not to watch or hear a masterpiece but to be in it! To unpick *Gerontius*, slowly work your way inside its complexities, to listen to the almost unbearably beautiful tunes of the altos – champions in the field – was a true pleasure; I once went on the Tube with a friend who still had a tear in their eye from rehearsing the end of Part One. To sing the *C Minor Mass* is to have genius rolled out before you, and (remarkably in my case) to have it actually come out of your mouth! And, of course, to turn all that into a public performance in such wonderful places was to give final purpose and form to the rehearsals, and I was fascinated by how the whole emerged from the painstaking process of building and connecting each brick. The light of a bright May afternoon through the windows of the Sheldonian, of a bleak November afternoon through the window of Coventry Cathedral, stays with me.

Michael Atherton wrote that one of the pleasures of opening the batting for England when he started as an international was to watch the best opener in the world, Graham Gooch, at the other end of the pitch. I'm certainly not international class, but I learnt a lot, from Nick, and also some of the singers around me – as ever the best way to learn is proximity to someone who knows what they're doing.

So thanks to all those who have made this such a lovely experience. You inspired me to set up a choir in my department, and I have already discovered a choir in the High Commission in Delhi. So there is much to look forward to, and I'll be back in three or four years.

I once went on the Tube with a friend who still had a tear in their eye from rehearsing the end of Part One.

Alex Ellis

Soloists

Dame Felicity Lott

I vividly remember the concert I took part in, back in 2003, to celebrate the Coronation Jubilee. We should have been in Westminster Hall and rehearsed there; I'd never been there before and it was glorious. Then part of the ceiling fell down and another venue had to be found, as I recall, within 24 hours. Fortunately, we could move to the Abbey. I can see the Choir – with a few extras – piled up on staging; I think I have a photo somewhere. You sang *Zadok the Priest*, guaranteed to make me weep, and so wonderful and appropriate in that setting. I think I sang some Mozart but remember more clearly the 'Brindisi' from *La Traviata*, which I'd never sung before. I fear my Italian may have sounded rather Cheltenham, but Alfredo was Gio Compario himself; Wynne Evans – Italian tenor par excellence. We were talking about it in Cardiff last year!

Jamie MacDougall

It's been my great pleasure to appear with the Parliament Choir over the years – given that the Houses of Parliament where they rehearse has a bar with its own brand whisky, who wouldn't? Seriously, I felt so privileged to be able to rehearse deep in the heart of Parliament in that beautiful Chapel – what a gem.

Music is a great leveller. It unites people with a common purpose or, in the case of the Choir, perhaps that should be a Commons purpose.
Jamie MacDougall

I first sang with the Choir at Gray's Inn, in a concert entitled 'Shore to Shore.' I was drafted in to sing some Scottish songs by Ronald Center, James Naughtie's former music teacher. I think he was there to translate to the audience: after all, I don't think Gray's Inn has heard a rolled 'R' for quite some time. The Choir was very welcoming. I think wearing my kilt helped break the ice on that first encounter – it certainly helped me get a taxi after the event.

My next role was as soloist and quasi-choir ambassador, or perhaps mascot would be a better description, when I was asked to go to South Korea to sing in Mendelssohn's *Lobgesang* with the Choir of the National Assembly of Korea. It was an experience I will never forget: the vastness of the cities and the beautiful concert hall just a few miles away from the world's most protected and guarded border. Accompanied by Simon Over and Lord German, we did our bit for East–West relations. The concert was repeated in London with the UK Parliament Choir and Korean Choir joining forces. It was a truly memorable evening.

But my fondest memory was of the large concert at the Queen Elizabeth Hall. The Choir really showed its fun side, letting its hair down with numbers from opera and musicals. We got to do some G&S and the G&Ts in the interval helped that. But Bernstein's 'Let Our Garden Grow' from *Candide* at the end really showed the mettle of the Choir and was a fitting climax to the night.

It's wonderful to know that there's a choir in the Houses of Parliament. In a place that appears, from the outside, to be so adversarial and confrontational, it's good to know that music is helping so show the way. Music is a great leveller. It unites people with a common purpose or, in the case of the Choir, perhaps that should be a Commons purpose.

Congratulations, and I wish you all many more years of singing together and I hope to share a stage with you in the future.

Soraya Mafi

It has been a pleasure to work with the Parliament Choir both at the Anghiari Festival, and the memorable and moving concert to mark the 100th anniversary of the Armistice at Westminster Hall.

Not only are the Choir a wonderful group of musicians, but they are also a welcoming ensemble, whose warmth not only encompassed me as a visiting soloist, but my family who came to Anghiari and fell in love with the festival, the town, and the people involved in the music-making. The Choir's passion for the music they perform is infectious, and has made the Anghiari Festival a musical event that always holds a place in my heart.

To have performed with the Choir at Westminster, in celebration and reflection of the 100th anniversary of Remembrance Day, was a true honour and an event I will never forget. To see people of different political beliefs stand beside one another and unite through music, in order to remember those lost in World War One was incredibly moving and, to me, truly reflected why singing in choirs and ensembles is such a wonderful and important part of our culture.

Soraya Mafi

Composers

John Rutter

The only question to be asked in the House about the Parliament Choir is why there wasn't one long ago, followed by a vote to decide which of their recent concerts has been the most inspiring. They always say that the really valuable work in the Palace of Westminster

John Rutter

happens behind the scenes, and here is a prime example – except that the Choir, under Simon Over's leadership, is gaining increasing and well-deserved prominence. Here's to many more years of the harmony it brings. The Parliament Choir symbolises something in our world which lies beyond (and, dare I say, above) politics.

Brian Hughes

I was invited by Simon Over to take a rehearsal in London with The Parliament Choir in preparation for a performance of my work, *The Bells of Paradise* which was to take place at Gray's Inn. As the choristers entered the rehearsal venue in ones and twos, I tried to work out whether they were indeed members of the great and good, or secretaries or porters and the like. In the event, it did not matter one jot: the large assembly of singers was as one, and sang with enthusiastic zeal and commitment – a most enjoyable experience.

Live concerts and broadcasts have taken place in Britain and Europe over the last 20 years; I am sure this unique choir will continue to thrive and prosper in this new world of challenges.

For so long as people within the Palace of Westminster can work together in mastering complex scores, in intensive rehearsal, and in coming together as a chorus to produce a body of sound that stirs the hearts of the audience, there is hope for our politics.

Mark Hill QC

Audience

Mark Hill QC

From its inaugural recital of Handel's *Messiah* at St Margaret's Church, Westminster, in December 2000, I have been in musical lockstep with the Parliament Choir for two decades, hearing it perform in venues such as the grandeur of Westminster Hall, the lofty etherealness of Westminster Cathedral, and the war-ravaged and restored cathedral in Coventry. The Parliament Choir has consistently delivered barnstorming performances of major works by, amongst others, Britten, Verdi, Mozart and Elgar, supported by the dynamic Southbank Sinfonia and a host of world-renowned soloists, under the benevolent baton of Simon Over, its charismatic conductor. Concerts fizz with excitement, including the annual Westminster Christmas with its lighter seasonal repertoire.

In the febrile political climate post-Brexit, it is comforting to find harmony amongst parliamentarians and egalitarianism with Peers of the Realm, elected MPs and a wide range of dedicated staff, putting political divides and hierarchies aside in the pursuit of 'one equal music'. The incalculable benefits of soft power through international co-operation, such as with the German Bundestag Choir marking the anniversary of the Armistice, contribute hugely to the comity of nations. For so long as people within the Palace of Westminster can work together in mastering complex scores, in intensive rehearsal, and in coming together as a chorus to produce a body of sound that stirs the hearts of the audience, there is hope for our politics.

Sir Oliver Heald QC MP

Footballers famously have their WAGs and the Parliament Choir has its non-singing followers, often HAPs – Husbands And Partners. A camaraderie has developed at the concerts and as we have got to know each other in Anghiari. We have enjoyed the Choir's programme and Southbank Sinfonia and had a lot of fun.

The Choir has had memorable occasions such as the visit of the Bundestag Choir to Westminster and the concert at Notre-Dame. The German President of the Bundestag, in high emotion, described his feelings about mutual understanding between our nations and the French were very moved that our Parliament Choir was showing solidarity shortly after the Paris terror outrages. The attendance of Foreign Minister and choir stalwart David Lidington enabled the Ambassador to put on a fine reception at our Embassy in rue du Faubourg Saint-Honoré.

The singing is front of house and I pay tribute to my colleagues such as Cheryl Gillan, Bernard Jenkin, Sue Hayman, our Noble Friends, my wife Christine and all singers, performers and the professional team, but there are good moments in the audience too. When the Choir was singing the 'Hallelujah Chorus' at the cloistered nunnery in Anghiari, Tony Ronald and I rose to our feet, honouring King George II's example, to the astonishment of the Italians, wondering what the mad English were up to now.

Some HAPs were a little nervous ahead of the Notre-Dame gig, about Nicholas O'Neill's piece *Tu es Petrus*. At the Cadogan Hall preview, one or two of the less knowledgeable HAPs felt they heard silences in the music. O ye of little faith! When performed at the great Cathedral, the silences disappeared to be filled with the deep echo of the ancient walls. Nick had studied Notre-Dame composers and the gaps were a feature. It was so sad that the Cathedral suffered a terrible fire; let's hope to see it restored to its best, as happened after the Windsor Castle fire.

There is a relaxed atmosphere at the Anghiari Festival with the Choir and Southbank Sinfonia: moments in the Pizzeria, ice cream, occasions such as Sir Thomas Allen singing in Piazza del Popolo, the Wednesday market, where every street is filled with music. There are some wonderful conversations with followers such as Jim Naughtie (singer too) Tony Hall (ex-BBC) and the author of *Ecclesiastical Law*, Mark Hill QC, as well as HAPs such as tunnelling expert Bill Grose, Tony and James; and then after the concerts chatting into the night with the Choir singers – reliving their triumphs and singing songs from *South Pacific* with Veronica, Lady German and Dr Tony Burch in the garden of Il Sasso.

The regular events at Cadogan Hall, St John's Smith Square and Westminster Cathedral have resulted in the discovery of nearby pubs and eateries to celebrate the Choir's successes. We have missed so much with COVID-19, I would love to hope that we can have a grand concert followed by pasta and Chianti as soon as possible.

The German President of the Bundestag, in high emotion, described his feelings about mutual understanding between our nations and the French were very moved that our Parliament Choir was showing solidarity shortly after the Paris terror outrages.

Sir Oliver Heald MP

3. Choir Life

Arriving in Parliament

Vivian Widgery traces the route through Parliament to the Chapel of St Mary Undercroft.

You might not think that Oliver Cromwell, the most puritan of Puritans, the man who banned not just Christmas carols but mince pies, would have anything to do with a choir, even if it were based in his stronghold of Parliament, but you would be wrong. For those who sing in the Choir but do not work there, and are therefore not in possession of a pass, the journey into the hallowed precincts starts under his stern, and no doubt disapproving, gaze. Clutching the invitation that shows that they are members of the Choir, they line up, along with many others, on the slope that leads from St Stephen's entrance (passholders only) down past the magnificent statue of Cromwell, standing tall above them, sword in hand (no fancy horse for the Lord Protector – he leaves them to King Richard the Lionheart, next along), into the security room where they and their possessions are dusted down, scanned and X-rayed before being released through the glass door into what is known as the Parliamentary Estate.

Now that they have been through the modern part of their journey, they find themselves first in the mid-nineteenth century, as they go into the lovely New Palace Yard, with a green and a fountain, the Elizabeth Tower to the far left and, on the right, their next set of doors, the huge and heavy arched oak doors that lead into the magnificence of Westminster Hall. This is the oldest building on the Estate, and virtually the only part of the ancient Palace of Westminster that survives in its original form. No matter how many people are scurrying around, no matter how many times one sees it, this marvel of medieval architecture, with its stupendous hammer beam roof, the largest medieval timber roof in Northern Europe, catches one's breath. Its soaring height, amazing carvings and flagged floor, not just worn by the feet of centuries of visitors but studded with plaques commemorating outstanding events in Britain's history, including the trials of King Charles I and Warren Hastings and the lying-in-state of monarchs and Prime Ministers, up to the addresses given by modern statesmen such as Nelson Mandela, awe the visitor (and the worker) as much the hundredth time as they did the first. We remember, too, the sell-out concerts the Parliament Choir has given there to commemorate the beginning and the end of the First World War, a century after its horrors.

At the far end, a flight of stairs leads up to St Stephen's Hall, and most visitors will go up those stairs and on to their ultimate destination – meetings with MPs, Peers and staff, attendance at Committee meetings or, more likely at 6pm on a Monday evening, a social occasion. Choir members start off on those stairs but then head to the far left hand side, where there is a small, unassuming oak door leading to the glories of St Stephen's Chapel (about which more later). Through the door (generally locked), and down a small staircase they go, ready for another evening of beautiful music and hard work. In a brief journey, the singers have moved through centuries of history on their way to rehearse with the Parliament Choir, and that brief journey is by no means the least of the pleasures of being part of this unique Choir.

The roof of Westminster Hall under restoration 2019

Repertoire and Location: How What and Where We Sing Is Decided

Elizabeth Mann

In the early years, a pattern was established that the Parliament Choir would perform two or three public concerts a year, one of a larger scale than the others, and some private concerts for our then generous sponsors, BT. There are certain peculiarities of this choir, notably the uncertainties caused by general elections, which may mean Members – and members – losing their parliamentary seats. And it is difficult to rehearse in the run-up to an election when Parliament is dissolved. Added complications are the long parliamentary recesses and the party conference season which do not allow very much time for rehearsal for an autumn concert. Consequently, for our major concerts such as *War Requiem*, *Belshazzar's Feast* and *The Dream of Gerontius*, our Music Director wisely allows plenty of lead time, so we are not caught short.

Simon Over is fond of saying, 'Take what the universe gives you and make something of it!'

Simon Over is fond of saying, 'Take what the universe gives you and make something of it!' While the Parliament Choir has many advantages, it has always to be aware of costs. With the high-profile concerts it is easier to find sponsorship and afford the large orchestral forces a Verdi *Requiem* may require. At the other end of the scale, in order to stay within budget, when a piece may be scored for a harp – for example, in a particular arrangement of *Greensleeves* – the harp may have to be ditched and its part played by winds. Not quite the same effect.

Nicholas O'Neill has been the Choir's Composer-in-Residence since 2011, adding that to his roles of Chorus Master and rehearsal accompanist. The Palace of Westminster had not had a composer since Ludford in the sixteenth century, who wrote for the court there. Even so, when you hear we have a Composer-in-Residence it must sound like an absolute luxury and, of course, we know as a choir that we are exceptionally lucky to have pieces specially written for us. Paradoxically, a lot of what Nick does for the Choir is adaptation and arrangement, and this can often save the Choir money. Also, if Nick is writing a new work for us, he will be aware of any other work we will be singing in a particular concert, and of its orchestration. We have sung his setting of the parliamentary prayers *Of All Persons and Estates* in three concerts, and he has re-scored that piece to use the orchestra and soloists to hand. (For example, the Mozart *Requiem* requires two basset horns and three trombones.) And he can also simplify: the double fugue of the *Osanna* in Mozart's *Mass in C minor* appears frighteningly complicated on paper, but when reorganised by Nick (rather than rewritten or rearranged) becomes quite straightforward.

Of course, this is cutting the coat according to the cloth, but it also makes sense overall in putting together a programme. Imaginative concert planning leads to very enjoyable experiences for audience and choir alike. Simon and Nick might find, for example, a Mozart piano concerto which uses similar orchestral forces to the *Requiem* and this can make a delightful concert, especially when the piano soloist is the superb Alessio Bax. Or, in programming what Simon calls 'a carrier bag concert' (because it requires so many different scores to be taken onto the platform), such as the Cadogan Hall celebration of coronation music for HM The Queen becoming our longest-reigning monarch, there is something for everyone and it is great fun to sing.

Also fun to sing and, according to Nick, fun to write are his arrangements of hymns and carols for the Christmas concerts in St John's Smith Square: perhaps particularly *We Three Kings* with its swirling harmonies 'full of Eastern promise' and its insistent bass rhythms – like galumphing camels. This has become an annual hit. Other pieces written to perform at these concerts have been poignant and passionate, notably *This Light of Reason*, commissioned by a choir member after the murder of Jo Cox MP, which sets the luminous imagery of John Donne's prose and offers some hope in a dark world.

Another necessary consideration is what works where. Because of the particular

'Renaissance Rebirth' at St John's Smith Square, 18 March 2015

Rehearsing in Notre-Dame, May 2016

circumstances of the Choir, it is essential that any concert venue is within easy access of Parliament. Central London offers many options: St John's Smith Square, Cadogan Hall, the concert halls of the South Bank and Westminster Cathedral for the largest-scale works. For the RAF centenary concert, we went to the RAF church, St Clement Danes in the Strand. This was so successful that in the following season we tried the Guards' Chapel in Birdcage Walk. There, the Choir sang Nick's new piece *A Certain Everlasting Polyphony*, Haydn's *St Nicholas Mass* and *Te Deum* and Erika Curbelo played the *Trumpet Concerto* with a small orchestra of ten players plus organ. This programme beautifully fitted the acoustic and the scale of the Chapel.

For the Paris concert in Notre-Dame, a programme was devised which Simon describes as an 'English sandwich': Poulenc's *Gloria* and Gounod's *St Cecilia Mass* wrapping Vaughan Williams's *Five Variants of Dives and Lazarus*, Howells' *Behold, O God our Defender* and Nick's new piece *Tu es Petrus*. Nick talks of writing for a particular place, the need to balance clear harmonic progressions with the size of the acoustic. The eight-second delay in Notre-Dame, because of the length and height of the Cathedral, meant him leaving gaps in the music for the sound to catch up. As he said, his use of medieval rhythmic modes, Pérotin's melodies and the sheer weight of eight centuries led to a feeling of 'if stones could speak' and of all sorts of strands coming together. Many members of the Choir attest to an extraordinary sense of the numinous, some even claiming to have seen the ghost of Pérotin. This was not the experience, however, of the London run-through a week before, in the comfortable, well-upholstered Cadogan Hall – a very different acoustic with no echo. *Tu es Petrus* in Notre-Dame, however, was a triumph.

Something to Look Forward to

Mari Takayanagi

I work in the Parliamentary Archives and usually my Monday before a rehearsal consists of a wide variety of public services and outreach tasks. I might be supervising researchers looking at documents in our search room, answering enquiries, or preparing for an exhibition or display. We hold the historic records of the House of Commons and House of Lords going back 500 years, which include a wealth of material on every subject under the sun; we hold the Act of Parliament that naturalised the composer Handel as a British citizen, for example. Then at 6.10pm I realise it's time for choir, and usually end up running along the House of Lords West Front Corridor to make it (more or less!) on time.

Christine Judd

We spend most weekends at our home in Cumbria, so Mondays generally begin with packing, closing up the house and driving to Penrith, usually for the 10.03 train to Euston. In London, Frank would usually go straight to the Lords and I would open up the flat and catch up on work, but would always try to devote at least an hour to go over whatever work we were rehearsing before making my way to Parliament and the Crypt.

Libby Dewdney-Herbert

Mondays are long days – I travel by early train up from Dorset in the morning before rushing to work in Millbank House. There's always masses to catch up on after the weekend and it doesn't take long before 6pm comes and it's time to walk over to the Crypt Chapel for a rehearsal. I've been extraordinarily lucky to have worked in the Palace of Westminster for more than 25 years but walking down the spiral staircase into the Chapel still gives me a thrill.

Rehearsals

Many is the rehearsal that has been interrupted by a policeman, having run down the rather narrow stairs to the Crypt, shouting loudly, 'Division in the Lords' or 'Division in the Commons', with the result that Members of whichever House is having the division then have run back up the stairs to do their democratic duty and vote in the Lobbies.

Of all the pleasures of working in Parliament, singing in the Choir must be near the top, and of all the pleasures of singing in the Choir, rehearsing in the Crypt (or, to give it its proper title, the Chapel of St Mary Undercroft) must be near the top. Just to sit in there admiring its over-the-top decoration is a balm to the soul after a hard-working day. Of course, the style is not to everyone's taste, and I remember being horrified when the soprano sitting next to me one day committed the lèse majesté of saying, 'I really hate all this Victorian excess.'

Of course, you do not turn up faithfully every Monday evening just for the décor, no matter how much you like it. Quite apart from the fact that membership of a choir means that rehearsals are essential, it is such a pleasure, after a long hard day at work, to be doing something different, something both physical and mental, something that challenges the brain in a completely different way from the day job, something that makes you almost a different person from the one working long hours in relative anonymity. A House of Lords Clerk, who spent much of his working day hidden under a wig in the Lords' Chamber, said that it was wonderful to take off that wig and come out of hiding, to meet people who are all in the Choir on the same basis – they love music.

Alas for the poor Members of Parliament, whether they belong to the Upper or Lower House. They are the only ones who can never switch off, as they are always on duty, and have to be ready to vote whenever a division is called. Many is the rehearsal that has been interrupted by a policeman, having run down the rather narrow stairs to the Crypt, shouting loudly, 'Division in the Lords' or 'Division in the Commons', with the result that Members of whichever House is having the division then have run back up the stairs to do their democratic duty and vote in the Lobbies. They nearly always return, though! Such are the demands of singing while representing your country.

Another wonderful thing about rehearsals is the sheer pleasure of working with musicians of an incredibly high calibre, who challenge you to do better every time. Simon's patience, as he coaxes out the best from his amateur choir, is amazing, with only the occasional cry of, 'Look at me, please!' He helps his singers by giving them strong beats, making sure they come in at the right time, explaining what the composer is aiming for. Simon is always ready with a joke or anecdote to keep us going. Mind you, the sopranos still haven't quite forgiven him for the following: 'What's the difference between a soprano and a Rottweiler? Jewellery.'

There is the privilege of working with the Composer-in-Residence for Parliament, of hearing about the thinking behind his latest piece, of understanding what he is trying to do. I have never worked with another composer, but if they are all as intelligent and well-read as Nick, they are clearly a breed apart. He explains the music so well that it helps you to get to the heart of what he is trying to say. Occasionally, he takes a rehearsal: he is a bit harder on us than Simon, and can be quite rude, but we always take it in good part, usually because he's funny about it, and because he's always right! And of course, as an accompanist, Nick helps us so much as we learn the piece.

With the two of them driving us and encouraging us, getting an understanding of a piece of music and learning to sing it go hand in hand, and if the cries of 'Watch' grow a little more frequent as the date of the concert comes nearer, we know that, thanks to their work and ours, the rehearsals have prepared us to face our public and present them with music that they will love, as we have learnt to love it over our months of patient rehearsing.
VW

Study Days

At some point in the lead-up to each major concert a Saturday is found in the calendar where the Choir comes together with its redoubtable and inspiring double act of Simon and Nick, Music Director and Chorus Master, for a whole day of singing (10–4 with a lunch break). This is a wonderful opportunity to explore the music for our next concert with more time and leisure and energy than at the weekly two-hour Monday

That first evening, I discovered that Nick's warm-up regime requires effective breathing and mental agility from singing numbers to days of the week with lots in between. I had to wonder later 'Are you really there?'
Gillian Perry

A study day at St Katherine Cree in the City of London

night rehearsals, and without the interruptions of the Division Bell.

It has huge advantages (and I am sure our maestri see the improvement the following week) as we come to rehearsal fresh and relaxed, not at the end of a stressful working day. The atmosphere is concentrated, dedicated and fun. There is time for sectionals, there is time for note bashing, and there is time to go over and over those tricky passages in the more challenging works, and there is also time to work on the more refined details of dynamics and colour.

To give us a different perspective, occasionally members of the Choir are encouraged to take part in practice days organised by other choirs, such as the 'Come and Sing' days with the Vasari Singers or the Bach Choir. Those of us who took part in it enjoyed an excellent and illuminating day in preparation for *The Dream of Gerontius*, led by the renowned choral conductor David Hill. We were also treated to a day of rehearsal with John Rutter who really showed the Choir how to bring a fresh aspect to the familiar.

Our study days have taken place in various London churches: St Peter's, Vere Street; St Matthew's, Westminster; St Anne and St Agnes, Gresham Street – the headquarters of VOCES8; Pepys's church – St Olave's, Hart Street; St John's, Waterloo; and now, when it is available, St Clement Danes, the RAF church, whose Music Director is none other than our own Simon Over. For our biggest concerts where we are joined by other choirs – Coventry Cathedral Chorus and St Albans Bach Choir, for instance – we have been outside London to a Methodist church in St Albans, convenient for the Midlanders and not at all inconvenient for the Londoners.

I have made many good friends in the Choir. And along with working hard there is, of course, time to socialise over lunches and teas and coffees; these all sweetened by Vivian Widgery's cakes and biscuits which she bakes to raise money for her local food bank. EM

Concert Management

Michael Switsur describes the sometimes challenging business of getting the Choir on stage.

Getting a choir which includes busy Parliamentarians into the right concert seating arrangements at the right time requires organisation. When I was first asked to wrangle the distinguished ranks of Choir members into their concert formations, I thought I would have to draw on the best practices of diplomacy. But there was no reason to be nervous. Unity in working together to deliver the best performances we can is the overwhelming spirit of all the Choir members. There are certainly no prima donnas of a non-musical variety: in the Choir you are a soprano, alto, tenor or bass, regardless that some may be in the Cabinet or sit on the Opposition Front Bench.

Organising one or two hundred singers to line up and process in some of the most awe-inspiring venues has been a joy. Before a concert, the crypts, libraries and vestries of historic buildings such as Notre-Dame Cathedral, Paris, become the spaces where the

Choir draws breath before coming on to perform. In Notre-Dame, I remember leading the Choir to the seemingly never-ending side aisles before processing. Seeing the seraphic looks on people's faces as they took in the surroundings that we were about to fill with astounding music will stay with me forever.

Historic buildings are not without their challenges for performing concerts, but they are well worth the price. Singing the RAF 100 Concert in Sir Christopher Wren's St Clement Danes church meant constructing staging for the Choir to stand on that had to avoid the splendour of Grinling Gibbon's 300-year-old carved wooden pulpit. Wren also provided a sublime setting for us in the Sheldonian Theatre in Oxford. My skills were tested, however, when the evening sun came through the upper clerestory windows, directly into the eyes of the sopranos and altos. I was asked what I could do about it and had to reply that unfortunately, Sir Christopher Wren had not fitted blinds to the windows in 1669. Fortunately, the earth had turned a few degrees before the singing began and all was well.

Behind the Scenes

As with all choirs. there is a huge amount of organisation that goes both into general administration and behind the scenes for every concert successive Choir Managers and Secretaries as well as volunteers have done amazing work over the years, resulting in a well-run choir and culminating in great concerts in some amazing locations.

The Parliament Choir is truly fortunate in its talented and ambitious Music Director and Chorus Master. To keep the Choir running smoothly, the Choir also benefits from the services of a CEO, a Choir Secretary, and volunteer members of the Choir, who contribute to rehearsal and study day arrangements, newsletter production, website maintenance, Choir social events, and Friends Scheme administration.

The Secretary role is a pivotal one: acting as a central communications point. It is hugely rewarding, as secretaries get to work closely with the Music Director, Chorus Master, CEO and Trustees, and they get to know all members of the Choir.

At the beginning Jane Jacomb-Hood was appointed Choir Secretary to work for two days a week. She worked from her home in Aldeburgh, coming up to London weekly for rehearsals. She never missed one in more than eleven years. As the scope of the role increased Denise, on secondment from BT, became Choir Manager and took over some of Jane's responsibilities. When Jane retired in 2012, Fiona Lamming became Secretary, followed in 2014 by Holly Haines, Denise's daughter, a recent graduate who moved on to a full-time job in Parliament. When this happened the Choir no longer had the support of BT and money was short. Christine Heald came to the rescue, offered to take on the administration as a volunteer and her great friend Diana Thompson joined in to help her out. Both were enormously efficient, and Diana took it on herself for one year.

Next came Aileen Walker, who had worked in Parliament for 30 years, becoming Director of Public Engagement in the House of Commons. With apparently effortless professionalism, for two years she combined the role of Secretary with consultancy to parliaments in Africa and elsewhere. At the beginning of 2021 she returned to her native Scotland and the Choir has once again been very fortunate in recruiting Virginia Hawkins who has become our new Choir Manager. She joined the Choir at the start of 2015 when she was seconded to the House of Lords from the National Assembly for Wales. Although she retired from Parliament in 2016, she still loves singing with the Choir and travels in every Monday from the Cotswolds for rehearsals.

Meanwhile Anna Yallop had become Choir Manager and in 2016 was appointed the Choir's first Chief Executive – a role she continues to fulfil with great charm and generosity (as she has not only given freely of her time, but also been very generous financially). She has worked in Parliament since 1997, but her background in law and in the media brings enormous experience and expertise to the work of the Choir. These have proved invaluable in bringing about some of the Choir's most ambitious concerts.

Not least, mention must be made of Val Goss who, with her husband Paul, a fellow tenor, after their first visit to Anghiari bought a house in the town and the following year took on the enormous task of liaison between the Italian organizers and the English contingent, Southbank Sinfonia and the Parliament Choir. She modestly calls this 'helping to strengthen the link with Anghiari', but she has played an essential part in making the Festival run smoothly, in the process learning Italian from scratch, and making the Festival unforgettable for those members of the Choir who have taken up the invitation to sing there. EM

Baroness McIntosh of Hudnall pays tribute to Jane Jacomb-Hood, the Choir's first Secretary, who died in 2021

If you put Jane Jacomb-Hood's name into Google, a small but illuminating collection of references come up which together tell you a lot about who Jane was. There's a link to the Britten-Pears Foundation archive which notes two letters from Jane to Benjamin Britten, dated 1971. There are photographs credited to

Val Goss

Jane Jacomb-Hood with Lord German at her retirement presentation

Jane of Britten and Pears at the piano and of Pears in the first performance of Death in Venice at Snape Maltings in 1973, and charming pictures she took of Imogen Holst's home in Aldeburgh. You can also find evidence of her work in the film and television industry in the 90s, including as Company Secretary to Handbag Television Limited – who knew?

These glimpses reveal three hugely important aspects of Jane's life: her deep connection to Aldeburgh, its music and its most illustrious musicians; her skill as a photographer; and her lifelong love of film. Sadly, there is no link to the Parliament Choir – perhaps we should put that right?

The other great love of Jane's life was her family, particularly her sister Susie and her nephew Ben. Google helps us to understand that too – an obituary for Susie, who died in 2018, shows the depth and warmth of their bond.

Of course, there was much more to Jane than Google can tell. I met her 40 years ago when she became the first-ever Sponsorship Manager at the RSC where I was working at the time, and we remained friends after we'd both moved on. We even set up a film production company together. The film never got made but we had a good time trying! Some years later, when Simon Over and Geoff Filkin were looking for help with administration for the newly formed Parliament Choir, I remembered that Jane, by that time back in her beloved Aldeburgh, might have some time available. The introduction was made and she joined the team where she remained for more than ten years.

Jane was remarkable in many ways. She was charming, talented and well-connected, but also exceptionally modest. Above all she had a gift for friendship, as many Parliament Choir colleagues will testify. She was generous, loyal and always more interested in others than in herself. She loved the Choir. In one of her last emails to me she said, 'Administering the Choir and my time at the RSC were the best times of my life.' We have lost someone very special.

Helen Wilkins recounts some of her more unexpected duties as verger:

When I first arrived as verger, the lighting used for Choir rehearsals was not safe so needed setting up before and removing after rehearsals. I helped oversee the implementation of new lighting that was aesthetically acceptable to the heritage department and acceptable to all stakeholders. This was the legacy of former Black Rod, David Leakey, a great musician and supportive member of the Choir. I also provided fans when it was too hot and heaters when it was too cold. However, this was all done as part of a wider team – I remember Nick O'Neill being infinitely patient on the days he would arrive and the porters had not set up the lighting, or the perseverance of all the members the time they arrived to find a huge flood had blocked the entrance, so with others I ferried and led groups through the 'secret' back entrance to the Chapel!

Friends

Maggy Dean

As the Choir has gone from strength to strength, so the importance of the Friends of the Choir has grown. The Choir now has more than 100 loyal supporters, from across Parliament and beyond. Some Friends sing with the Choir, others have sung with the Choir in the past. Some are parliamentarians, some staff; others are family members or friends. They are all people who value and appreciate the opportunity to hear the Parliament Choir sing fabulous music in amazing venues. Friends commit to making a regular donation to the Choir at a Bronze, Silver, Gold or Platinum level. Their great generosity allows the Choir to plan for the future. Friends receive regular updates about the Choir. In 2018, as a gesture of appreciation, a reception for Friends was held in the Lord Speaker's Apartments.

5. Connections

British Telecom

John Anderson, formerly Managing Director of BT Government describes the exciting journey of BT's relationship with the Choir

It is often said that many great enterprises or achievements start from humble beginnings. For me, that is certainly true when looking back at the history of the Parliament Choir. A phone call from Lord Filkin one autumn day in 2000 led to an association with the Choir lasting almost 15 years – equal measures of involvement, support and enjoyment both for BT and myself with the Parliament Choir and, of course, with Simon Over and Southbank Sinfonia who are so closely linked.

I recognised the pleasure music brings to so many people and it seemed fitting at the beginning of a new millennium that a choir based in the Palace of Westminster could indeed fill a gap in such an august but often adversarial setting!

John Anderson

The telephone call with Lord Filkin was quite short and straightforward: he was thinking of forming a choir based in the Palace of Westminster (possibly the first in the venerable history of Parliament) and although they had plenty of aspiring singers, they required financial support to book venues, pay for an orchestra (and conductor) plus soloists if they were to make the venture a success. Although I am not musical myself, I remember very clearly in my early childhood hearing aspiring (and very talented) pianists playing on our Bechstein piano in the front room, music echoing through the house, as they practised for the Leeds Pianoforte competition, founded by Fanny Waterman and supported by Lady Harewood in the early 1960s. In particular, even then, I recognised the pleasure music brings to so many people and it seemed fitting at the beginning of a new millennium that a choir based in the Palace of Westminster could indeed fill a gap in such an august but often adversarial setting!

John Anderson and Simon Over

The first concert (*Messiah*) was held at St Margaret's Church in Westminster in December 2000. None of us knew what to expect but the initial concert was an instant success and set the platform for BT's initial twelve-month sponsorship to continue for over 15 years. The attraction of working with the Choir over so many years was, of course, inextricably linked to the inspiration and expertise provided by Simon Over and the formation of Southbank Sinfonia, which were fundamental to the success of the new venture. A group of committed choristers (but from different political persuasions and roles), with young but extremely talented musicians at the very start of their musical careers, supported by a dedicated and inspirational conductor/musical 'mentor and guru' were very powerful ingredients.

The opportunity to perform in marvellous auditoriums and settings was a bonus. Concerts were held in many different venues – ranging from Westminster Abbey, the Banqueting House in Whitehall, the Foreign Office, Westminster Cathedral, the State

Apartments, York Minster, and the National Railway Museum to overseas venues in Paris, Berlin and Tuscany – which gave both the Choir and Southbank Sinfonia a unique offering and position in our musical heritage.

There were many highlights during these early years. Some were grand occasions – the Mozart *Coronation Mass* at the Banqueting House in 2002, the Coronation Jubilee concert at Westminster Abbey (attended by Prince Charles) in 2003 both spring to mind, followed by concerts at Westminster Cathedral, Westminster Hall and nearer to home for me, at York Minister. Others had more mundane settings but were just as enjoyable and inspiring nevertheless, such as the musical reception at the top of BT Tower in London, the concert for North Yorkshire school children at the National Railway Museum in York plus numerous musical classes held in local schools in the South-East, North-East and beyond. This is a legacy that has brought much pleasure to many people over many years and has acted as an inspiration for a generation of young musicians as well as building relationships – whether political, commercial or purely social in such a competitive world!

Judy and I attended nearly all of the concerts during this period and actively participated in some of the planning for future concerts and programmes. In particular, we are very proud to have introduced Lady Walton, William Walton's widow, who established the fabulous garden La Mortella in Ischia. This led to the Walton Foundation sponsoring the performance of *Belshazzar's Feast* in the Festival Hall with Southbank Sinfonia. We are delighted that this relationship has flourished. We have also made many friends over the years, including Baroness Cohen, Lord and Lady Filkin, Baroness Hollis, Baroness McIntosh, Lord Thomas and Baroness Walmsley, Alan Beith MP, Bernard Jenkin MP and many others, and are indebted to them for helping make the concerts so enjoyable for us and our guests as they mingled with us at pre- and post-concert receptions. Mention should also be given to the contribution made by Denise Westbury, who acted as the liaison between BT and the Choir for many years and whose endeavour and support was fundamental in maintaining the close relationships we all benefited from and enjoyed.

So that initial phone call led to such a wonderful experience for all those involved right from the start to the present day – both for participants, performers and audiences alike. The continued inspiration of Simon Over during this period goes without saying; whether mentoring young musicians, supporting more elderly politicians or arranging and conducting marvellous concerts, all leave a legacy that will be safe and secure for the next 20 years and beyond, and have helped to make the Parliament Choir and Southbank Sinfonia unique and so very special.

Denise Westbury

Denise Westbury has been involved with the Choir since its earliest days and has a unique, all-round experience of it. She was working with John Anderson when he asked her to act as liaison between BT and the Choir and she organised all the events around the Choir's

BT private concert in the Speaker's State Apartments

What was great in the relationship between BT and the Choir is that we were prepared to take risks and to go places one wouldn't immediately think of, which made concerts fun.

Denise Westbury

private concerts. It is generally acknowledged that the Choir could not have got to where it was without BT's support and Denise did much to smooth the path of the relationship. Then as the Choir's programme became ever more ambitious and BT clients more and more interested, Denise was seconded from BT for one day a week to help manage the Choir. When John Anderson retired, she continued to work with his successors. She came back as Choir Manager for a time and started to sing in the soprano section, which she still does, and is now a Trustee of the Choir.

Early on, the Choir took part in the BT Christmas Concert at the Albert Hall. Whilst it was exciting to be singing there, the Choir had only a very small role in the concert, which we decided wasn't a good use of people's time, considering the membership of the Choir and the difficulty for Parliamentarians to attend. What was great in the relationship between BT and the Choir is that we were prepared to take risks and to go places one wouldn't immediately think of, which made concerts fun. Then there was the Greenwich concert, which was a huge success, although we were trying out something that was different and out of people's comfort zone. Some one hundred guests went by boat down to the old Royal Naval College at Greenwich, as would have happened in earlier days, docked and walked to the Chapel where we listened to the *Nelson Mass*, and then had dinner in the Painted Hall. It really was a magical evening. The format of private events was repeated a few times, for example in the concert in the Locarno Suite in the Foreign and Commonwealth Office, when the Clerk to the Parliaments gave a fascinating insight into his working day. He described what a relief it was to go down into the chapel and sing after sitting silently all day wearing a wig. Making it specific to an audience was something different, and showed the ability of the Choir to perform in different places, which is what it does wonderfully well.

It made a complete package – it ticked all the boxes that people were looking for: professionalism, extending the Choir into something richer and greater, enhancing the ethos behind what the Choir was trying to do. The partnership with Southbank Sinfonia used the synergy between prominent parliamentarians and what Simon was doing with the orchestra and made something great come out of it.

When Pierre Danon was CEO of BT Retail, he was ambitious to put the Choir front and centre of London events, with everyone wanting to be at its concerts. Without him we would not have done the Westminster Hall concert (transferred to Westminster Abbey) with the Prince of Wales in attendance. Pierre Danon had 350 guests – so many that we had to take on several different venues for drinks parties to entertain them all before and after the concert. He wanted it to be the stand-out event of the London season.

With each change of leadership at BT, I managed to get John Anderson's successors to buy into what had been created as a package. It was generally outside their experience, but they stayed with it. But then, things changed, as BT became more focused on global ambitions. It was just the result of time and place – nothing to do with lack of desire to support the Choir. Things just became different. I'm proud of the fact that this is the longest support that BT has given to any organisation – 17 years in total, when normally there was a maximum of a five-year contract. It was a real partnership, we worked closely together.

For me performing in the Queen Elizabeth Hall with Jamie MacDougall and Janis Kelly was fantastic. There, it was not only a privilege for the audience to have that expertise and entertainment but a privilege for Choir members to be able to sing with soloists of that calibre, who are not only gifted but also givers – inspiring confidence, so that the event becomes a spectacular experience for everybody. I had amazing feedback after that concert. The professional singers and Southbank Sinfonia lifted the Choir to a different place.

Airbus

Katherine Bennett tells how she involved the Choir in the centenary celebrations of the RAF with the RAF100 concert in St Clement Danes

On 10 July 2018, the nation looked up to the sky to watch 103 RAF aircraft fly over Buckingham Palace, ending with a magnificent finale of over 20 Typhoons flying in formation to spell out 100. This was one of many national occasions held to mark the centenary of the Royal Air Force that year. One pilot said that one of their most moving memories was seeing East London primary school children – lined up in the form of 100 – waving up from their playground. The RAF100

Lining up before the concert (Katherine Bennett 2nd left)

The RAF100 concert in St Clement Danes

theme was 'Commemorate, Celebrate, Inspire' and it became a catalyst for a wonderful year of events.

The Air Force Bill, laid down by David Lloyd George's Government, received the Royal Assent in November 1917, thus uniquely bringing into being a Service within the Armed Forces by an Act of Parliament. Lord Trenchard, the first Chief of the Air Staff, said at the time, 'We intend to make an Air Force worthy of the name; we must create an Air Force spirit, or rather foster this spirit… by every means in our power.'

I joined the Parliament Choir in 2016. Being aware through my work at Airbus of the RAF100 planning, perhaps some of this same spirit helped inspire our concert. As Simon Over is also Director of Music at St Clement Danes, the Central Church of the RAF, the planning very quickly became a reality.

Our concert was held on 25 April 2018 at St Clement Danes and we were honoured to have numerous special guests in the audience. These included Air Vice-Marshall Alison Mardell representing the Chief of the Air Staff; descendants of Lord Trenchard; the Rt Hon David Lidington MP, then Chancellor of the Duchy of Lancaster; numerous MPs and Peers; and RAF Benevolent Fund representatives. Many of these guests also delivered readings linked to RAF100. Air cadets from the 444 (Shoreditch) Squadron provided the guard of honour.

Simon Over put together a superb programme of music. The Parliament Choir were joined by some of the members of the St Clement Danes Choir and I will never forget their part in our performance of Allegri's *Miserere mei, Deus* from beyond the door of the gallery as we looked over the mahogany pews and beautiful church floor interspersed with 800 insets of Welsh slate shaped into RAF unit badges.

The concert included uplifting national pieces such as *I Was Glad* by Sir C Hubert H Parry, *God Be in My Head* by Sir H Walford Davies (who was the RAF's first composer), Ron Goodwin's *Those Magnificent Men in Their Flying Machines* and the first performance of *High Flight*, a new commission by Nicholas O'Neill with text from John Gillespie Magee. Another particular highlight was singing *Te Deum on Oranges and Lemons* by Paul Leddington Wright which features the bells of St Clement Danes.

Airbus was very proud to support the concert; we are a provider of aircraft to the RAF and, significantly, our site in Broughton built Wellington bombers (the builders were mainly women) during WWII. Interestingly, this site holds the record of building one entire aircraft in 24 hours during that period.

I would encourage the Choir to continue to mark significant national milestones such as this in the future.

As Walton's *Spitfire Prelude* was also part of our concert, it is perhaps fitting to finish with the words of Pilot Officer John Gillespie Magee, who described his experience as a Spitfire pilot during WW2:

With silent, lifting mind I've trod
The high untrespassed sanctity of space,
Put out my hand and touched the face of God.

Southbank Sinfonia

The Parliament Choir arose out of the Antioch Singers, a choir set up at St Margaret's for members of the congregation when Simon Over was Director of Music, as he and Geoff Filkin have described elsewhere. For their first concert Simon assembled an orchestra of young instrumentalists who had either just completed or were in their last year of studies at London conservatoires.

Struck by the quality of their playing, Simon was dismayed to discover they were pessimistic about their chances of employment in orchestras, and even more dismayed when some months later he met by chance one of the cellists whose talent had particularly impressed him. To get by in London she was doing temporary work, she no longer had time and energy to practise and was considering having to abandon her musical ambitions. It set him thinking how these excellent young musicians could be helped into professional life. Together with Michael Berman, a parent of a St Margaret's chorister, and a successful entrepreneur who has a particular interest in developing people's talents to the full, he began to come up with a scheme to offer a programme of playing and professional development to help players bridge the gap from music college to the profession.

Southbank Sinfonia, the 2020-21 cohort

The result was Southbank Sinfonia, which Simon and Michael and Katherine Verney started in 2001. Every year since, it has offered nine months of intensive orchestral experience, links with many different orchestras, opportunities to explore all kinds of repertoire, new interaction with audiences, and outreach with schools and opportunities for all sorts of relationships, all of which help the players in their future careers. Every year 32 new players are chosen by audition to take part in this unique programme. Twenty years on its participants are employed in leading orchestras all over the world, and more than 600 musicians have now taken part.

Southbank Sinfonia's relationship with the Parliament Choir is truly symbiotic and of great mutual benefit. Since it was adopted as 'the house band', the orchestra has played for every one of the Choir's concerts when an orchestra is called for. The Choir always appreciates the enthusiasm and freshness of their playing, and they probably bring the Choir's performance up a notch or two. However, the partnership also fulfils one of the Choir's main charitable aims: to support young musicians. Members of the Choir have come to enjoy getting to know the musicians and many support the orchestra financially. The Choir, corporately, supports the bursary of one player each year in line with its charitable aims. EM

Rebecca Crawshaw

Every year the Parliament Choir sponsors a chair in Southbank Sinfonia, and it has become something of a tradition, though not an invariable one, that we sponsor a trumpet player. Janet Cohen, when she pioneered this declared, 'I do like a trumpeter to call my own.' In 2014 Rebecca Crawshaw was the beneficiary. She has since gone on to enjoy a busy and varied freelance career, playing with many of the UK's leading orchestras, as a chamber musician and for West End musicals. She tells how remarkably positive was the experience of her year in Southbank Sinfonia

My experience in Southbank Sinfonia in 2014 was nothing short of life changing. After music college and before joining the orchestra, I struggled to find freelance work and was seriously considering giving up my dream of playing professionally. The ten months I spent playing weekly concerts of challenging music, surrounded by inspiring colleagues was a catalyst for my own improvement and helped me find the joy in playing again. The opportunities Southbank gave me have led to lasting working relationships with orchestras and ensembles, and perhaps most importantly the whole experience gave me the confidence to pursue a career in music.

My trumpet chair in the orchestra was very kindly sponsored by the Parliament Choir and without their support I would not have had this wonderful year. I was lucky enough to perform regularly with the Choir both during 2014 and the years afterwards and these joint endeavours were always brilliant concerts. The Verdi Requiem in Westminster Cathedral to mark the close of the 2014 season was a particular highlight for me as a trumpet player! As was the beautiful and historic concert of Handel's Coronation Anthems in Westminster Hall with the Parliament Choir and the Bundestag Choir. It was always a joy to meet members of the Choir at rehearsals and performances whilst I was in Southbank, and I am always thrilled to see these friends at concerts now.

Rebecca Crawshaw

James Murphy, who for six years was Managing Director of Southbank Sinfonia before becoming Chief Executive of the Royal Philharmonic Society, reflects on a relationship highly valued by both sides

When you run a classical music organisation, people often ask, 'What's your public affairs strategy?' meaning, 'How are you making your presence felt in Westminster?' It's any Chief Executive's least favourite question, mine included. At least until I became the Managing Director of the Southbank Sinfonia orchestra in 2011. Then, when anyone asked me the question, the answer was simply this: 'The Parliament Choir.' Through the Choir I was blessed suddenly to know dozens of people from across the parliamentary firmament who not only adore music, but adore making it, putting their all into ambitious concerts each year with our humble orchestra. Each time we got together I could see how much it meant to everyone in the Choir that our graduate players – all with their eyes set on bright futures at the highest musical level – would take time to perform with them. I like to think the orchestra roused the Choir to reach for greater heights themselves and, in turn, I think the orchestra cherished the sheer 'oomph', the sheer ballast and blast of joy that the Choir collectively invests in every possible quaver. I yet wonder how Simon Over miraculously created both entities within a year of one another, and some of my happiest moments running the orchestra were seeing him at the centre of it all, like the captain of a giant galleon, rousing the very best from singers and players alike on a bracing voyage. I have a new role now, but feel fortunate to have discovered and savoured this brightly beating musical heart at the very centre of Westminster, vibrantly striving for harmony.

Classic FM

Phil Noyce, Managing Editor of Classic FM, considers an opportunity which has turned out to be a good fit.

The Palace of Westminster may not always be known for political harmony but happily, thanks to the Parliament Choir, musical harmony is far easier to find within its walls.

It has been our great pleasure at Classic FM to broadcast the Choir's concerts for many of its twenty years. As part of Global, the media and entertainment group that also operates radio stations such as LBC, Heart and Capital, Classic FM is proud to have been able to share the Parliament Choir's choral performances with our five-and-a-half million listeners in constituencies across the length and breadth of the United Kingdom.

When we were first offered the opportunity of broadcasting one of the Parliament Choir's concerts on Classic FM, the fit seemed particularly appropriate. After all, here was a choir whose singers were drawn from the membership of the House of Commons and the House of Lords, and from among the many individuals who work with MPs and Peers on the Parliamentary estate. Since Classic FM's transmitters were first switched on back in 1992, we have been passionate about democratising classical music by making what is surely the greatest of all art forms available to the widest possible audience. So, we jumped at the chance of broadcasting concerts that radiated out from the home of parliamentary democracy.

Right from the start, it felt like a neat fit and our relationship has never looked back. Under the keen direction of Simon Over and Nicholas O'Neill, the Parliament Choir continues to hit the musical high notes and has developed and grown in stature over the past two decades. The parliamentarians' love of the world's greatest music clearly shines through each of their performances, which are never less than joyous occasions.

On behalf of all of my colleagues at Global, Classic FM, and all of our listeners, I wish the Parliament choristers past and present the happiest of anniversaries. We look forward to sharing many more wonderful moments of musical harmony with you in the decades to come.

Other Choirs

In the Choir's third year a rather special performance of *Messiah* took place in Central Hall, Westminster, when MPs and Peers invited singers from their constituencies and local areas to join forces with the Choir. An enormous choir was formed – 284 singers in total, 68 of whom were members of the Parliament Choir, the others drawn from 38 other choirs from all over the nation, from Ashford to Banchory and from

Huddersfield to Winchester. For BT, which so generously supported the Choir, this instance of the Choir reaching out nationwide reflected an important part of their contribution.

Other collaborations have been with the Malcolm Sargent Festival Choir, the Deutscher Chor London, the St Albans Bach Choir and Chorus, the Anghiari Choir and the Bundestag Choir. Members of the Bach Choir and the London Concert Choir have also joined us on occasion, as have the Bar Choral Society, Croydon Philharmonic Choir, Barts Academic Festival Chorus & Orchestra (BAFCO), Deansbank Singers, DfES Choir, Goldsmiths Choral Union, Treasury Singers and the Sussex Chorus. Our most important and long-lasting association, however, has been with the Coventry Cathedral Chorus (formerly Saint Michael's Singers).

Alison Baverstock reflects on taking part in the Jo Cox Choir

MP4 is a pop group consisting of four MPs. One of their number, Kevin Brennan (MP for Cardiff West) came up with the idea of recording a song to mark the memory of Jo Cox MP and raise money for the causes she supported. He asked for volunteers from the Parliament Choir to be part of the venture. Several high-profile contributors were promised, and I signed up to sing with Steve Harley (Cockney Rebel), Suzi Quatro and KT Tunstall, the whole thing to be conducted by Suzi Digby OBE, who has been credited with being able to teach stones to sing! It was to be recorded in The Backstage Centre at Thurrock, an educational initiative enabling wider access to careers in the performing arts, and which I was eager to see.

We got onto a bus outside Parliament opposite the statue of Boadicea and I was almost immediately handed my very first recording contract (a waiver of my rights). The song we were to sing ('You can't always get what you want' by Mick Jagger and Keith Richards) is specifically orchestrated for the inclusion of a community choir, and all were keen to wrest the music back from its recent adoption by US President-Elect Donald Trump.

The recording process itself was surprising – we never actually sang the whole thing through. Rather, we recorded phrases, waited for conductor Suzi to get approval via her headphones, and then progressed to the next one. Presumably it was later melded together by the producers, and the voices of the soloists added. Regular recordings of our choir concerts (including the one of the music commissioned in her memory) have felt more musical.

To be honest I felt pretty conflicted all day. It's a great cause, and the guided tours of both The Backstage Centre and the Royal Opera House costume and scenery departments were fascinating. But the reason for all this jollity was with us throughout – a young woman had been butchered in broad daylight while hearing the concerns of those she represented. The recording took place just before the trial of her attacker, and the more information that came out about the heroic way in which she had behaved that day, the greater the sense of injustice.

Even though it didn't make the Christmas number one, I hope it raises lots of money for charities close to Jo Cox's heart. But I hope too that people think about just how much we expect from those who represent us.

The Coventry Connection

Saint Michael's Singers (since renamed Coventry Cathedral Chorus) and the Parliament Choir shared the concert platform for the first time in 2003 at a Golden Jubilee celebration of HM The Queen's 1953 coronation in Westminster Abbey. The link between the two choirs was instigated through Simon Over, a Coventrian with close ties to the city and its cathedral, and Paul Leddington Wright, Musical Director of Coventry Cathedral Chorus. Since that first joint venture, the two choirs have enjoyed a close working relationship, performing many of the major works of the choral repertoire, including Walton's *Belshazzar's Feast*, Verdi's *Requiem*, Mendelssohn's *Elijah*, Brahms' *German Requiem*, Elgar's *The Dream of Gerontius* and, perhaps most memorably, Britten's *War Requiem*, commissioned for the festival to celebrate the consecration of the new Coventry Cathedral in 1962. These concerts are performed every two years or so, normally at two venues: Coventry Cathedral and Westminster Cathedral, but have also taken place at the Royal Festival Hall and Westminster Abbey. The two choirs came together in 2010 to celebrate the tenth anniversary of the Parliament Choir in a performance of Mozart's *Requiem* which was, uniquely, the first concert of its kind to be performed in the historic Westminster Hall at the Houses of Parliament

Paul Leddington Wright

I first met Simon Over in the late 1970s when he was 14 and keen to progress his organ studies. I started giving him organ lessons at

The Coventry Cathedral Chorus perform in the cathedral

Coventry Cathedral. His subsequent career has been distinguished, and forming the Parliament Choir was a great and imaginative achievement which complimented the wonderful work he has done with Southbank Sinfonia. As conductor of Coventry Cathedral Chorus, formerly Saint Michael's Singers, it has been exciting for us to join with the Parliament Choir both in Coventry Cathedral and eminent London venues for joint performances of some of the greatest choral works. Simon and I have coxed and boxed with the conducting, and also worked together on several performances of Britten's *War Requiem*. We look forward to our continued relationship with the Parliament Choir and Simon.

Members of Coventry Cathedral Chorus send warm congratulations to Simon and their friends in the Parliament Choir as they celebrate their 20th anniversary, and hope that their close relationship will continue and thrive in the years to come.

Barrie Rogers

We are so fortunate to have this wonderful relationship with the Parliament Choir. It allows us all to perform the larger works of the choral repertoire. It's always a great pleasure to share the concert platform with our friends and to renew old acquaintances. I've been lucky enough to be involved in many of our joint ventures, including performances of Verdi's *Requiem*, Mendelssohn's *Elijah*, Elgar's *The Dream of Gerontius* and Britten's *War Requiem*; this, particularly, in our 'home' venue, Coventry Cathedral (the building for which the work was commissioned in 1962). As well as Coventry, there have been memorable performances in Westminster Abbey, Westminster Cathedral and, uniquely, Westminster Hall in the Houses of Parliament. One event that stands out in my memory was singing to a packed Royal Festival Hall in May 2017 in a performance of Walton's brilliant and exciting *Belshazzar's Feast* with the terrific Southbank Sinfonia. My niece and her husband were in the audience that evening and were totally blown away by the experience! Let's look forward to the continuing friendship.

The first 20 years of the Parliament Choir have been a harmonious triumph of parts over the partisan. Here's to the next score.
Gary Watt

Gary Watt

As a tenor in Saint Michael's Singers and (the same choir with a new name) Coventry Cathedral Chorus, I have memories of three special concerts in which we sang alongside the Parliament Choir. The memories were made special by the people (writing in the pandemic lockdown, it's comforting to recall a time when we were pleased to be crammed together uncomfortably on a crowded stage), but also by factors of time and space. Time was of the essence ten years ago when we sang Britten's *War Requiem* in Coventry Cathedral on the eve of the 70th anniversary of the wartime bombing of the old cathedral. Timing was similarly special and surreal on 13 November 2019, when we performed the high harmonies of Elgar's *The Dream of Gerontius* in Westminster Cathedral while, in the background, the Brexit dispute in Parliament was hitting its deepest pitch of discord. The special space in my memory is Westminster Hall. In 2010, the Parliament Choir celebrated its 10th anniversary there with a performance of Mozart's *Requiem* and a first performance of Nick O'Neill's *Of All Persons and Estates*. It might have been, so I've been told, the first public concert ever held in that space. As a professor of law, it was a special privilege for me to perform in the very hall which, for seven centuries of our national history, had been home to the legal business of the realm. The first 20 years of the Parliament Choir have been a harmonious triumph of parts over the partisan. Here's to the next score.

Michael Switsur

Amongst many goosebump moments, the most personal came in Coventry Cathedral when we joined Saint Michael's Singers in Mozart's *Requiem* for the 75th Anniversary of the burning of that city. My father had told me of when, as an 11-year-old in November 1940, he had seen from many miles away, the night sky red with the destroying fires that followed the bombing. The poignancy of Mozart's great *Requiem* has never been greater for me, singing one year after my father's passing in that great Phoenix of a Cathedral, in partnership with friends old and new.

St Albans Bach Choir

Mike Taylor

'Would anybody like to sing Brahms' *German Requiem* with the Parliament Choir in a month's time?' Thus began a wonderful relationship with the Parliament Choir nearly eight years ago. It was during a St Albans Bach Choir (SABC) rehearsal that Jo Likierman, a member of both SABC and the Parliament Choir, was seeking experienced singers to join a performance of *A German Requiem* in Westminster Cathedral. The concert was to be recorded by Classic FM. 'They call us Stiffeners,' she continued in her recruitment drive, at Simon Over's behest. 'People who know the work well can attend the final few rehearsals, and then support the Parliament Choir in its concert performance. We'll also be performing with the wonderful orchestra, Southbank Sinfonia, with an additional performance in Coventry Cathedral a few days before with the Saint Michael's Singers.'

This set the path for what has followed since, the opportunity to sing marvellous music on wonderful occasions in iconic venues and form a very close bond with new friends in Westminster.

I confess to some trepidation at the outset. I knew no one in the Palace of Westminster and had some concern that our arrival at the last minute might irritate singers who'd been preparing for several months. Both fears were dispelled immediately, with a warm welcome from everyone for confident singers with good knowledge of a difficult work arriving to join the ranks. The story of the succeeding years reads very well.

However, it's not just about the big occasions – rehearsals are terrific fun too. Simon Over and Nick O'Neill are quite a double act. Simon's vision and ambition for the Choir are truly inspirational, and Nick's musicianship beggars belief at times. (I recall Nick playing the fiendish *Belshazzar* score on the organ in a rehearsal, simultaneously

The poignancy of Mozart's great Requiem *has never been greater for me, singing one year after my father's passing in that great Phoenix of a Cathedral, in partnership with friends old and new.*
Michael Switsur

playing the accompaniment and bringing out difficult bits for each voice part. A mesmeric performance worthy alone of the annual membership fee to hear.)

My personal favourite, however, adds yet more to the international flavour and music-making joy way beyond initial expectations from Jo's original invitation: singing Verdi's *Requiem* in the open air at the Anghiari Festival in Tuscany in 2015 with fellow SABC, Parliament Choir, Firenze and Anghiari friends. The sounds of the trumpets off stage in Anghiari's main Piazza will remain with me forever.

I'm privileged to wear two hats in all this: an individual member of the Parliament Choir and SABC's member leading the alliance we enjoy hugely. Since that first invitation, SABC members await eagerly my announcing the next concert alliance with the Parliament Choir. Many congratulations to my and our parliamentarian friends in reaching this 20th anniversary. We look forward to making more memorable musical joy together in future.

Children's Choirs

One of the charitable aims of the Parliament Choir is to support and encourage young musicians. From time to time, the Choir has been joined in its concerts by children, notably in its performance of *Carmina Burana* at Cadogan Hall in 2017. Frideswide Voices, an Oxford-based girls' choir, was the first to regularly sing the liturgy for services in Christ Church Cathedral where it is now the resident choir. Founded only in 2014, the girl choristers' participation in the Parliament Choir's concert was a landmark for them. Members of the Choir were very touched to

Carmina Burana at Cadogan Hall with Nicholas O'Neill and James Longford on pianos, O Duo with five percussionists from Southbank Sinfonia and Frideswide Voices on the balcony

receive handwritten notes from each of the girls expressing their delight and excitement at taking part.

Other collaborations have been with the girl choristers of Coventry Cathedral, who performed Britten's *War Requiem* with the Parliament Choir both in Coventry and in Westminster Cathedral in 2010; the North Yorkshire County Youth Choir took part in the splendid performance of *Messiah* in York Minster in 2009; and the boy choristers of St Margaret's Church, Westminster Abbey joined the Choir for the first large-scale Christmas concert at Westminster Hall in 2011, broadcast by Classic FM.

One Thing Leads to Another

Other people describe elsewhere how things come about in the Parliament Choir – a chance conversation, an allusion to a piece of music they would particularly like to hear or perform, the search for people and companies generous enough to help fund the Choir's concerts – and by way of illustration here is the story of the involvement with the Choir of two Liberal Democrat Peers.

Joan, Baroness Walmsley, and Martin, Lord Thomas of Gresford, are perhaps the earliest examples of romance within the Parliament Choir, and certainly the first choir members to marry each other. She sang in the first concert and became the third Chairman of the Choir. He joined the Choir for the second concert. They were married in the Chapel of St Mary Undercroft in 2005 and some members of the Choir were privileged to sing for the service. Both Joan and Martin gave tremendous support to the emerging Southbank Sinfonia, by now established as the Choir's own orchestra. Members of the Choir were invited to their pre-wedding concert performed by the orchestra and the London Welsh Chorale in St John's, Waterloo. A fervent Welshman, Lord Thomas commissioned from the Welsh composer Brian Hughes' *Bells of Paradise* for his beautiful local Gresford parish church, whose bells are considered one of the Seven Wonders of Wales. *Bells of Paradise* is a work originally written for choir, orchestra and church bells, where a local choir sang and Southbank Sinfonia played as part of a tour of the local area arranged by Joan and Martin.

Moving on to 2011, *Bells of Paradise* was repeated and performed by the Parliament Choir – though without the challenge of synchronising with church bells – at a BT private concert in Gray's Inn, 'From Shore to Shore', a programme of works representing all four corners of the United Kingdom. Lord Thomas is a QC who specialised in criminal cases and is a Bencher of Gray's Inn. The Choir and BT were very grateful to him for arranging this special evening in his own Inn of Court.

After this, some barrister singers formed the Bar Choral Society, now flourishing, which is a rather special workplace choir for the legal profession, just as the Parliament Choir is for Parliamentarians. The Choir has been very pleased to welcome members of the Bar Choral Society who have joined them in their larger concerts. Particularly poignant was one member who, though terribly unwell, in conversation with Simon Over said he would die happy if he could sing *Belshazzar's Feast*.

'From Shore to Shore' in Gray's Inn

A perusal copy was acquired, which had German and English translations, so 150 copies were ordered. Unfortunately, when they arrived (just in time for the first rehearsal) these copies had only a German translation. Lady Luce (wife of Richard, former Minister for the Arts and Lord Chamberlain) who sang with us at the time, put us on to Jarmila Kamas, who coaches singers in Czech at Glyndebourne. She came to teach us pronunciation and meaning and we set about singing it in Czech. Jarmila knew some high-profile people in the Czech Republic so managed to get some Senators to the performance in Cadogan Hall (and also some sponsorship in kind from Pilsner Lager). As a result, they started a Czech Senators' choir and invited the Parliament Choir to Prague in December 2010 to sing it with them in St Vitus Cathedral. And Jarmila joined the soprano section of the Parliament Choir. EM

And this was one of the impulses behind our performance in the Festival Hall in 2017.

Another intricate web of contacts began through a different conversation with Simon Over. Harvey Cole, a supporter of Southbank Sinfonia, happened to mention before he died how much he would like to hear a piece he had heard broadcast on the Third Programme in the 1950s and never since, though he had tried to persuade the BBC to repeat it. This was *Czech Christmas Mass* by Jan Jakub Ryba, a piece well loved by the Czech people. When Simon was invited to Mr and Mrs Cole's aggregate 150th birthday party, on top of the Gherkin building in the City, he thought he had better oblige by performing it.

Alixe Buckerfield de la Roche

One of the remarkable elements of the Parliament Choir is the huge diversity of talents and expertise reflected in its membership. It is one of the many characteristics which makes the Choir the unique musical community it is, composed of so many members collaboratively striving for musical excellence across all four sections. One such member was David Caron, a distinguished and popular member of the bass section, and a global expert on International Maritime Law. Professor Caron hailed from UCLA in Berkeley, California, and was appointed Executive Dean of the Dickson Poon School of Law at King's College,

University of London. David's dynamic and popular personality endeared him to many in the Parliament Choir, and his passion for musical excellence was much valued, sadly cut short by a premature death. At David's memorial service in Inner Temple, at the Inns of Court on 23 March 2018, our Choir Conductor, Simon Over, was invited to participate along with other eminent international colleagues paying tribute to David and his remarkable life. Simon's rendition of a Schumann composition was very powerful, and left a lasting impression on many of those attending that day. As well, the fact that the family requested that Simon close the service with *Amazing Grace* was very moving: it was an ending which David himself would have enjoyed greatly.

Soft Diplomacy

One of the important features of the Parliament Choir is that it is not just a workplace choir but an integral part of the life of Parliament, and makes a contribution to that life. The first example of that was the concert to mark the Queen's Coronation Golden Jubilee in 2003. In 2005, a concert was held in the Royal Gallery to mark the 200th anniversary of Trafalgar Day, in the presence of His Royal Highness Prince Andrew, featuring a special arrangement of sea shanties, by Nicholas O'Neill. Of great importance to Parliament and the nation were the two concerts held in Westminster Hall in 2014 to mark the 100th anniversary of the start of the First World War and 2018 to mark the 100th anniversary of the end of the First World War. In these two concerts, the Choir was joined by the Bundestag Choir. The President of the Bundestag, Norbert Lambert, also attended and spoke movingly about reconciliation at the 2014 concert. On a smaller scale, members of the Choir have taken part in musical events taking place in the Palace, such as the Commonwealth Festival and an event with a group of disabled singers from Colchester.

Although the Choir started life as an all-party group, it has recently become a unique body, under the direct patronage of the Speaker of the House of Commons and the Lord Speaker, and that has strengthened its role as an integral part of life and music of Parliament.

Sir David Lidington

After 2010, when I went to the Foreign Office as Minister for Europe, I had to scale back my choral commitments, but I saw a new side of the Choir – its potential diplomatic role. First in Paris, on a glorious evening in Notre-Dame, then in Berlin, in an atrium of the Bundestag festooned with Christmas lights, in a joint concert with the Bundestag Choir, I saw and heard how a shared love of music could, in some small way, help to ease bruised international relationships and remind us all of our common cultural inheritance.

Alixe Buckerfield de la Roche

At their very best, international collaborations can expand the dimensions of a nation's powers of expression and musical interpretation: they can foster internationalist musical initiatives and creative ventures for

Christmas concert 2016 in Paul-Löbe-Haus in Bundestag, Berlin

the future, and they can also prove an invaluable 'soft power' lever in a nation's toolbox of diplomacy. Our Parliament Choir's joint Christmas concert with the Bundestag Choir on 12 December 2016, delivered all these elements and more! Musically it was a delight – to fuse two differing musical traditions into a single celebration of Christmas, and it offered the opportunity for both choirs to experience the training and focus of two rather different conductors. On the wider European stage, the Berlin Christmas concert came at a critical moment, shortly after the UK had voted to leave the European Union, when forging long-term ties of a new kind were to be important.

In personal terms, the Christmas concert also opened a separate door: in 2016, I had been a Defence and Security specialist for over two decades, and so it was both a surprise and a delight to meet a colleague in the Bundestag Choir, Claudia Bülter, working across an allied domain in Germany. As we all know, the thrill of developing precision and excellence in musical expression, and refining our capacity to 'sing as one' while simultaneously blending as a whole are constantly evolving skills. We love music-making because, at our best, we catch a glimpse of the sublime and it makes our hearts fly! But when we can do that in international collaborations, it elevates the whole process to a new level. And when we can do that as part of a wider building of international friendships and long-term partnerships, it achieves something much larger than the original objective. At the post-concert reception, I thanked our impressive British Ambassador, Sir Sebastian Wood, for his hospitality during our stay in Berlin, and with great clarity he made a compelling case for an ongoing 'soft power' role for artists such as the Parliament Choir in carving out new arenas post-Brexit, for reciprocal European relationships. In listening to him, I recognised that while all we who sing delight in the music we bring to audiences, there are also larger long-term results which may well emerge from the initiatives in which we're engaged. It's a wonderful spur to all of us in the Parliament Choir to new ventures!

Dr Ruth Moeller

Choral diplomacy – singing connects

It is 20 years since the British Parliament Choir was founded and likewise 20 years since the choir of the Music Association of the German Bundestag was brought back to life in Berlin. Six years ago, both choirs performed together for the first time.

The President of the German Bundestag, Dr Wolfgang Schäuble, made this statement on the occasion of the joint performance of the two Parliament Choirs on 31 October 2018:

'The joint performance of our two Parliament Choirs brings an audible sign of harmony into Westminster Hall. This harmony can be achieved musically more easily than politically. One hundred years ago, lamentations prevailed over the unnamed suffering of a world war that shook a whole continent. Times have changed into happier ones. Still today the shrill and nationalistic sounds within a Europe of multiple voices

Foreign and
Commonwealth
Office

Sir Simon McDonald KCMG KCVO
Permanent Under-Secretary of State
King Charles Street
London
SW1A 2AH

Tel: 020 7008 2150
Email: pus.action@fco.gov.uk
www.fco.gov.uk

The Rt Hon Dame Caroline Spelman DBE MP
House of Commons
London
SW1A 0AA

5 May 2017

Dear Caroline,

PARLIAMENTARY CHOIR

Thank you for your letter. I have heard great things about your performances in Paris and in Berlin. And I am very happy to endorse your work, on both artistic and diplomatic grounds. I am sure that you will continue to go from strength to strength.

Do keep us in touch, including on your future trips.

Yours sincerely,

Simon

Simon McDonald

Rehearsing in the Bundestag: Nicholas O'Neill marooned, seeking a way in, and members of the Choir waiting

Miloš Bulajić

never lead to their political goal. The moving concert to commemorate the end of the First World War also reminds us of this.'

For the choir of the German Bundestag this was already the second joint concert with the choir of the British Parliament in Westminster Hall. And it was just as exciting, moving and impressive as the first time to sing in this historic building and environment in front of so many people. A concert in Westminster Hall with the British Parliament Choir remains something very special – a real goosebumps experience.

The choirs of the British Parliament and the German Bundestag had already sung together in 2014 to commemorate the 100th anniversary of the outbreak of the First World War. In his foreword to the programme, Prince Charles reminded us of the truce on Christmas Eve in 1914, when Christmas carols united British and German soldiers across the trenches of the Western Front. The two choirs picked up on this sentiment in 2016 when they invited their audience to sing Christmas carols together in the hall of the Paul-Löbe-Haus in Berlin in front of delegates and the international public.

Singing connects, and creates friendships that members of both choirs foster with enthusiasm when they meet annually in Anghiari (Italy) at the invitation of Simon Over for joint concerts with like-minded people from many countries all over the world.

We were not only deeply moved by the concerts themselves, but also by the hospitality that we were shown. We were given tours of the Parliament rooms in the House of Lords and House of Commons with all their historical and magical splendour; right there *in situ* we listened to the history and to stories and were reminded of the joint foundations of our democracies; and we were even received by the Speaker of the House of Commons in his private rooms and by the Foreign and Commonwealth Office.

The visits to London and the return visits to Berlin were short, but still seem as though they were much longer. They were so full of impressions and experiences. The memory is still very vivid, and it is our wish that we will be able to repeat these joint experiences many more times in both our countries. Singing is fun! Singing connects! Singing creates friendships – even across borders!

Karin Guenther, tenor

Still today I think back with immense joy to our three joint concerts. It was an indescribable experience to sing such challenging pieces together with so many other people. The two performances in London in Westminster Hall, this significant historical building, have left a lasting impression on me. And our joint Christmas concert in Berlin in the German Bundestag has shown how two choirs can harmonise together in a performance even though they rehearsed separately. Singing provides joy and brings people together. We ought to preserve this treasure.

Aileen Walker

The Paul Löbe Haus in Berlin (the Bundestag's equivalent of Portcullis House) was a large space to fill, but the capacity audience appreciated the Advent concert performed on

Music connects – across all borders! Our concerts will remain unforgotten, all of you will be forever in our hearts! We can hardly wait to see you again here in Berlin, in London or maybe in Anghiari!

Claudia Bülter, soprano, Bundestag Choir

Before the concert, Nicholas O'Neill warms up the Choir

Exploring the Bundestag, looking down into the chamber

12 December by a joint choir of the German Bundestag and the UK Parliament. The combined choir sang some pieces together, emphasising the international nature of the event by singing in English, German, and French. The Bundestag Choir sang two pieces on their own — a lively 'Cantate Domino' and an unusual and haunting version of 'Stille Nacht', and the Parliament Choir sang 'The Angel Gabriel' and Nick O'Neill's lovely arrangements of 'Sweet Was The Song' and 'We Three Kings'. With two choirs, two conductors, and two pianists all working in such harmony, the official speeches naturally alluded to the political situation and the ties between our countries. Musical diplomacy.

Dr Norbert Lammert, former Presdent of the Bundestag, welcomes the Parliament Choir to Berlin

A joyous occasion: Žarko Bulajić (top) and Simon Over at the Bundestag

Dagmar Linnemann-Gaedtke, soprano
Being allowed to sing in Westminster Hall in London and in the Paul-Löbe-Haus of the German Bundestag was an overwhelming experience for me. When I remember the entry into Westminster Hall I am always overcome with unbelievable joy and emotion. What a privilege!

Dr Jutta Struck
We recall wonderful days in London and look forward to our next choir performance. Together we are stronger!

Žarko Bulajić, conductor; Dr Kerstin Bode, soprano; Dr Yvonne Gall, soprano
In the sun, clouds and rain, in Berlin, London and Anghiari, we sang from Mozart to O'Neill, talked and laughed a lot, and every time we met, our friendship and reunion was filled with more joy, deeper understanding and higher appreciation. Thank you for all these great moments we had together and congratulations! We congratulate the Parliament Choir on its 20th anniversary and hope that we will all stay healthy, meet again soon and sing together!

6. Concerts

A selection of significant and special concerts from the Choir's first twenty years, how they have come about and what they have meant to members of the Choir.

2000 St Margaret's Church, Westminster Abbey. First concert, *Messiah*

Jane Gordon-Cumming

How could we not succeed after opening with *Messiah*, our first Parliamentary performance, held most fittingly in St Margaret's, the Parliamentary church. I was thrilled to join the fledgling choir in 2000, with my great pal Tricia Gray who worked for David Lidington – an esteemed tenor – and a member of the Choir from those earliest rehearsals. Simon's baton coaxed out unexpected top Cs, and from the very start there was a sense of purpose, a *joie de vivr*e, with an attractive blend of voices from all corners of the Parliamentary estate. We grew in size and confidence and, unsurprisingly, ambition (our sight reading also improving).

Libby Dewdney-Herbert

One of my top three concerts: I was particularly struck by the sense of occasion and sheer joy of that *Messiah*, my first concert.

Susan Ruckes

I had been working in the telephone switch room since 1997 when I attended, with two friends, the Choir's first concert, Handel's *Messiah*, in St Margaret's Westminster in 2000. In 2003 a friend and I attended the concert in Westminster Abbey that should have been in Westminster Hall. Later that year I spoke to Simon Over after the carol singing in Portcullis

Messiah *in St Margaret's Church, Westminster Abbey, 6 December 2000. The chorus 'Glory to God' with* trombe lontane *(trumpets in the distance) as indicated by Handel.*

House, and in January my contralto colleague, Luzy Bertorelli and I began attending rehearsals in the Chapel. Our first concert was the Brahms *Requiem* in St John's Smith Square.

2003 Westminster Abbey Coronation Jubilee concert

Susan Craig

On 18 June 2003, the Parliament Choir was to have sung in Westminster Hall for the first time. Three days before, after the rehearsal a piece of wood fell from the roof and landed in the area where the Prince of Wales would have been seated. I was Director of Human Resource Management in Parliament at the time and the Occupational Health, Safety and Welfare Service (OHSWS) reported to me. Consequently, I had to inform the Parliamentary authorities that on the advice of the Safety Officer it was not safe to hold the performance in Westminster Hall.

Alone in the hall, I could have gathered up the pieces, put them in my bag and said nothing, but good sense prevailed, not least because the place where they had fallen was where the Prince of Wales was due to be seated and the word 'regicide' flashed through my head!

Simon Over

Simon Over

This was to have been the first public concert in Westminster Hall in the 900 years of its significant national history. On the Sunday prior, we assembled everybody in the hall; a 300 strong choir, orchestra of 70, State Trumpeters, and soloists from British Youth Opera alongside world-famous soloists Sir Thomas Allen & Dame Felicity Lott. We hired an eighteen-speaker electronic organ for the occasion as well as many timpani and bass drums for the cannon fire in the *Te Deum* from *Tosca*. After everybody had left that Sunday afternoon rehearsal, I was standing on the podium alone in the hall, organising my thoughts and music, making notes, reflecting on the rehearsal before leaving, when there was a loud crash behind me. I turned round and saw some small pieces of wood on the floor that had fallen from the ceiling. I looked at the wood and considered what to do next. Alone in the hall, I could have gathered up the pieces, put them in my bag and said nothing, but good sense prevailed, not least because the place where they had fallen was where the Prince of Wales was due to be seated and the word 'regicide' flashed through my head! I went to find a security officer who, after hearing my account of what had happened replied, 'Well, what do you expect me to do about it?' We subsequently discovered that it was war damage that had probably dislodged the timbers originally and that the vibrations of our strong musical forces had completed the job! I like to think that we did the Palace a service; if that had happened later when there were many people in the hall, it could have been tragic!

By the following evening when we all met again for a Dress Rehearsal, there was a huge crane in the hall and at the end of the rehearsal, the Serjeant-at-Arms and Black Rod appeared, to tell the whole company that the concert would not be able to take place in that hall! We immediately got onto the Dean of Westminster who, having thought he'd finally got rid of me (I had worked for ten years at the Abbey as Director of Music at St Margaret's) found me causing trouble again. He opined that where the state fails, the church comes to the rescue, and he agreed to host the concert. Of course, as reserve venues for a Coronation concert go, Westminster

HRH The Prince of Wales at Coronation Jubilee concert 18 June 2003

Abbey isn't bad! The next three days involved all sorts of activity; building a platform and installing more than 20 plasma screens around the Abbey for people to be able to see, in a building not designed for concerts. At nearly midnight the night before the concert, the Dean rang: 'So you've brought the roof down in Parliament and you're about to go through the thirteenth century 'Cosmati Pavement' in the Abbey; when will you be satisfied?!' I had my team there early the next morning, watching as the stage was constructed and it was completed just after the two o'clock rehearsal began.

I've been involved in some nerve-wracking performances across 40 years in the music profession, but this was on a different level.

Fifteen minutes before the concert was due to begin (and I had dared to think that everything was in place), I received a message that the Prince of Wales had dispensed with his motorcade for the evening, believing he could get from home to the Abbey easily, and was unfortunately delayed by a demonstration *en route*. The atmosphere in the Deanery (our Green Room) was very tense; you prepare yourself for a start time but when that time comes and goes and half-an-hour later you're still waiting, it's very difficult to know how to deal with your nervous energy. Tom Allen was not on until the second half of the programme and so when we finally began the procession from the west end to the east of the Abbey, he said he was off to the pub. His first item in the programme was 'Largo al factotum' from *The Barber of Seville* (Rossini). When we arrived at that point in the programme, he was nowhere to be seen. I looked round and asked the Leader of the orchestra where he was, but he shrugged. A few long seconds passed, and it occurred to me that sometimes people enter the stage singing that aria, so I risked it and started the introduction with my heart pumping madly. I've never before or since experienced such relief as when I heard him singing from the other side of the screen dashing up the aisle in Figaro style. When he arrived at his place, he nodded and smiled in my direction. I'm not sure what my expression conveyed to him, but it was a lot more than 'I'm pleased to see you'!

There were many musical highlights in that programme. The first half was coronation-related, the second an opera celebration, and at the request of BT's Pierre Danon, we did the 'Te Deum' from *Tosca*. I'd asked around various opera houses about how best to effect the cannon fire in this excerpt and one suggestion was to approach the Moscow Militia! Many sets of timpani and bass drums seemed more likely to get through Parliamentary security (perhaps those drums had in fact been responsible for the ceiling in Westminster Hall), but whilst there was plenty of room for them there, in Westminster Abbey they had to be set up in the side aisles above memorial stones; Dame Sybil Thorndike in the south, Purcell and Vaughan Williams in the north, with all the players watching me via screens. The moment when Scarpia sings, 'Tosca, you make me forget God', immediately swamped by the chorus's full-throated unison 'Te Deum' (a canticle that has probably been said or sung in that place every day for ten millennia) was a moment I shall never forget.

Jonathan Sayeed MP, who was the Chairman at the time, had booked a filming company to make a DVD of the concert; in the end a very different (perhaps more entertaining) DVD was made, describing all the different stages in the process between the rehearsal in Westminster Hall and the concert in Westminster Abbey.

Hugh Merrill played an essential part in that concert and has been a great friend to the Choir ever since. In the early 1990s he served as a private secretary to The Prince of Wales, responsible among other things for HRH's contact with industry, and then for BT he was at various times chief of staff to the Chairman and the Chief Executive, so he was responsible for bringing together some of the principal elements of this concert. The concert was also the moment when I introduced Hugh to British Youth Opera, and for some years thereafter he was their Chairman. Now a member of the Choir and also a Trustee, Hugh's contacts have helped enormously to connect the Choir to all sorts of people who have shaped our 20-year journey.

Maggie Ronald

The Golden Jubilee June 2003 concert was very memorable, for lots of reasons. The move to the Abbey from Westminster Hall seemed to happen very smoothly. Only listening to Simon's recollections of the work involved in changing the venue did I realise the amount of effort it took to rearrange everything in the space of three days. My favourite part of the whole concert was Tom Allen coming down the aisle singing Figaro's aria 'Largo al Factotum'. I thought it was a wonderful bit of planned theatre to arrive in that way, singing as he walked towards us, so to learn that Simon didn't know if he was back in the building when he started the piece makes it even better!

2009 York Minster *Messiah*

John Anderson, by now Managing Director, BT Regions, is a Yorkshireman and always an enthusiast for the possibilities of technology and its ability to connect people. Hence this ambitious collaboration: the Parliament Choir went north and was joined in concert by the York Teachers' Choir and the North Yorkshire County Youth Choir. During the preceding week Simon Over, with members of Southbank Sinfonia, worked with pupils from 11 schools in the York area, four of which were connected by NYnet's state of the art (for 2009) technology. Their week ended with a performance in York's National Railway Museum. This was also the Choir's first concert to be recorded by Classic FM and was broadcast on Christmas Day.

Messiah *in York Minster, 2009*

Annalise Pask

My number one concert would be Handel's *Messiah* at York Minster, my inaugural Choir concert. I didn't really know any of my fellow singers until the journey up, when some fortuitous seating arrangement in the train carriage got me talking to a spirited bunch of Choir members whom I now count as some of my dearest friends! Singing the *Messiah* in such a majestic setting was a complete joy.

2010 Coventry Cathedral *War Requiem*

Simon Over

As a Coventrian, *War Requiem* is a work very close to my heart. My organ teacher in the Netherlands knew about Coventry through this extraordinary work and yet I fear very few residents of the city know about it and its significance, let alone know it well. It has been my privilege to be involved (as pianist, organist and conductor) in many different performances, each monumental in its way.

One of my predecessors as Organ Scholar in Oxford was Meredith Davies who had been Conductor of the City of Birmingham Symphony Orchestra in the 1950s and as such was preparing the chorus for the premiere of *War Requiem*. He told me that the quality of the chorus (which included other singers from around the diocese) was so bad that Britten lost confidence in the performance. Apparently, there was a woman in the chorus with a red leather-bound score which caught his eye during a rehearsal. In the break he asked to see it and discovered it was in fact the Verdi *Requiem*. She explained that she'd been to the local library and asked for a *Requiem* and they gave her that one! In addition to the poor quality of some of the choir, the difficulty of the cathedral's acoustic, along with other minor snags like the Soviet government's refusal, on political grounds, to allow the intended soprano soloist Galina Vishnevskaya to take part, and her part having to be learned at ten days' notice by Heather Harper, were overwhelming to Britten who arrived in Coventry for rehearsals following a minor operation. He therefore suggested that Meredith conduct the symphony orchestra and chorus while he directed the Melos Ensemble and two male soloists, Peter Pears and Dietrich Fischer-Diskau, who aptly represented an English and a German soldier, a significant statement so soon after the war.

Meredith Davies came to speak at a dinner for me in Oxford and we discussed the possibility of his conducting the work in our college, to mark the tenth anniversary of Britten's death, with his orchestra and chorus from Trinity College of Music (where he was at that time Director) together with my chorus and choir, and I would play the organ. He managed to persuade Heather Harper to sing the soprano solo. A consummate professional, she was chauffeur-driven into the quad in a Rolls Royce where I met her and escorted her to her place on the platform. She had only a handbag over her arm and appeared not even to have a score with her. Davies said 'From Figure 32,' and she was right there without even needing a note. It was fascinating going through his score with Davies, seeing Britten's handwritten notes and hearing his reminiscences. I went back into the chapel about an hour after the performance (which had had great impact, not having been conceived for a building the size of an Oxford

War Requiem in Coventry Cathedral, 13 November 2010, performed from the south screen with the ruins of the old cathedral behind. Coventry Cathedral has a very unusual north-south alignment, necessary so that the ruins could be incorporated into the new cathedral. That the new is perpendicular to the old indicates that God is all around.

college chapel) and saw Davies seated on the podium with his head in his hands. I asked if he was all right and he responded that he was just living with his memories.

Subsequent to that, I played the piano part in a performance in Wells Cathedral, the organ parts (chamber and 'grand') in Coventry Cathedral, and toured Germany in a set of performances which drew together a Russian symphony orchestra, Polish chamber orchestra, the chorus of the place where the concert was being held (Potsdam, Hamburg and Schleswig Holstein) with soloists from three different countries and the Coventry boys' choir (which I was accompanying on the organ).

We're working on some cool music by Benjamin Button.
Schoolboy from the Midlands

Saint Michael's Singers, now Coventry Cathedral Chorus, was formed in 1963, a year after the premiere of *War Requiem* (its early membership included a number of people who sang in the premiere) and has been a regular and much-valued partner to the Parliament Choir over the last 20 years. When its director, Paul Leddington Wright (also my former teacher) invited us to join them in a performance to mark the 70th anniversary of the bombing of the old cathedral, I was thrilled and started thinking about a reciprocal performance in Westminster. It also struck me then that it would be a good moment to make the work better known in and around the city. There were people like my father still around who could remember seeing the cathedral ablaze on that awful night and it occurred to me that the schools of the city should join together for this project. History departments could look at the world wars; the poetry of *War Requiem* is from World War One and the bombing relates to World War Two. English departments could study the poetry of Owen and Sassoon and the music departments war-related composers, Britten, Bliss, Bax, Butterworth, and others not beginning with B!

The plan was that Southbank Sinfonia players (trained in running workshops to inspire school students) would be resident in the city for a week and, with the children, interview people like my father about their memories, look at the *War Requiem* and understand its message and significance, then write their own *War Requiem* with their own poetry and music to be performed in the cathedral the day before. They would have free tickets for the Saturday performance and could bring along their parents for a nominal ticket price. I visited Geoffrey Robinson, then still MP for Coventry North West. I remembered him coming to my school when I was twelve (he clocked up 43 years before retiring in 2019). It was the most fruitful fundraising visit I've ever made. He spoke of approaching the Coventry Building Society and other major institutions in the city and I suggested he call them whilst I was there. I left his room with £20,000 pledged. I'd imagined that was the difficult part, but in fact persuading the schools to join the project was much harder. 'Will it benefit our A Level results?' I was asked more than once. I protested that whilst it might or might not, it would be something memorable for the children and give them the opportunity to know and appreciate this crucial work and important part of their city's history. Thankfully Bluecoat C of E school saw the potential value and hosted the project.

It all happened according to plan. One of my favourite moments was when the BBC

Midlands Today came to the schools' performance and interviewed a local boy with a deep Midlands accent. 'We're working on some cool music by Benjamin Button.' I think Britten would have loved that.

For the performance on the Saturday evening the inside of the cathedral was turned around to have the ruins of the old cathedral as a backdrop through John Hutton's glass screen. I conducted the chamber orchestra and soloists on the steps of the Chapel of Unity (which seemed appropriate), and Paul conducted the symphony orchestra and chorus (we swapped roles a few days later in Westminster Cathedral). Before the concert the German Ambassador rang the Peace Bell (inscribed 'Peace, *Friede*', it had been presented to HM Queen Elizabeth The Queen Mother at a service 20 years before, which marked 50 years since the bombing).

The particular significance of these performances for me was having politicians (inextricably connected to wars) singing alongside the young players of Southbank Sinfonia, themselves the same sort of age as the soldiers who went off to fight, never to return. Also, having the girls' choir of the cathedral singing (at both performances), instead of the usual boys, made the point that it wasn't just boys, soon to be young men, who suffer in wars; girlfriends, wives, mothers all had to live for the rest of their lives confronting the effects the atrocities of war had on their loved ones. One of the politicians in the Choir at the time was Admiral Lord West, Parliamentary Under-Secretary of State for Security and Counter-Terrorism and a former First Sea Lord and Chief of the Naval Staff. His

presence necessitated a full closure of the building before the concert, including a dog search; a vivid reminder of the significance of politicians singing in *War Requiem*.

Maggie Ronald

Our performance in Coventry Cathedral of Britten's *War Requiem* in November 2010 to mark the 70th anniversary of the bombing was very moving. We sang at the back of the building, with the ruins of the old cathedral behind us and finished with a long silence, no applause.

Annalise Pask

I couldn't choose between the Coventry concerts. I adore the cathedral and it has been such a privilege to perform there three times. The *War Requiem* was particularly difficult (I am sure it had Simon and Nick on the edge of a breakdown at times), but it felt like a huge achievement musically and it was a real honour to be able to perform it in such an important place. My Choir friends and I have developed a huge affection for the city!

Baroness Jolly

Singing Britten's *War Requiem* in Coventry Cathedral was special as I had attended the second performance of that, conducted by Britten, in 1963.

St Vitus Cathedral, Prague, was most memorable for being the coldest I have ever been in my entire life.
Annalise Pask

Christine Judd

I think Britten's *War Requiem* was the most memorable concert, especially the performance in Coventry Cathedral looking out onto the remains of the old cathedral. It is such a deeply moving work.

2010 St Vitus Cathedral Prague

The *Czech Christmas Mass* is sung all over the Czech Republic every Christmas and is known and loved by all Czechs. Ryba means fish, and carp is at the heart of the traditional Christmas dinner. This performance with the Senators' Choir was broadcast live on Czech television

Maggie Ronald

We sang Ryba's *Czech Christmas Mass* in Prague's St Vitus Cathedral in December 2010, an exciting but extremely chilly experience. Snow boots helped as did fingerless gloves bought for all by Denise. Luckily generous helpings of glühwein before the concert helped to keep the internal temperature up! Afterwards there was a brilliant deep and crisp and even walk through thick snow to a reception at the nearby Bishop's Palace where we sang (briefly!) for our wonderful supper. The Zither Carol went down well. Among many other treats in Prague, we were given a special tour and reception in the original town hall, an *art nouveau* gem, and also a private tour of Alphonse Mucha's house. We were looked after very well. Despite the problems getting home, it was a great trip!

Annalise Pask

St Vitus Cathedral, Prague, was most memorable for being the coldest I have ever been in my entire life. We also nearly didn't make it there or back due to the extreme weather, but it was such an amazing experience and the discovery of a rather lethal spirit called Becherovka helped us defrost!

Prague, Archbishop's Palace reception

Well wrapped up: singing in St Vitus' Cathedral at -8 degrees

Jean Guise

A totally unexpected aspect of our visit was being marooned in Prague for three extra days.

The visit was anyway memorable for performing in a venue – Prague Cathedral – that was several degrees colder inside than outside. We in the choir would have been unable even to hold our scores without the fingerless gloves provided by our prescient Choir Manager. The tankards of mulled wine presented to us on arriving at the splendid Archbishop's Palace for the 'after party' could not have been more welcome – or appreciated.

A freak snowstorm at Heathrow meant that our return flight was cancelled, and the first available flight went to Gatwick three days later. The tour company booked our comfortable hotel for three further nights. On the bright side, there are worse places to be marooned than Prague during the Christmas season! We enjoyed our 'bonus' days exploring the city's Christmas markets and visiting beautiful buildings such as Obecni Dum, Prague's finest Art Nouveau Building. And plenty of good robust winter-warming food. Another highlight was a mainly Mozart concert on the magnificent grand entrance hall staircase of the National Museum in Wenceslas Square.

All the same, it was a huge relief to touch down at Gatwick and get home in time for Christmas.

2012 Cadogan Hall

***Lobgesang* with Korean Parliament Choir**

Eugene Lee, the violin soloist in this concert, is a South Korean New Zealander who took part in the Southbank Sinfonia annual programme in 2009, and subsequently has become the orchestra's Associate Leader. He is Assistant Leader of the Philharmonia Orchestra and is married to the soprano soloist for this concert, Sung Eun Seo. They had performed this same concert together in Seoul in January 2012 with Jamie MacDougall as the tenor soloist and Simon Over again conducting. Lord German, who was also on the trip describes his experience below Eugene's.

Eugene Lee

When I first heard of the 'Parli Choir' I had no clue as to what it was by the sound of it. Now, it's as familiar as the 'ROH' or the 'LSO'.

It was 2009 when I met and heard the Choir for the first time and it was clear that this was not just another 'hobby' choir. I belonged to Southbank Sinfonia, an internationally-recognised orchestral training programme, which takes pride in its partnership with the Parliament Choir over many years. The two share a unique key which creates a special connection when they meet. I am fortunate enough to have performed with them over the last ten years and have many fond memories which I will treasure for a long time, both on- and off-stage. To me, the idea of being inclusive and sharing one's passion with another, without social hierarchies and prejudice, is what epitomises the Parliament Choir. Perhaps this is what draws my fascination and allows their enthusiasm to be meaningful.

Eugene Lee, conductor as well as violinist

Michael German

The Korean (Ad)venture

The Choir's desire to link with other parliament choirs across the globe led the link with the Choir of the National Assembly of Korea (that's South Korea of course). As usual a two-way concert was planned, though it was eventually one way only, with the Korean Choir coming to London to join us performing Mendelssohn's *Lobgesang* (*Hymn of Praise*) in a concert at Cadogan Hall. This interesting work, which became known as Mendelssohn's 2nd Symphony, was composed to celebrate the 400th anniversary of Gutenberg's invention of the printing press.

The planning for this joint venture was scheduled to take place in Seoul alongside a performance of the work, with Simon Over conducting the National Assembly's Choir and a local orchestra, in a Friendship Concert in the Aram Concert Hall, Seoul, on 12 January 2012.

As Choir Chair at the time, I joined Simon, and soloist Jamie MacDougall on this visit. My role was to deal with the organisational, political and diplomatic parts of the proposed joint concerts, and to deal with the not insignificant financial arrangements which make such a large venture feasible.

Sometimes you get a sixth sense about whether these major events can be made to work. Increasingly my personal antenna picked up these vibes from the start. The Korean Choir had offered to pay all the expenses for our visit, including the fees charged by Simon and Jamie for their musical activities whilst in Korea. The reality struck home when Simon, Jamie and I were faced with the hotel bills at the end of our stay, when we had been assured that these would be covered. And it became even clearer when Simon and Jamie's fees were not paid either. For both of these professional musicians, conductor and soloist fees are their livelihoods. Travelling halfway around the world and not being paid is a very serious matter and a failure to meet pre-agreed contractual arrangements.

The failure was caused by the Choir's Director, Professor Kim, who had made these financial commitments without securing the funds to back them up. This turned out to be a feature of his activity as demonstrated by an incident in a local shopping mall. Simon and I had joined Professor Kim for a meeting in a coffee bar in a sort of market stall. Suddenly two men appeared and grabbed Professor Kim by his jacket collar, hauling him out of his seat and physically and verbally remonstrating with him in Korean. I attempted to get some sense of what was happening and tried to calm the situation. Eventually after a 'conversation' of which I understood nothing, the men dumped Professor Kim back in his chair, with a warning to us 'not to trust this man' and then left. A Korean colleague then gave us a resumé of what had just happened. The men were trying to recover money which was owed by Professor Kim, and which he had failed to repay. So, what followed was inevitable, the Korean Choir Director was operating outside the relationship with the National Assembly, and certainly the Choir itself knew nothing of these financial arrangements. Our choir sought eventual recourse via the Korean Embassy in London and the funds owed were eventually repaid. This in turn led to the National Assembly Choir being disbanded and Professor Kim dismissed as its Director. But thankfully this did not happen until after the Choir (minus Professor Kim) at their own personal expense had performed with us in London.

But there is a musical silver lining to this story, the concert in the Aram Concert Hall went ahead, I sang with the National Assembly Choir, and also made a speech extolling the virtues of parliamentary choir links to an audience which included ministers and other prominent politicians. The concert featured not only the incredible Jamie MacDougall as a soloist, but also Southbank Sinfonia star violinist Eugene Lee, now Assistant Leader of the Philharmonia Orchestra. And Eugene's talented wife, Sung Eun Seo, was the second soprano soloist in the *Lobgesang*. I have a vivid memory of the dress rehearsal with Sung Eun Seo sitting on the stage floor at the feet of her husband watching him play so beautifully the Bruch Violin Concerto. True love in public view! And it was a feature of our visit as well. Eugene's father had travelled to Korea from New Zealand to hear his son's performance, and Sung Eun Seo's family all lived in Seoul, so we spent a wonderful few days in the company of them all – seeing the sights of Seoul and enjoying meals together.

However, the backdrop lesson of this Korean visit is that preparations for any Parliamentary links have to be built on a solid organisational and financial footing. However, music transcends everything –- which is, I suppose, the reason why we love our Choir so much.

2014 Cadogan Hall
Haydn *The Creation*
Lord Filkin

A Choir cannot be a democracy, even though we try to be open and inclusive. Simon, as Music Director, must choose the works we perform, balancing complexity, scale and cost with the opportunity of diverse venues. This did not stop some of us trying to persuade him to choose a work we wanted. So it was for me with Haydn's *Creation*, a work I had first heard when I was 15 years old performed at my school, and I was overwhelmed by the beauty of the ideas, Haydn's music and the words of Milton and the King James Bible, and by its inspiring optimism.

Eventually, after many years of nagging, Simon decided we were ready to perform this great work. Doing so linked back to our first concert, as Haydn, late in his life, heard *Messiah* performed in London and was moved by it to want to write a great choral work, which became *The Creation*.

We performed it to our great enjoyment and to the satisfaction of Simon and Nick O'Neill and hopefully also the audience in Cadogan Hall. This unusual hall has been one of our homes for many years – there are still some members of the Choir lost in its backstage labyrinths! Thank you, Simon, Nick and Cadogan Hall!

Nick's notes in programme:
His 'pictorial' writing engages with von Swieten's rather literal Germanic text, and illustrates in music the 'soaring eagles' and 'great whales' and all kinds of other birds – lark, dove and nightingale – and wild and domestic and lowly animals – lion, tiger stag and horse to cattle, sheep insects and worms.

And after the performance, in the Choir's newsletter, praise from our Chorus Master:
'The Choir really enjoyed performing *The Creation*, Haydn's masterpiece… a performance of wit, vitality and verve, Haydn would definitely have approved.'

Susan Ruckes

My aunt passed away in December 2018, just before her 100th birthday. For the last few years, she was blind and unable to move unaided, but her mind and memory were as sharp as ever. Her radio was permanently tuned to Classic FM. My aunt enjoyed listening to the Parliament Choir concerts, especially the Christmas concerts from St John's Smith Square. Unfortunately, one of her favourite oratorios, Haydn's *Creation*, was not transmitted, so she was unable to hear that wonderful elephant portrayed by the contra bassoon – 'By heavy beasts the land is trod.'

The Creation *at Cadogan Hall , 2014*

2016 Cathedral of Notre-Dame de Paris
Poulenc, O'Neill, Howells, Vaughan Williams, Gounod

Alan Walker

Having travelled to Paris on the Eurostar with Caroline Spelman and Jeremy Lefroy, whom I had met in the queue at St Pancras, I was drawn into work matters after checking into my hotel. Rather delayed by this, I arrived at the side gate at Notre-Dame somewhat after the appointed time for Choir entry to the rehearsal session to find it firmly locked shut.

Fortunately I was able to use my Serjeant-at-Arms pass to attract the attention of the gatekeeper, and a liberal helping of apologetic French to persuade him that I should really be inside the building and singing rather than outside the railings and talking – I was very relieved to be let in after only a short (but stern) lecture on punctuality.

On the day of the performance, and I think unbeknownst to my voice rep (sorry Michael), I fitted in a business day trip to Nyon, along the lake from Geneva – out by an early train and then back to France on a flight to Orly with a slightly undignified gallop through the airport to catch the RER back to central Paris – and all this with my dinner suit in my hand baggage in case of delays.

The experience of singing in Notre-Dame was an indelible one, especially the great wave of sound of Nick's *Tu es Petrus*, echoing round the very building he had written it to be performed in – the memories all the more poignant now given the terrible damage later wrought by fire in 2019. I hope we may have chance to sing there again some day.

The experience of singing in Notre-Dame was an indelible one, especially the great wave of sound of Nick's Tu es Petrus, *echoing round the very building he had written it to be performed in – the memories all the more poignant now given the terrible damage later wrought by fire in 2019.*

Alan Walker

Notre-Dame, 2016

Maggie Ronald

Our concert in Notre-Dame in May 2016 was splendid and we all felt very honoured to have been given the opportunity to sing there. However, for me the best moment was the night before when our rehearsal had finished and the cathedral was empty. To walk round, enjoy the silence and drink in the past of this iconic building was a unique experience.

Christine Judd

Since I first got to know Paris in my student days, Notre-Dame and St Chapelle have been amongst my favourite buildings and I always try to visit them when I am there. It was therefore a thrilling privilege to sing there. Nick's fascinating references to Pérotin made singing *Tu es Petrus* there a very special experience. I cannot swear that I saw Pérotin, but (and I have been a history teacher) I deeply felt the emotional experience of singing music in the style sung there so many years ago.

Notre-Dame, 2016, rehearsals and performance

Notre-Dame, 2016

2017 Royal Festival Hall *Belshazzar's Feast*
SbS promotion, its 15th birthday celebration
Jean Guise
A highlight for me was *Belshazzar's Feast*, one of my all-time favourite choral works, in the Royal Festival Hall. I love it because of the sharp contrast between the tender lamenting passages and the no-holds barred blaze of orchestral colour in the central Feast section.

Mari Takayanagi
My favourite concert was *Belshazzar's Feast* at the Royal Festival Hall, because I thought it was the best we ever sang – it was a difficult piece, we practised hard, and it all paid off. At the end I felt jubilant – we'd nailed it! – and I was delighted that such a large hall of people had witnessed it.

Susan Madel
During *Belshazzar's Feast* in the Festival Hall in May 2017, I most remember guiding a young blind woman through the concert, she lived her life through music and singing. Such an inspiration compared with the decadent Belshazzar.

2018 Sheldonian Theatre and Queen Elizabeth Hall
Mari Takayanagi
The concert that moved me most was *From Gallipoli to the Somme*, the First World War concert at the Sheldonian. There is a movement when the male parts belt out a chorus and then the voices drop out gradually, until none are left but the conductor is still beating time – and you realise they have all fallen, every last one.

Anthony Ritchie, composer *Gallipoli to the Somme*
It was one of the highlights of my career to travel to London and Oxford for the performances of *Gallipoli to the Somme*. The Parliament Choir was superb and I enjoyed meeting members of the Choir and attending rehearsals. Simon was the glue that held these performances together as well as the world premiere in Dunedin, New Zealand. I am a loyal Otago man but for me the UK performances were a nose ahead of the Dunedin one, just for sheer exhilaration and crackling atmosphere. It was extraordinary, too, to have so many City Choir of Dunedin members present, along with Tessa (violin) and Anna (soprano). I will never forget the kind comments of parliamentarians and others associated with the Choir, and also meeting with returned servicemen and women after the concerts.

Simon Over
Creative New Zealand, the national arts development agency, had a five-year commemoration programme marking the centenary of World War One which offered funding for the creation of projects to add new perspectives on the war. One stipulation was that there be another country involved. Philippa Harris, General Manager of the Dunedin Symphony Orchestra, of which I am the Principal Guest Conductor, suggested that we commission a work that could then be performed in the UK by Southbank Sinfonia.

Often on my visits to New Zealand I also work with City Choir Dunedin and it occurred to me that if we were to commission a choral

Gallipoli to the Somme, with City Choir, Dunedin, New Zealand at Sheldonian Theatre,Oxford, 2 June 2018

And at Queen Elizabeth Hall, 13 June 2018

work, the Dunedin Choir would sing it there and the Parliament Choir could sing it in this country. The New Zealand connection comes through Anna Yallop, so I discussed it with her and she was of course enthusiastic to work on a project with musicians from her homeland. Having conducted the premiere of Anthony Ritchie's third symphony in Dunedin and his *Remember Parihaka* in Japan, I was keen for him to be the composer. My suggestion was something along the lines of *War Requiem*, but with a text representing other countries (especially the Antipodes). It should be written for soloists, chorus and orchestra, and should not require the huge forces demanded by *War Requiem*. Anthony agreed to write for a chamber orchestra, the size of Southbank Sinfonia, and he listened to clips of the Parliament Choir to be sure to write appropriately for them (he knows City Choir Dunedin well).

Kate Kennedy, a lecturer in music inspired by World War One at Oxford, advised Anthony on suitable texts and then travelled with me to do a programme for Radio New Zealand and interview Anthony Ritchie in a pre-concert talk for the premiere on 1 October 2016. Parliament Choir tenor Mike Meur (who has family in New Zealand) came to sing in this first performance, representing the Choir, and the City Choir was joined by the Southern Youth Choir. City Choir's excellent director David Burchell had his choir learn the whole of the last movement – words from the Ataturk Memorial in Turkey – from memory:

> *You, the mothers who sent your sons*
> *from far away countries, wipe away*

your tears. Your sons are now lying in our bosoms and are in peace. After having lost their lives on this land, they become our sons as well.

The feeling the Choir projected while singing these poignant words from memory is something that will stay with me for ever.

It was a great joy two years later to start rehearsing this work with the Parliament Choir. In Dunedin the previous year, speaking to the audience at the beginning of the concert, I suggested that the composer, the choir and its director, the orchestra's Concert Master and members of the audience might consider coming to join us, hardly daring to believe they would, so I was thrilled when all of that happened. For so many to travel at their own expense from just about as far away as it's possible to be, made the first performance in the Northern Hemisphere a momentous occasion.

The Choir didn't find it easy at first. The atrocities that the text and music describe so vividly made for heavy-going early rehearsals in London. As ever, I was extremely grateful to those open-minded members of the Choir who could see from the start that it was worth the investment of effort. I remember getting quite cross with one MP who told me in front of a large number of the Choir that they found it too depressing. I swiftly pointed out that it was probably fairly depressing for a lot of the soldiers involved and their families too, to whom they never returned. The job of art is not to make something so barbaric seem like fun.

Early in the rehearsal process I was driving the aforementioned Kate Kennedy (by now my wife) to a meeting with her colleague Kate McLoughlin in the English Faculty at Oxford. Professor McLoughlin has written many books on war-related literature and was in 2017-18 the co-convenor of a Mellon-Sawyer international seminar series: Post-War: Commemoration, Reconstruction, Reconciliation. Kate McLoughlin had asked Kate Kennedy to advise on possibilities for the series and as we discussed it on the car journey, it occurred to her that I should invite myself to the meeting and suggest *Gallipoli to the Somme*. Professor McLoughlin (a fine musician herself) was interested and, once she'd heard the work, agreed to promote a concert at the Sheldonian Theatre (a place dear to Nick and me, as we'd both received our degrees in that historic hall). The Mellon-Sawyer support for that concert together with that of Creative New Zealand for the UK part of the project, as well as the financial partnership with Southbank Sinfonia, all enabled us to take the risk on a Southbank Centre event and it was a particular joy to be able to offer our friends from Down Under two concerts (as well as a reception on the Master's lawn of Trinity College before the Oxford concert, and another in the penthouse of the New Zealand High Commission before the London performance) to honour their commitment in travelling so far. We were also grateful to FANZA (Foundation for Australia and New Zealand Arts) for their support for the project.

The two performances were quite different: both began with Dunedin violinist (and member of that year's Southbank Sinfonia) Annabel Drummond playing *The Lark Ascending* by Vaughan Williams, composed in 1914 and based on George Meredith's poem.

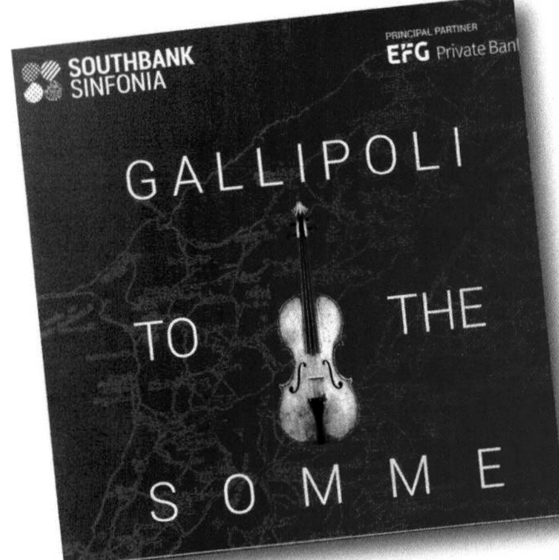

During the first few minutes at the Sheldonian, there was a busker outside competing strongly with the solo violin, effectively – and perhaps appropriately at a war commemoration concert – sabotaging our idyll.

The Queen Elizabeth Hall makes up for its lesser elegance with the convenience of being purpose-built for classical concerts, as well as for its generous hospitality space. The post-war brutalist architecture of the auditorium allows nothing to detract from the power of the performance and, having already performed *Gallipoli to the Somme* in the Sheldonian, as is so often the case, I think everybody felt more confident in this second performance to be bold on the South Bank (where of course the best artists in the world regularly perform).

The soloists for both performances were Anna Leese (also from Dunedin and a former student of Anthony Ritchie) and Jon Stainsby, who had won a prize in Southbank Sinfonia's Peter Hulsen Orchestral Song Award. Peter Hulsen, himself a war victim, had come to the UK on the Kindertransport and left provision in his estate for this award. I should also mention another great friend and supporter of Southbank Sinfonia: Elman Poole from the South Island of New Zealand who, over twelve years, funded around 15 Kiwi players (like Annabel Drummond) to take part in the SbS annual programme. He was with us at the Sheldonian performance and that was one of his last outings before his death the following year. His will has provided South bank Sinfonia with enough to fund a New Zealand player for 50 years.

Scott Blackwell, Secretary of the City Choir Dunedin, writes:

I'm writing on behalf of City Choir Dunedin to thank you, the Parliament Choir and Southbank Sinfonia for making our recent visit an unforgettable experience for our singers. We had such a wonderful time singing with you, we feel blessed and honoured for the chance to share your talent, your time and your hospitality.

This generosity extended to welcoming visiting singers into the Choir and into your homes and to the delight which many of your members expressed in singing Anthony Ritchie's evocative music and text.

For our part, we were made to feel so welcome and comfortable in these extraordinary venues and by this extraordinary and august company.

I wish we had some opportunity to reciprocate your hospitality but understand that many of your members would be unable to spare the time to travel to New Zealand. If, however, any of your members were in New Zealand (for example, for the 12th World Symposium on Choral Music, to be held in Auckland, New Zealand in July 2020) we would be delighted to extend some Kiwi hospitality.

2019 Westminster Cathedral
The Dream of Gerontius

Simon Over on a long-held dream

'Do you think we would ever be able to tackle *Gerontius*?' asked Baroness Hollis some time during the Choir's first year. 'One day,' I replied, determined and desperate to do it in equal measure.

We approached Westminster Cathedral about performing it in 2008, but the 150th anniversary of Elgar's birth had been the previous year and several performances had taken place there, so the Administrator recommended we sing another of Elgar's great works, *The Apostles*.

Between the general rehearsal and the performance of *The Apostles*, the Chaplain at the time escorted me to his office to use as a Green Room. Seated at his desk, contemplating the privilege and responsibility of the task I was about to undertake, I noticed some of his cards and without conscious thought, took one. For reasons I can hardly explain, the following day I phoned him and asked whether I might talk to him about joining the Roman Catholic church. He put me in touch with Father Michael Durand from whom some years before I had bought the complete works of Mozart in the Bärenreiter edition (from which I've conducted a number of works in Parliament Choir concerts: *Coronation Mass*, *Requiem*, *C Minor Mass* as well as various arias, concertos and opera excerpts).

Father Michael prepared me in six sessions, after which I was received into the Catholic Church in the cathedral the following summer, since when the cathedral (which I've loved since my teens, when I came to London for organ lessons with Stephen Cleobury, Director of Music at the time) has been my spiritual home.

So, the desire to perform *Gerontius* there grew ever stronger, and when James Murphy, Managing Director of SbS at the time, suggested to Anna Yallop, after the success of the partnership with the orchestra in presenting *Belshazzar's Feast* that *Gerontius* would be a good next project, I was delighted. The subsequent discovery that Cardinal Newman, whose poem Elgar used as his text, was to be canonised by Pope Francis on 13 October 2019, exactly a month before our scheduled performance, only heightened the excitement and my determination to make it work.

My first experience of the work was, as a boy, hearing Saint Michael's Singers perform it in Coventry, so I asked Paul Leddington Wright whether we could do another shared project with a performance in Coventry Cathedral as well as the one in Westminster, and it was planned for 9 November.

The Westminster performance became significant in a number of ways: as well as the building's relationship to St John Henry Newman, it was where Elgar had himself conducted the first London performance. It was for the players of last year's Southbank Sinfonia the final concert of their year. For a number of MPs who were not standing at the forthcoming Brexit-dominated election, it was their last concert with the Choir, and it was a finale too for one of our patrons, Sir Thomas Allen, who had sung it early in his career and then, after huge farewells from Covent Garden just months before, decided that this would be his 'Gerontic' farewell to performance. The combination of his mighty Priest, sung from the pulpit of the cathedral together with the Angel, Catherine Wyn-Rogers, who has sung it countless times, and the brilliant Gerontius, Robert Murray, who decided just before the performance that they should sing it from memory (which was terrifying for the rest of us), was unforgettable for me; I can't imagine a better group of soloists. The addition to the Parliament Choir and Coventry Cathedral Chorus of friends from the St Alban's Bach Choir (organised by Mike Taylor) and the chamber group Mosaic, who provided a glorious semi-chorus, completed a stellar cast.

Before the concert I asked the audience to remember Gil Magill for whose funeral the previous year the final section 'Softly and Gently' had been played, and Lord Jenkin of Roding, one of the first Trustees of the Choir who loved the work dearly. He was a true elder statesman, from whom I learnt a great deal.

Westminster Cathedral was packed, with many unable to get a ticket, and the responses to the performance were numerous and extraordinary. A member of the audience who spoke to me afterwards commented that one could not imagine a better place to perform such a work. The following day I received an email from the British Ambassador to the Holy See inviting me to take the whole cast to the Vatican in October 2020 (a year after the canonisation of Newman). Lord German and I undertook a trip to the Vatican in January 2020 to discuss logistics, after which we were very optimistic about it happening. COVID-19 prevented that year, but at the time of writing, this has just been confirmed for October 2022. After all that Italy and the UK have suffered through this awful time, the need for such collaboration is greater than ever.

The Dream of Gerontius, *Westminster Cathedral, 13 November 2019*

Alan Walker

Our first performance of the work, on a dark and rainy Saturday evening, was an intense experience, with the audience remaining seated and silent during the short interval and almost unwilling to break the atmosphere with applause after the thrilling conclusion. Sir Thomas Allen's silent ascent to the pulpit beside the Choir to sing 'Go Forth' rendered that movement even more effective for me by him being only feet away – unforgettable.

For the Westminster Cathedral performance, I was fortunate to secure tickets for my parents who travelled to London to join my mother-in-law in the audience. My father had accompanied my mother to a performance of the *Dream* on a date almost 50 years earlier. That version was sung on a rainy day in a marquee, which sprang a leak and whose drips were eventually diverted into a surprisingly resonant metal bin. Our performance lacked that essential element but happily was adjudged to have been of better quality all round. High praise indeed!

Christmas

Vivian Widgery

Where would Christmas be without choirs, big, small, medium, good, not quite so good? Who doesn't enjoy singing Christmas carols, whether as part of a choir or just in the audience or congregation? So it is with the Parliament Choir – Christmas has always been important to us, although it took us a while to settle into the best venue and format.

We started with a bang – and why not? – when we sang the Bach *Christmas Oratorio* in the Methodist Central Hall in December 2001, where La Serenissima played with us and Lorna Anderson, Richard Wyn Roberts, James Gilchrist and Michael George were the soloists. The following year was even bigger and better: the Royal Albert Hall, no less – the only time that the Choir has sung there. This was a massive event, with other choirs taking part and Dame Esther Rantzen compering. She took the time to lobby the parliamentarians in the Choir on behalf of Childline, quite understandably, while the conductor, Richard Cooke, asked male Peers to jump in the air at the line 'Ten lords a-leaping', a request that was not taken up.

Perhaps because this was a hard act or two to follow, there was a hiatus of one year before, in December 2004, the Choir started a series of five small carol concerts in the atrium of Portcullis House, the parliamentary building across the road from the Palace. Here, we gave some short but fun concerts, with audience participation from Members and staff of both Houses, who came and went, often having their supper while watching and taking part.

Christmas 2010 was the year of Ryba's *Czech Christmas Mass*, and the occasion of the Choir's first overseas performance, in Prague, an expedition that those who took part in remember very well – references to it will be found elsewhere in the book. And the next year we were back in Central Hall, this time partly to celebrate the fact that the organ had recently been restored. Unfortunately, it broke down halfway through and the organist and Nick O'Neill disappeared into its bowels and did some tinkering to persuade it to start again. Luckily, it worked. Although Simon Over conducted and Southbank Sinfonia played with us, Howard Goodall conducted the Choir for his lovely setting of *Stella, quam viderant Magi*. The programme was entitled 'A Westminster Christmas' and both David Cameron, then Prime Minister, and Ed Miliband, then Leader of the Opposition, did readings, albeit via recordings. This was the first time that Classic FM recorded one of the Choir's concerts, and broadcast it on Christmas Eve: a great honour.

Various venues and various different programmes had been tried, and it was felt that the 'Westminster Christmas' format – a mixture of choir-only pieces and audience carols, sprinkled with readings about Christmas – worked very well… so now to find a venue. What could be more appropriate than St John's Smith Square, just around the corner from Parliament, and the right size for our audience? Thus, 2012 saw the start of our Christmas association with SJSS, and it is now a tradition, even in 2020, in pandemic conditions, socially distanced and streamed to its audience.

Something else that has become a tradition is Nick O'Neill composing or arranging a carol each year, taking a fresh look at old classics or writing the tender and inexpressively moving *This Light of Reason* in 2016, commissioned in memory of Jo Cox, and the equally moving *Carol for Jane* in 2017, after the death of a choir member. In 2014, to commemorate the start of the First World War, Nick's arrangement of two carols in combination, 'It came upon the midnight clear' and 'Stille Nacht' provided another poignant moment, with one choir up in the gallery and a trumpet playing to evoke the Christmas truce. There have been various different accompanying musicians, including a Slovenian conductor, the Bundestag Choir and their conductor Žarko Bulajić, London Festival Brass, the RAF Salon Orchestra, the trumpeter Crispian Steele-Perkins, percussionists and, of course, Nick O'Neill. One year, Nick and Simon played a piano duet, a bravura rendition of 'Brasileira' from Milhaud's *Suite for Two Pianos*.

Christmas will always be part of the Choir now.

Alastair, Lord Aberdare

As a passionate Berlioz fan, I was delighted that the Choir sang 'The Shepherds' Farewell' from *The Childhood of Christ* in our 2019 Christmas concert. In introducing the piece, Simon

kindly mentioned that I am the Chairman of the Berlioz Society. Despite having listened to virtually all Berlioz's works countless times, this was actually the first piece by him that I had actually sung. So I was rather embarrassed to discover for myself the truth of what I have always told people about why I love Berlioz: that one of the features of his music is unexpectedness, and that much of it is difficult to perform. Despite my knowing the piece so well, I felt I failed dismally to do it justice in my attempts to sing the bass part.

Alison Baverstock

A fine Christmas present – the chance to sing in St John's Smith Square...

When the Christmas decorations come down in January, I always find the associated sudden and close contact with all that tinsel feels a bit *de trop*. It's not just food and alcohol we have had too much of, there's also the decorations and compulsory jollity. So January is when people start on diets and detoxing, estate agents prepare for the desire for change that fuels the spring selling bonanza, and publishers launch all their new 'how to' books. But before we consign our own memories of 'Christmas just past' to the recycling, it's worth pausing to think about the Parliament Choir's final concert of 2014, in St John's Smith Square.

To start with, it's a building that always takes me by surprise. Walking towards the church from Westminster, it seems to have just landed centre-square; the staircases that lead up to the doors function like the panels that supported the craft that took ET home. They appear precisely locked into position, ready to fold up again at short notice. Lit up against the night sky, the building seems to hover slightly, as if primed for take-off. For those who enter from the box office and restaurant the transformation is equally striking – from low ceilinged bustle to high church baroque; from talking emphatically across a tight space in order to make yourself heard to a pressing silence – sudden and self-imposed.

This year the concert marked a high for the Choir in several ways. Firstly, there was the surprise of finding oneself on stage, all dressed up and ready to perform with at least some voice, for the second time within a week. Not all of us made it. Some had opted for either one concert or the other – or laryngitis had made the choice for them.

But whether you were in the audience or on stage, the music was just beautiful. From the rousing opening strains of a hymn in which all participated to the eerie serenity of *Stille Nacht*, wafting over the space from the organ loft towards the Choir, reaching us just in time for a reply. The singing was of a high quality throughout, and it was pleasing to have friends say they had heard – and enjoyed – the concert when broadcast on Classic FM on Christmas Day.

For the Choir, Smith Square also provided the year's most comfortable venue – and as this was our fourth major concert of the year, we had a variety of useful comparators. The plump red cushions and significant leg room are a pleasure, notwithstanding the charms of origami covers and crush of the massed choirs in Westminster Cathedral, and the abiding summer chill of Westminster Hall. Certainly no one seemed in a rush to go home afterwards.

There were many who just stood around and chatted, and the bar downstairs did a roaring trade, even though Caroline had warned that staying on might mean you were likely to be asked about sponsorship.

Overall, what stands out from 2014? Perhaps that a choir matures with movement. This year we have been reordered, recombined, sung in various languages and in a range of locations – and as a result perhaps become more engaged with those around us. All the parties that surrounded the German choir's visits helped us to recognise more faces, and the early sing-throughs of new music are sounding stronger. Due to Nick's warm-ups, I can hold my breath for much longer.

There are certain associated stresses. Lining up a large number of people in a small space involves a snaking procession, folding back on itself – perhaps last experienced at school. There is an accompanying anxiety I had forgotten about since. No one is quite sure where they are supposed to be, and whether the people we were standing next to now are indeed those we spotted at the rehearsal, given the transformative effect of choir costumes.

But however tired we were by early December, the dazzle of a concert night is always an uplifting experience. And although we had just a week between our two final performances, looking back there is a lot to be said for an early Christmas concert. Ours set the scene for the time ahead – distilling quiet and beauty before the final seasonal rush and plunder began. In short, a hopeful presage of Christmases to come.

A socially-distanced Christmas concert 2020, St John's Smith Square

Nicholas O'Neill's compositions and arrangements for the Choir's Christmas concerts:

'Sweet Was the Song' – 15 December 2005
'Silent Night' – 7 December 2011
'Awhile A'wandering' – 5 December 2012
'We Three Kings' – 5 December 2012
'The Angel Gabriel' – 3 December 2014
'It Came Upon The Midnight Clear' (Christmas truce) – 3 December 2014
'Westminster Wassail' – 9 December 2015
'This Light of Reason' – 7 December 2016
'Carol for Jane' – 6 December 2017
'Gabriel, That Angel Bright' – 5 December 2018
'The Oxen' – 4 December 2019
VW

Anghiari and the Parliament Choir: The Development of a Tradition

The Anghiari Festival has evolved over almost two decades, since 2003, when Simon Over was invited to take over the singing school Studio Lirico after the death of its Director. In the process of founding Southbank Sinfonia he could not take this on but volunteered to bring the orchestra over to perform some concerts. When Simon went to recce this exquisite little Tuscan walled town, situated between the upper Tiber and the Arno, he saw all sorts of possibilities for concerts in its various churches and gardens, in the town and countryside around, and for chamber groups to play in its *piazze*, *piazzette* and *angoli*. If he were to bring the orchestra to Italy for one concert then why not make a week of it? With the wonderful support of the *comune* (town council), over a few years that first *settimana musicale* became the Anghiari Festival, a magical week for those who have attended and performed there and a widely acknowledged benefit to the town.

Sally Cantello, with contributions from Val Goss and Nicholas O'Neill

The Anghiari Festival has become for many Parliament Choir singers an integral part of the Choir's annual programme.

At first a small number of choir members spotted the opportunity to satisfy their love of music and all things Italian with a trip to the festival. Eventually, as word got out about the joys of the festival, numbers grew until, in the latter years, 30 or more choir members not only regularly attended the festival but took an active part in performances, together with a growing number of their friends and family.

This active participation came about gradually over a number of years as relationships developed between individual choir members and local music aficionados. One in particular, Jo Harvey, an English woman who married an Italian and settled and raised a family in Anghiari, acted as a key protagonist in the building of these links.

The festival generally includes a wide variety of symphonic, chamber, choral and operatic music. Young opera artists have visited from the British Youth Opera, the Dutch National Opera Academy, the Royal Opera House Jette Parker Young Artists Programme and Bury Court Opera, while choral performances have generally been by Vox Musica, the talented ensemble directed by Michael Berman, one of the founders of Southbank Sinfonia. In addition to these performances, the local amateur Anghiari Chorus would generally put on a choral work.

It was in 2010, with a performance of the Fauré *Requiem* scheduled, that the local singers realised they had some UK singers in the town attending the festival and invited them to join their ranks.

Scores were borrowed, a few hasty rehearsals organised and on 21 July, about six or seven members of the Parliament Choir joined their Italian friends in a moving rendition of the *Requiem* in the beautiful sixteenth century church of Carmine, a former Carmelite monastery in the hills outside the town, with soloists from the Dutch National Opera Company. And so a tradition was born that has intensified the links between the *Anghiaresi* and those who attend the festival, and led to strong friendships, new skills and

perspectives, and some outstanding collaborative international performances.

The following year, in 2011, a larger number of Parliament Choir members attended the festival as word got around about the experience. After all, what's not to like about listening to music in the warmth of a Tuscan evening, in locations steeped in history and surrounded by stunning scenery (complemented, of course, by delicious food and wine)? And as for actually taking part in a performance in such magical venues....

And so, on 23 July 2011, Choir members lined up again with the locals, this time in the Piazza del Popolo, to sing the Mozart *Coronation Mass*. The combined singer numbers having grown with the addition of the UK singers, the staging didn't offer enough space for all to line up. The solution was to station the bass singers in the building behind and have them sing out of the windows. This allowed them to be fully heard but not fully seen, affording the opportunity for a bottle or two of local red to be consumed clandestinely during proceedings (or so it is rumoured...).

By this time, the local Anghiari choir had morphed into the *Maratona Corale*, so-called from the long weekend of intensive rehearsals held in May of the same year to prepare for the concert. Once the timing of these Maratona weekends had been changed from February to May (after a particularly snowy weekend hampered plans to attend) they quickly became a feature of Parliament Choir life, with many choir

Anghiari from outside the town walls

Verdi Requiem *in Piazza Baldaccio, Anghiari*

members adding a pleasantly warm off-season weekend in Tuscany to their holiday schedule.

Smart planning on the part of Simon Over meant that the repertoire for the Anghiari and UK concerts was coordinated, so both UK and Italian singers could support each other's performances with increasing confidence and minimal rehearsals.

In 2012, on the 10th anniversary of the festival, 25 Parliament Choir members joined the *Anghiaresi* (and were individually named in the programme for the first time) to sing the Vivaldi *Magnificat* and *Gloria*, this time in the cloisters of the Carmine monastery. Before the production, locals displayed their customary hospitality by providing a delicious supper eaten in the evening sunshine with glorious views of the hills and valleys surrounding the old monastery.

By 2013, the concerts and their associated rehearsals had become a regular part of the festival. The first rehearsal would be held on the Friday evening before the start of the festival and kicked off by an *al fresco* supper provided by the local singers, giving participants a chance to catch up on the year's events and gossip. Friends and family (FAFs!) who weren't taking part in rehearsals used the free time afforded by these to continue lounging by the pool or, in the words of an MP accompanying his wife to the festival, spend happy times 'FAFing' around at the pizzeria.

The Anghiari singers were directed by Bruno Sannai and Giulio Camaiti but by this point Nick O'Neill, the Parliament Choir's Chorus Master, had become heavily involved in both rehearsals and performance, giving the benefit of his deep experience of the English choral tradition. This sometimes sat at odds with the Italians who had a more idiosyncratic approach to practice but Nick, whose mother tongue is Italian, was able to overcome language difficulties or cultural differences and directed many barbs of gentle sarcasm at the UK singers contrasting with a more vocal approach to upbraiding the Italians. Stiff-upper-lip Brits looked on in amazement at Nick's impassioned berating of the Italians for too much chatter in rehearsals, only to see him laughing with them over a shared beer in Bar Baldaccio an hour later.

The performance of 2013 was Handel's *Messiah*, with 24 members of the Parliament Choir singing (and one of them being attacked by an enormous maybug attracted by the bright lights), and an enthusiastic audience seated picturesquely around the old well of the monastery, perhaps contemplating, in the quieter arias, the former Carmelite inhabitants going about their daily tasks.

Anghiari is in a mountainous part of Italy so the weather can be unpredictable, even in summer. Particularly stormy weather, complete with torrential rain and lightning strikes, affected the whole 2014 festival, including the joint UK/Italian performance of the Mendelssohn *Hymn of Praise*, for which Nick O'Neill had provided a Latin text, once again held at the Carmine monastery. The rain, or the imminent threat of it, lent a 'hokey-cokey' aspect to the concert. With instruments insured for tens of thousands of pounds, the string players could be forgiven for wanting to avoid the damage a single drop of rain can do to a treasured patina. As a result, orchestra, singers and audience moved from the outside

The performance was watched by an audience of over 800, added to by scores of onlookers crowding down the steep hill to the piazza, *enjoying the spectacle for free, and even today they say the town has never seen anything like it.*

courtyard and cloisters to the inside of the church and back out again several times until the final decision was made to perform inside. The acoustic of the church was less than perfect for the choral piece but proved beneficial for Nick O'Neill's string piece *Against the Pull of Silence* (commissioned by a choir member) which sounded sonorous and moving in the more confined setting of the church.

In September of that year, a number of Parliament Choir singers left the UK in 26°C of heat to join the Maratona Chorus in a surprisingly chilly Anghiari for a 'Come and Sing' weekend prior to the Choir's own performance of the Verdi *Requiem*, with 60 of the *Maratona Corale* joining the UK singers in Westminster Cathedral in November 2014.

The increasing skills and confidence of the combined festival chorus and the success of the Verdi concert in London led to the most exciting UK/Anghiari joint venture yet, in 2015: the Verdi *Requiem* held in Piazza Baldaccio, the main square of the town, with the main road through town closed off to traffic – the importance accorded to cultural events in Italy! Val Goss from the Parliament Choir, who had so fallen in love with the town after previous visits that she and her husband Paul bought an apartment there, volunteered to do much of the organisation and James Naughtie, an enthusiastic supporter of the festival (and singer in the combined performances, along with his wife Eleanor Updale) spearheaded the necessary fund-raising effort.

The 30 or so choir members and family and friends who took part will never forget that performance. The hot, sticky, bilingual, tutti rehearsals held in the 30°C heat of a glass-roofed sports hall tested everyone's stamina, patience and powers of concentration. The same sweltering sports hall was also the fallback option in the event of inclement weather, so the organisers were fervently hoping (and probably praying hard) that the weather stayed dry. On the day itself performers and organisers alike looked nervously at the gathering clouds but after a brief shower the sky cleared in time for the final rehearsal and 170 singers came together in the newly-styled Anghiari Festival Chorus in a spectacular and exhilarating rendition of this monumental work. Audience and singers alike were thrilled by eight off-stage trumpets stationed in upper windows round the square and two spine-tingling bass drums thundering through the 'Dies Irae', played by local musicians.

The performance was watched by an audience of over 800, added to by scores of onlookers crowding down the steep hill to the *piazza*, enjoying the spectacle for free, and even today they say the town has never seen anything like it.

In 2016, choir members joined their Italian colleagues to sing the Gounod *Messe Solennelle* and Nick O'Neill's *Tu es Petrus*, inspired by the Parliament Choir's performance of these two pieces in April of that year in Notre-Dame. Some singers went direct from Paris to the Maratona weekend which took place just a week after the Notre-Dame concert, attracted by the opportunity to spend a few more days in Paris and then cross Europe by train. The July concert was the first of these to take place in the Cathedral of Sansepolcro, an historic town in the Tiber valley known for its Piero della Francesca frescoes (not to mention its excellent market) and reached from the top of Anghiari by a hair-raising drive down a 1 in 4 dead-straight hill. The town provided a magnificent buffet before the concert and the concert was so popular and the Cathedral so full that the Mayor had nowhere to sit. Nick O'Neill sprang into action to find a chair for him, only to discover that by the time he had located the Mayor and got him to the right spot, the empty chair had been nabbed by an enthusiastic Italian lady. Discussions ensued and minutes before baton down order was restored, with all suitably seated.

2017's performance – this time the Mozart *Requiem* – also took place in the Cathedral of Sansepolcro. Over 30 members of the Parliament Choir sang in the Festival Chorus along with seven from the choir of the German Bundestag who had performed with the Parliament Choir in London in 2014 and in Berlin in 2016, including their director, Žarko Bulajić. An *al fresco* supper was again provided by the organisers and choir members sat in their 'concert black' on the steps of the Cathedral to enjoy it in the welcome shade. It was a particularly hot evening (resulting in one choir member succumbing to heat stroke during the performance), so delicious *gelati* were enjoyed after the concert by singers and audience alike, wandering around the square in the balmy temperatures of a late Italian evening talking excitedly about yet another stellar performance.

In 2018 it was the turn of the Mozart *Mass in C minor*. As a prelude to this, a large number of UK singers had joined their Italian counterparts in Anghiari for a Maratona weekend in May, finished off by a performance of the work in the newly refurbished seventeenth century Propositura church perched high on the Anghiari townscape.

Verdi Requiem *audience in Piazza Baldaccio*

The main performance of the work the following July was more challenging. Reverberations and a challenging acoustic of the church used in Sansepolcro for rehearsals of the large choir made practice difficult, particularly in regard to the tricky fugues (but did have the advantage of getting singers to develop their skills in relating to the beat not the sound).

On the day of the concert the forecast was grim and the event was nearly abandoned, owing not just to rain but a storm of near

In Anghiari, at festival time, music oozes through thick medieval walls, fills lofty cathedrals, rings around open squares, whispers in ancient village churches and springs from the Tiber! Even the sunflowers and tobacco plants dance and seem to sing in the breeze. It is a magical musical environment, which the Choir has made accessible to me.

Gillian Perry

Summer storm over Anghiari, and mopping up

biblical proportions that ripped up trees, smashed pots, destroyed awnings, shattered windows, scattered the carefully arranged chairs and left the Piazza Baldaccio awash. The heroic efforts of Simon's stepson Theo Kennedy and an army of helpers to press every mop in Anghiari into service to dry the deluged stage sufficiently for the string players to be satisfied no harm would come to their instruments (and singers' and audience bottoms wouldn't get too damp) enabled the concert to go ahead only slightly delayed, albeit with no final rehearsal or sound checks. When inclement weather strikes in Anghiari, concerts are usually moved indoors but no church in the town can accommodate the 800-strong audience held by the town's biggest piazza.

The Haydn *St Nicholas Mass* and *Te Deum* were additions to the UK/Italian programme in 2019, along with another rendition of Nick O'Neill's *Tu es Petrus* in the serene surroundings of the garden of Piero della Francesca in Sansepolcro. In stark contrast to the previous year this outdoor concert was notable for glorious but burningly hot sunshine. At 6pm when the rehearsal was due to start, it was still too hot for the delicate instruments to be out in the blazing sun, and waiting for the cooler part of the evening and for shade to come was a testing time for the performers. Parliament Choir singers, however, relished the chance to sing the Haydn in such a contrasting location to the Guards' Chapel where they had performed the work in the previous April and particularly enjoyed getting goosebumps hearing Erika Curbelo playing the Haydn *Trumpet Concerto* again.

Ciao Anghiari! Ci vediamo presto!

Virginia Hawkins

Anghiari is my happy place. It's where I go in my head when I want to get away from the trials and tribulations of day-to-day life. The festival experience is the perfect combination of everything that enriches life – wonderful company, good food and drink, amazing surroundings, perfect weather and, above all, beautiful, beautiful music. Being in Anghiari for the festival is just like being at home: the beautiful medieval town is friendly and welcoming and there are familiar faces from the Choir, friends from the UK and the town – made in previous visits everywhere – as well as new friends to make. My first visit in 2017 was an intensely emotional and life-enriching experience. The previous few months had been very challenging in many ways, culminating with the death of my father. The whole week, from boarding the early morning flight from Stansted with colleagues from the Parliament Choir to the final gala concert on the Friday night, was a truly magical experience. There are two things that really stand out from that week:

The Allegri Quartet, artistic partners of Southbank Sinfonia, played an intimate concert at the Santuario del Carmine in Combarbio on the Wednesday night of the festival. As they played the beautiful *Adagio for Strings* by Samuel Barber, tears stared to flow down my cheeks as I thought of my father who felt so far away. Towards the end of the piece, as I looked up into the night sky, a shooting star flashed across the heavens. In that moment, life suddenly seemed to make sense as the chaos of the past few months fell away and a great feeling of peace came over me.

Lady Judd, Pamela Currin and Christine Heald

The following evening was the Anghiari Festival Chorus' concert in the Duomo in Sansepolcro. The weather was very hot (over 40 degrees) and the afternoon rehearsal of Mozart's *Requiem* in the cool cathedral building was a welcome relief from the heat for all of us. In the evening, the cool of the afternoon had been replaced by the intense heat of hundreds of bodies packing into the building. The Italian love of music had brought the people of Sansepolcro out in droves. Those who couldn't find seats hung off pillars and sat on the floor, some at (and perhaps on) the soloists' feet. As the first few bars of the 'Requiem Aeternum' swelled towards our first entry, we tried to keep our minds off the heat and on the music. All was going well – we even managed the entries of the 'Kyrie' and 'Dies Irae' pretty successfully. During the 'Domine Jesu Christe', we noticed that the lady in front of us was succumbing to the heat and starting to wobble. Aileen, who was standing next to me, deftly caught her as she sank to the floor (there was no seating for the Choir) and passed her my fan and some water. After a few minutes she revived and stood up again to continue singing – not a good idea. She lasted a few bars of the 'Hostias' and then went down again. Aileen spent the rest of the performance propping her up whilst attempting to sing from my music and reassuring Simon that our colleague was ok. The lady was seen by a doctor at the end of the concert and fully recovered after a couple of days' rest. I expected the concert to be memorable for the music (and it was) but it has stuck in the memory for other reasons too.

The following year in Bar Baldaccio, after the choral concert being delayed by a tornado, thunder and lightning and torrential rain, Val Goss and I decided to declare singing in Anghiari an extreme sport!

I remember once singing the Italian national anthem, with appropriate Verdian gusto, leaning out of a window high above a square in Tuscany, under the stars, with a Peer of the Realm on either side of me, and another concealed behind the open shutters, busying himself with a bottle of Soave. It could only be the Parliament Choir.

James Naughtie

Margaret Lykiardopoulos

I recall being very ill in Anghiari and the kindness of one of the Choir members, who visited me in hospital and made sure that I had what I needed for recovery in time for the concert. Friendship is so important, and the Choir members support each other in many different ways.

James Naughtie

I remember once singing the Italian national anthem, with appropriate Verdian gusto, leaning out of a window high above a square in Tuscany, under the stars, with a Peer of the Realm on either side of me, and another concealed behind the open shutters, busying himself with a bottle of Soave. It could only be the Parliament Choir.

It was the climax to one of the wonderful Anghiari Festivals, where Simon Over's Southbank Sinfonia takes over the town for a week in the summer and where those of us who have followed the players there for years have enjoyed so much thrilling music-making and have made so many friends. And into that mix comes the Choir. Their ranks swelled by the lusty voices of the local ensemble – featuring impressive ranks of *bassi profundi* – and interlopers like me, the tradition has been to put on a choral evening in the square of Anghiari. The setting couldn't be better – an intimate piazza in a hilltop town with medieval walls and views down the valley to the Tiber as it begins its long meander to Rome. There are a couple of cafés, the friendly Bar Baldaccio where they've invented a Southbank pizza, a statue of Garibaldi, and lots of cats. The performance I remember best was the Verdi *Requiem* (you can still find it on YouTube) which turned into one of those perfect nights. Soloists came all the way from the Royal Opera House, and I think by the end of it we all felt that kind of exhilaration you get when you climb a mountain, or ski down a steep run without falling over.

This is a choir with spirit. You can't miss it. The first time I encountered it I wondered, naturally, if there would be much political talk. Of course, there wasn't. You could tell immediately that the joy of coming together in order to get away from the daily round – whether as a Member of either House, or a secretarial or research worker, or someone working in the library – was a liberation. When Simon first spoke about it, many years ago, I suspect he was a little apprehensive about the kind of atmosphere it would create. Because choirs have to develop a personality: if they don't, they quickly fall silent. It didn't take him long to discover that this one did. My own experiences, either just listening or happily joining in, is that its hallmark is enthusiasm. When they're singing, they are as happy as schoolchildren let off the leash for the evening. Not a single amendment to a Finance Bill is ever discussed.

The Italian nights hold special memories for me. Denied the chance to be in Anghiari during lockdown, I was thinking back to so many fun times there. Rehearsing in a schoolroom in sweltering heat with bats flying everywhere; worrying about scores that were picked up by a Tuscan breeze and blown away; trying to master some convoluted colloquial phrase with the locals; singing *Messiah* in the cloisters of an old monastery; having fun afterwards.

I can't wait to go back, and raise a glass to Southbank Sinfonia and the Parliament Choir.

Salute!

James Naughtie flanked by Lord Beith (then Sir Alan Beith MP) and Sir Paul Hayter at the Speaker's State Apartments

Southbank Sinfonia perform in Piazza del Popolo at the Anghiari Festival (photograph taken from the Gosses' balcony)

Lockdown: Carry on Singing

Aileen Walker was immediately aware of the importance of connection and continuity for the well-being of the Choir

The onset of the COVID-19 pandemic led to the cancellation of our planned 'Party Favourites' concert in the Queen Elizabeth Hall in May 2020. Our planned concert in February 2021 was postponed, but we shall perform Bach's *Mass in B Minor* in November 2021.

Lockdown restrictions introduced in 2020 gave rise to two particular challenges: how to keep Choir members singing when we could not physically meet together at rehearsals; but also – just as importantly – how to keep members feeling connected to the Choir.

I knew it was important to keep the weekly Choir email messages going. I also worked with Sally Martin-Brown, one of the Choir sopranos and a music teacher herself, to set up regular online opportunities to keep our voices in shape, continue to rehearse and to see fellow members' faces. Sally ran general sing-along sessions on Mondays via our private Facebook group and Zoom. We progressed to resuming our singing of the Bach *B Minor Mass* in separate voice part study sessions on Wednesdays, to keep developing our knowledge of that work. Even while on sabbatical our Chorus Master, Nick O'Neill, also filmed study sessions for us on different movements of the Bach *Mass in B Minor*. As the autumn term came round and we were still unable to meet together, Sally, Nick and Simon were running weekly Bach rehearsals for each voice part.

I know many Choir members have hugely appreciated these activities and the opportunity to keep in touch with each other.

Between the second lockdown and tightening of restrictions in December there was a tiny window of opportunity for some members of the Choir to perform a reduced version of 'A Westminster Christmas' in St John's Smith Square. There was no audience; the singers were spread out in the main body of the church and the concert went out on the St John's Youtube channel with tickets sold in aid of Shelter.

Sally Martin-Brown offers this reflection on lockdown

In weekly sessions we kept singing from April 2020 as the impact of the COVID-19 pandemic had its effect. When I started the rehearsals to keep us singing when others were unavailable, I never envisioned just how long they would go on for. I just knew it is so important to keep a singing community, well, singing!

Connecting via the internet was the only way. As the communication latency is too much we could not sing together, and so at first it was learning short Soprano, Alto, Tenor and Bass pieces, some songs, some sacred anthems that would then be sung with me and piano accompaniment from people's homes.

Once I worked out how to share the sound well via the newly learnt Zoom app (so many new words!), I also began to include recordings of other choirs, large and small, professional or keen amateur choral societies, that we could turn up the volume and sing along with. I wanted us to be able to have a sense of feeling and hearing our voices singing in harmony with others, something we were all aware of missing acutely. Songs from pop to jazz styles, hymns, anthems, madrigals, spirituals and folk songs. In the singsong choir Monday sessions, we explored and learnt many styles: from the 1500s to a 2021 composition, we covered a huge range to keep people singing and engaged.

There were many technical mishaps as we all learnt the new norm, and I'm proud of how we all stepped up and had a go to keep the music happening, even with extraneous 'noises off' from kettles to dogs. I think Simon would have liked the use of the mute button!

As the weeks progressed, we installed and got used to Zoom's idiosyncrasies as well as the Facebook Live. We learnt to sing in our own space while thinking ourselves internally as if in a bigger group, harmonising with me and with the many other singing groups from the recordings.

The recordings we sang with came from choral groups like The Sixteen, Voces 8, The Cambridge Singers under John Rutter, Union Chapel NYC, USA, to cathedral choirs like St Paul's or King's College Cambridge. As well as singing *a capella* on their own, members sang with my live piano or with me in four- or five-part harmony, with me prerecording some of the other parts such as when we sang the spiritual 'Wade in the Water' for which I rewrote some more positive words to lift us up:

I want to live freely while I live,
Show the world what I've got to give,
I want to live freely while I live.

Through the many weeks of singing new repertoire, continuing to learn the Bach *B Minor Mass*, and engaging with my warm-up exercises and stretches, I want to thank everyone for taking part in this extraordinary process and, on a weekly basis, keeping our choral dreams, community and the music alive. When I look back it was quite a ride!

Music doesn't exist without us performing it, as it is ephemeral and has to happen again the next time or it is lost. Mostly this can be seen through history as being caused by war or prohibition of the Arts, but this time a virus pandemic suddenly quietened the voices. We were delighted when live rehearsals began again in September 2021.

John Dawson

During lockdown due to the coronavirus, the Parliament Choir has demonstrated its modernity and adaptability, and I have enjoyed participating in the virtual choir practices via Zoom on Monday evenings. This has enabled me and other choir members to maintain our interest in the Choir as well as our enjoyment of singing and keeping in touch with each other.

The Future

When the pandemic struck early in 2020 and the Choir's activities were suspended, nobody could have envisaged quite the extent of disruption to all our lives nor the duration and uncertainty it would bring. Immediately our spring concert was cancelled, then it became clear that the Bach *B Minor Mass* planned for the autumn would also have to be postponed, first until February, then until June, and then again until autumn.

While we cannot be certain what the future holds, what is certain is that the Choir is in good heart, thanks to the efforts of Aileen, Sally, Nick and Simon and now Virginia to keep us all encouraged During the early part of 2021 the Choir learnt Duruflé's *Requiem* and continued to rehearse Bach's *B minor Mass*. The Bach performance will take place at St John's Smith Square in November. While a December trip to join the Choir of the Slovenian Parliament has had to be postponed, we hope to go there in 2022. An invitation to perform *The Dream of Gerontius* in Rome has been confirmed by the Vatican, and will take place next October in the Vatican Basilica of St Paul outside the walls. Further plans include a collaboration with the Bar Choral Society to sing a programme of Vaughan Williams, live performances of Duruflé at Keble College, Oxford and in London, and a December concert in the Victoria and Albert Museum. There is much to look forward to.

The interior of Keble College Chapel, location for planned concert in April 2022

Vatican Basilica of St Paul without the Walls in Rome (San Paolo fuori le mura), venue for planned concert in October 2022

Appendices

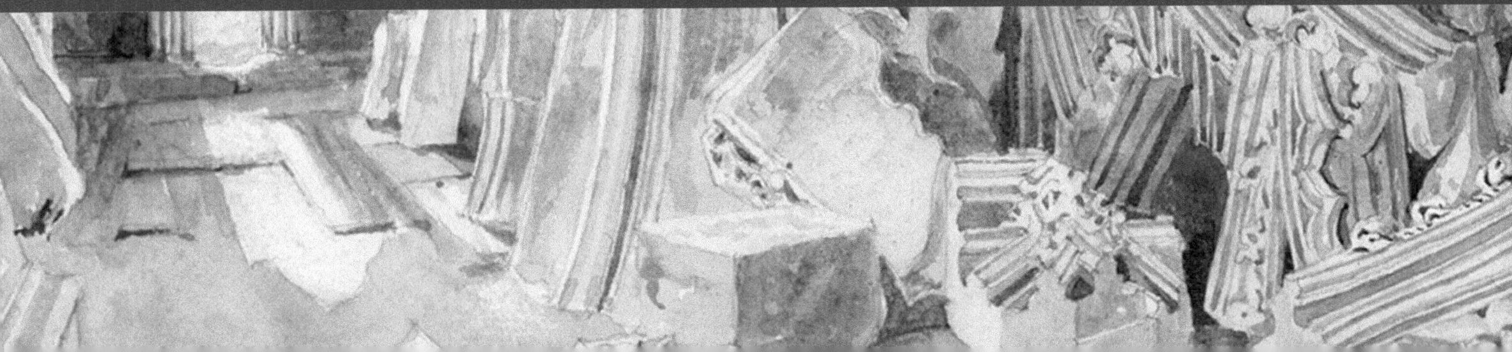

St Mary Undercroft, 1348-2020: The Improbable History of a Hidden Chapel

Elizabeth Hallam Smith

The Parliament Choir is privileged to have one of the most decorative rehearsal spaces in the country. St Mary Undercroft is the lower storey of the double-height royal chapel of St Stephen, completed in 1348, and renowned throughout England for its glittering splendour. It was as lavish as the Sainte-Chapelle in Paris, the Capetian kings' palace chapel which the Plantagenets hoped to upstage at Westminster.

In 1348 King Edward III founded a college at Westminster. It had 12 canons, 13 vicars, choristers and clerks who were housed in the area. Exceedingly wealthy and prestigious, the college was based in St Stephen's Chapel and, like the similar and still surviving college of St George's Chapel, Windsor, its role was to intercede for the crown and kingdom. At Westminster, services for the royal family were held in the upper chapel.

The undercroft housed the Chapel of St Mary in the Vaults, for the use of the royal household. Like the upper chapel, it was an important liturgical space. Verger and organist Nicholas Ludford – the last composer-in-residence until Nicholas O'Neill – composed a series of important masses for the chapel before c.1535, some dedicated to King Henry VIII. These have been brought back to life by

Rehearsing in St Mary Undercroft

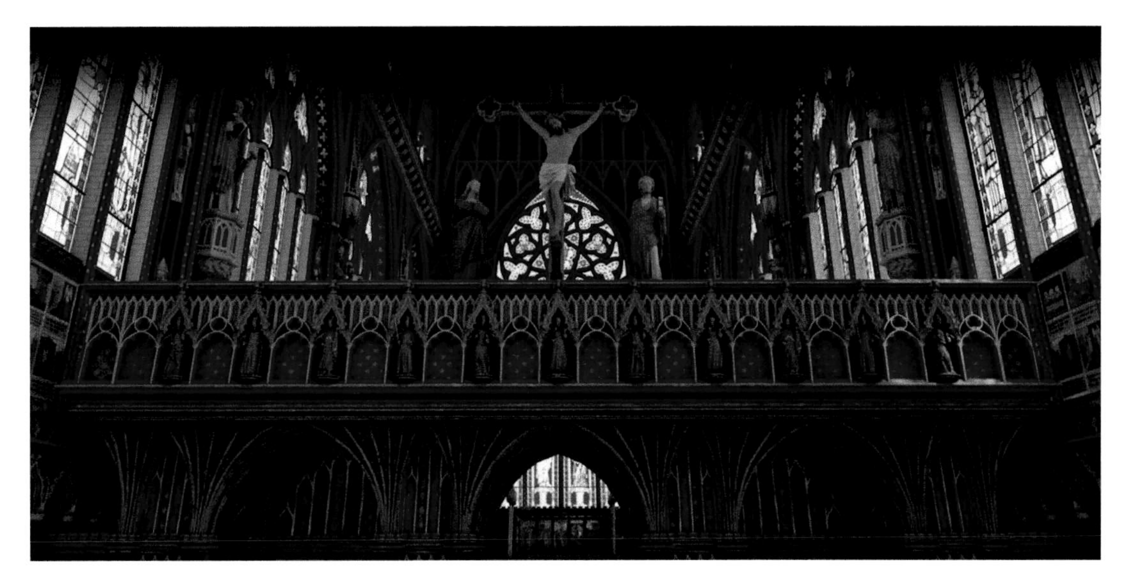

The upper storey of St Stephen's Chapel, a virtual reconstruction by the University of York

musicologists from the surviving service books of the college, and in 2015 were performed in St Stephen's Hall and St Mary Undercroft by the choir of Gonville and Caius College, Cambridge, conducted by Geoffrey Webber.

But St Stephen's College was dissolved in 1547. Edward VI gave St Stephen's Chapel – the upper level, where St Stephen's Hall now is – to the House of Commons as their chamber. From 1547 to 1750 the two bays at the east end of the undercroft were a 'great cellar', for general storage. Meanwhile the three western bays were fitted up to house the Burgess Court of the City of Westminster, there from 1583 to 1766.

Overseen by the vestry of St Margaret's Westminster, its functions were, according to a contemporary, 'to hear, examine, determine and punish... matters of incontinency, common scolds and common annoyances [in Westminster], and likewise to commit such persons as shall offend against the peace.' The Burgess Court perhaps gained from its proximity to the House of Commons in terms of influence, but his also caused problems. In 1650 the Commons attempted to take over its courtroom in the undercroft as a record store, a threat which the burgesses fended off with some difficulty. (This seems to rule out the oft-quoted though pleasing legend that the undercroft was used by Oliver Cromwell during the Civil War to stable his horse. Another reason to rule it out would be the sheer difficulty of getting horses in through the narrow doorways.) Worse still for the burgesses, the infamous Commons double-level lavatory, known as the bogghouse, was situated right next to the courthouse.

In c.1750 the two bays at the east end were converted from a storage cellar into the 'Grotto Room', styled no doubt as a quirky Gothic Revival reception room and attached to the house of the Auditor of the Exchequer. Royal confidante and artist Mary Granville,

Westminster in 1647 by Wenceslaus Hollar. St Stephen's Chapel, named 'Parliament House' at this time the Commons Chamber

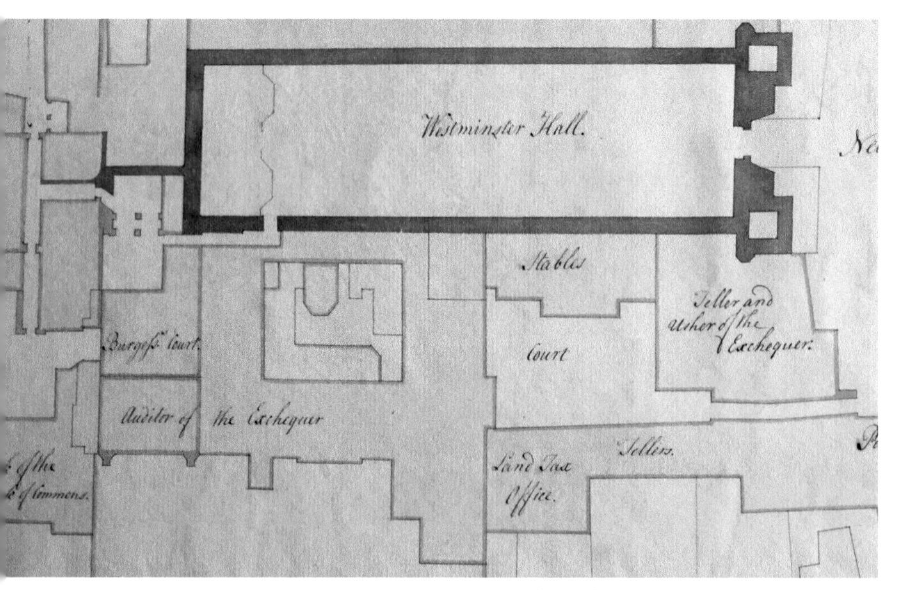

Plan of Westminster Hall, c.1760

Mrs Delany, attended a lavish party at the house, held by the incumbent Auditor, politician Henry Fiennes Clinton, Earl of Lincoln in 1756. She praised the 'crimson damask and very fine furnishings' with which his grand mansion was adorned. The fine old gothic room in the undercroft had, she thought, once been part of a monastery, but instead of monks wearing habits there were now female partygoers, 'wearing enormous hoops, gold and silver braid, exposed heads and shoulders, and numberless adornments for the head!'

The Commons Speakers and clerks, long confined to the immediate vicinity of the chamber, were in considerable need of additional space. Reforms to the Exchequer, which included the ejection of the Auditor of the Receipt from his house, enabled the Speaker to take it over in 1794. He decided to live on site, thus starting a practice which still survives. With the house came the Grotto Room section of the undercroft.

Speaker Henry Addington began to refurbish the house to reflect the prestige of his office, establishing grand state rooms in his north range. He soon began to use the Grotto Room for grand official banquets: his guest list for 1800, for example, included William Pitt the Younger, Charles James Fox and Richard Brinsley Sheridan. The antiquary John Carter, who a decade earlier had painstakingly recorded the roof bosses of the undercroft deeply lamented this use:

Surloins of beef and drinking glasses
Are here the only sight that passes,
Where erst in solemn pomp took post
The silver chalice, wafer'd host.

In 1802 Speaker Charles Abbott began a further programme of refurbishment of his house which transformed it into a spectacular Gothic revival palace by the Thames. All this was masterminded by celebrity architect James Wyatt, at vast expense. A key element was the extension of the Grotto Room by one bay and its adornment with chandeliers, crimson hangings and mahogany and black lacquer furniture.

But what of the undercroft's western bays, vacated by the Burgess Court? The contrasting uses of the two ends could not be greater. On the instructions of a Select Committee in quest of the holy grail of effective heating and ventilation for the Chamber, in 1791 a huge 'empyreal' [i.e. sublime] stove, 14 feet high, was installed. From it ran clay pipes, piercing the vaults and debouching hot air through the floor of the House above. So ineffective was this stove that in 1819 a huge new steam boiler replaced it, but was so dangerous that it was ripped out again within a few weeks. A less hazardous but still inefficient set up replaced it, which famously included the ventilator set above the Commons ceiling. This space became a very uncomfortable viewing gallery for ladies, barred from the chamber itself, but who could peer down on the proceedings below.

Returning to the undercroft, by 1822 the two bays became a wine cellar. The fire of 1834 badly damaged St Stephen's Chapel: its upper storey was demolished in 1838. The undercroft, though damaged was structurally intact and at first was used as a store, with the east end being used as Committee Rooms until 1845, when it was cleared out and Charles Barry

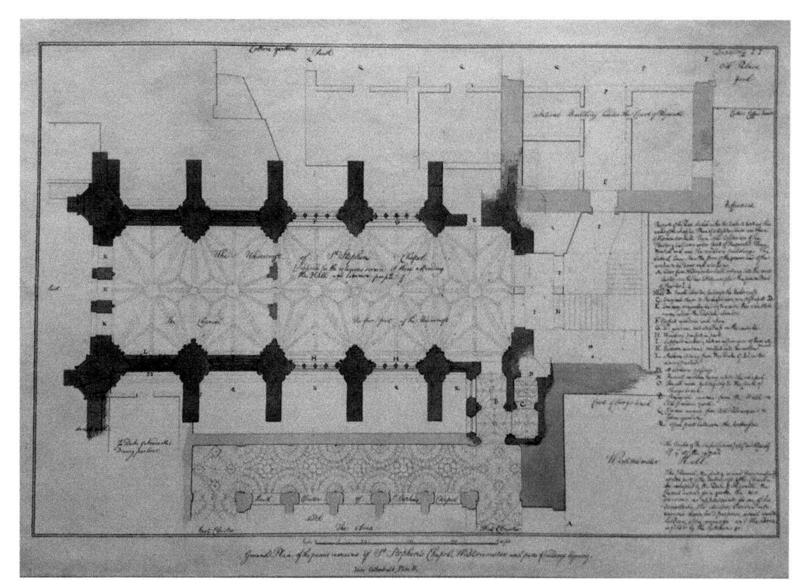

Plan of the undercroft, 1792

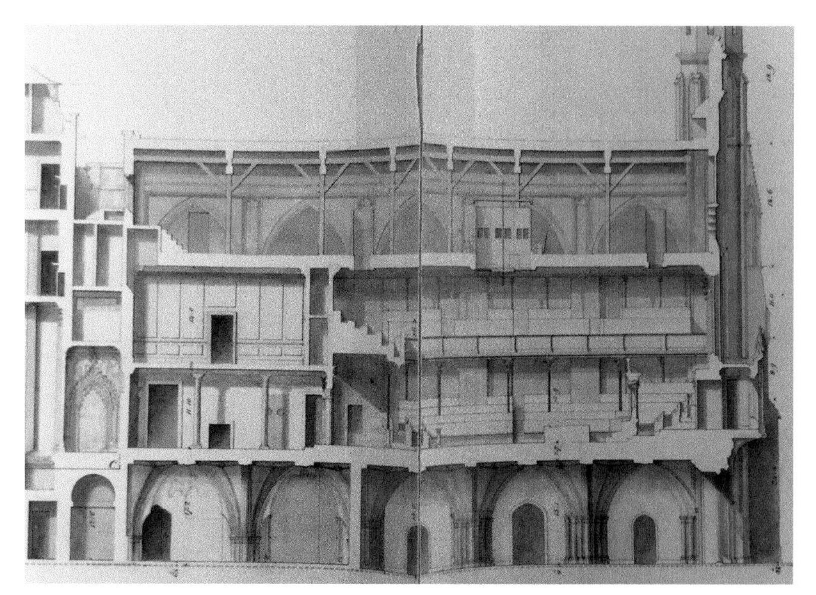

Section through the Chapel, 1884, showing undercroft at lower level

The House in session c.1822 showing the ventilator aperture

Watercolour (anon) 1834-5, painted soon after the fire which wrecked the upper chapel

began to repair it. From 1845 to 1850 Barry strengthened the foundations of the undercroft and built his brand-new St Stephen's Hall above. But it was not until 1858-60 that he was able to turn his attention to making good the stonework and repairing the vaults.

How much of the original fabric did Barry leave? Art historians agree that the doorway which today leads to the baptistery is fourteenth century. Opinion is far more divided on the bosses. Some think that the originals were retained and restored, others that they were discarded and re-carved. If the latter is the case, then the replacements were of exceptionally fine workmanship

We don't know what proportion of the ribs and vaulting is medieval and what is Victorian. The chapel's decoration is however all mid-Victorian. After Charles Barry's death in 1860 his son Edward Barry took over the project, embellishing the undercroft in a glittering Neo-Byzantine style. Largely completed by 1864, and signed off in 1869, this was done in a low-key way because of the predominance of low church sentiments in the House of Commons. The chapel's 'bedizening in gold' was much criticised by contemporaries, and its artistic merits have heavily polarised opinion ever since.

The Chapel of St Mary Undercroft now resumed its original function: a place of worship. Today it is used also for christenings, weddings and memorial services for Members, their families and Officers of Parliament. Regular services also take place there of different denominations, Anglican, Roman Catholic and non-conformist. Lady Thatcher's body lay there overnight before being taken to

A sketch of the ventilator

An engraving (1859) shows masons in action restoring stonework

Illustration c.1838 shows the undercroft used as storage, presumably for the Upper Chapel

Public tour of the chapel

Nicholas O'Neill conducting a Choir rehearsal in St Mary Undercroft

St Paul's Cathedral for her funeral. From the late 1890s MPs were allowed to take in visitors. In addition, public tours were permitted in the parliamentary recesses, the inappropriate behaviour of some visitors – who were keeping their hats on – occasioning hostile comment from members. Suffragette Emily Wilding Davidson entered the crypt with one of these groups, as a protest peeling off and famously secreting herself in an uncomfortable workman's cupboard at the west end of the undercroft for the night of the census – 2 April 1911 – in order to claim the right to vote. After this, public tours were stopped.

The chapel survived war damage in 1940 and major subsidence in the 1990s. A substantial repair project to its fabric and decoration is being planned, to safeguard the future of this extraordinary survivor of the old Palace of Westminster – and the home of the Parliament Choir.

The Organ

Vivian Widgery

I had been working in Hansard, the House of Commons, for 17 years, when I married in the late summer of 1996. We were lucky enough to be able to have our marriage blessed in the Chapel of St Mary Undercroft, and arrived there, fresh from the actual marriage ceremony in the rather less grand surroundings of the Chelsea register office, for a ceremony conducted by the Speaker's Chaplain, attended by our very small number of guests, some 18 in total.

We were somewhat surprised to find, as we walked in to the sound of the organist playing *The Arrival of the Queen of Sheba*, that in addition to those we expected, sitting right up by the altar, there were a further ten guests seated at the back of the Chapel. We had completely forgotten something that we had been told by the Chaplain's secretary: that the organ then used in the Chapel was less than satisfactory, and that a committee had been set up to investigate a new organ, more in keeping with the Chapel. She had asked whether we would mind if one or two of the committee members attended the blessing, and we said of course not. In the end, the entire committee turned up, hence the additional and unexpected guests.

The happy outcome (well, two, if you include the wedding!) was that a new organ was indeed commissioned, and it is that organ that now accompanies the Choir every week when we rehearse. What is more, the organist playing *The Arrival of the Queen of Sheba* (and making a very good job of it despite the inadequacies of the old organ) was none other than our own Simon Over! I always say that the organ should be named after us, but no one has taken me up on that.

Tom Mohan

The organ in the Chapel of St Mary Undercroft is one of the most striking recent works of art in the Palace of Westminster. It was dedicated in 1999, but fits so harmoniously into its surroundings that many visitors assume it is much older. Only the relative brightness of the paintwork and gilding hint at the organ's recent origins.

At the time of the restoration of the Chapel between 1860 and 1870, no organ was provided, and it was only in 1970 that a small organ was installed, primarily for use at weddings and baptisms. However, this proved to be musically ineffective and mechanically unreliable and in 1995 the Parliamentary Works Directorate decided to commission a new organ which would be worthy of the exceptional surroundings. An experienced organ consultant, John Norman, produced a brief for discussion in various committees of both Houses, and this launched a highly successful collaborative project.

The starting point for the brief was a drawing by A W Pugin of a small organ in an elaborate carved and painted Gothic case. Pugin was no organist, however, and his design as it stood was not entirely practical. It showed only one short keyboard, no pedalboard, and a rather unrealistic display of very narrow pipes. The organ builders invited to tender were therefore asked to produce workable proposals for an organ in the spirit of Pugin's design.

Pugin chapel organ

The location of the organ gave rise to disagreement between the Works of Art Committees which was only resolved after an unusual joint meeting on site, using a full-size mock-up to assess various locations. To reach a compromise, it was agreed that the organ should be provided with wheels, so that it could be moved if necessary. In practice, however, the location of the organ is entirely satisfactory from a visual and musical point of view, and over the last 20 years no-one has seriously suggested that it should be moved.

Following the tender exercise, the contract was awarded to William Drake Ltd, of Buckfastleigh, Devon. Founded by William (Bill) Drake in 1974, the firm quickly established a reputation both for exemplary craftsmanship and for expert knowledge of historic British organ building. Following Bill's untimely death in 2014, the firm has continued under the direction of his colleagues, and still produces new organs, and restores historic organs, to the highest standards.

The organ as built is a masterpiece of ingenuity and compression, fitting 696 pipes, a complex mechanism, an electric blower and wind reservoirs into a case with a footprint of only 1.83m by 1.14m. The voicing is modelled on surviving organs from the mid-nineteenth century. It is loud enough to lead a full congregation, and can perform a wide repertoire of music from many periods. It works particularly well as an accompanying instrument, blending well with voices and instruments, thanks to the natural, unforced speech of the pipes.

Organs are, however, seen much more than they are heard, and the appearance and decoration of the organ were an integral part of the project. John Bucknall, the architect responsible for the decorative scheme, drew together a team of artists and craftsmen, including Fleur Kelly, who painted the elegant, Van Eyck-inspired angels on the case doors, and Michael Painter, who carved the exquisite pipe shades and the angels which crown the organ. The rich decoration of the casework, including the gilding, was carried out using traditional methods by craftsmen from the firm of Howell and Bellion, who carefully matched the colour palette to the existing decorative scheme in the Chapel. The sturdy exterior metalwork of the case doors was made by Robert Hobbs.

The organ has been much admired since its installation, for both its visual and musical qualities, and it proves its musical worth in about 60 services a year. Groups of visiting organists from the United Kingdom and abroad also come on a regular basis. In addition, the organ displays its versatility every Monday evening during parliamentary terms, when it accompanies the Parliament Choir in a repertoire which ranges very widely indeed.

Graham Evans

One memory that I have is regarding the Undercroft where we have our rehearsals. A very special place, I am sure that you agree. When I was a Member of Parliament, I attended the funeral service for Margaret Thatcher which took place at St Paul's. However, the night before her coffin was brought to the Undercroft so that Members and Officers of the House to pay their respects. When I paid my respects to Mrs Thatcher, I hung back and observed the people who were also paying their respects. They included MPs of all parties, tearoom ladies, security staff and I particularly remember four police officers saluting the coffin, a very moving experience.

The Choir conductor stands on the exact spot where the coffin was positioned. So, when I look at him during the rehearsals, I always remember those four policemen and those that have gone before and say to myself how lucky are we to be in this special place.

Nicholas O'Neill and Jo Ramadan, an occasional deputy organist, in conversation at the organ

'It's a great change to be whipped by the conductor'

Peers, MPs and Westminster staff can find harmony once a week — at the Parliament Choir, reports
Emma Pomfret

Certain members of the Parliament Choir are limbering up more than others for their annual carol concert. "Ten Lords a-leaping ..." muses their music director Simon Over, "we're deciding what our Lords will do."

The Parliament Choir is a 120-strong mix of peers, MPs and staff from the Palace of Westminster; around a third of its members are politicians (the coalition slightly outnumbers Labour), while Parliament staff or pass-holders — the cooks, researchers, secretaries, doorkeepers and so on who keep the Houses running — make up the bulk. They've been singing on the quiet for ten years but with bigger concert venues booked for 2012, the Parliament Choir is out to be noticed.

On a Tuesday evening they are practising hard in the Chapel of St Mary Undercroft, beneath Westminster Hall. Upstairs, in the corridors of power, committees debate the new Welfare Reform Bill, Theresa May is preparing for a border-controls grilling and news breaks that Silvio

Parliament Choir in Westminster Hall, *right*. *Above*, Sarah Teather

Berlusconi will resign. But while Europe burns, the choir is focused on carols for its Christmas concert.

"Choir is my sanity," says Sarah Teather, the Minister for Children and Families. Ministerial responsibilities have elbowed regular choir practice out of Teather's diary, but she will sing a solo (*In the Bleak Midwinter*) at the carol concert. "For a while, Parliament Choir was the only way to include music in my life and I needed to carve out a space which wasn't politics," explains Teather, who before her Westminster life sang with the London Symphony Chorus. She still takes singing lessons. "You have to have some hinterland or you'd go a bit nuts."

The Parliament Choir was founded to accommodate MPs and peers for whom parliamentary life made a "normal" choir impossible. Parliament sits until

TIMES PHOTOGRAPHER, DAVID BEBBER

on some days and choristers have to dive out of rehearsals to For many, the weekly rehearsal is ractive role reversal. "We're used ng bossed around by the party ," says Lord German, the choir's man, "but it's a great change to put our swords against each other be 'whipped' by the conductor." er takes no-nonsense control of hearsal. "Words, words, words!" ps. "Ten-nine-eight ... it doesn't o sound like a football team," he s, berating their oikish *Twelve of Christmas* countdown.

hat they love is they don't have to esponsibility," says Over. "For they can sit back and do as they're rather than having to think on feet, being in fear of attack."

tical ballyhoo is left at the ch box; apart from some mild -Commons joshing, nobody talks "We're much more likely to gossip who's going out with whom and you did at the weekend," says er. Before you rush to google ament Choir" and "expenses", pers pay an annual subscription £60 to £120 depending on salary)

Listen to the Parliament Choir perform at **thetimes.co.uk/classical**

and, thanks to some hefty sponsorship from BT (to the tune of £60,000 per year), it uses no taxpayers' money. Nobody auditions and the standard ranges from trained ex-choristers to enthusiasts who "like a sing". For those who can't read music, O'Neill helps to fill the gap with one-to-one lessons; he's coaching several choristers through their Grade 1 singing exams.

Continuity is another challenge. Choir members can go Awol for months while a demanding piece of legislation is passed. Rehearsals are also disrupted by the division bell: there can be as many as three votes in a single rehearsal. Come election time there is some turnover of members — and a lot of distraction. In 2010 Lord Filkin, the choir's founder chairman, resumed his duties for a year. "Members of the House of Lords are not afraid of an election," explains Alun Michael, MP, "and it doesn't disrupt their lives at all."

As politicians rise up the ministerial ranks they tend to disappear from the choir. "I sang all through Opposition," says Caroline Spelman, Secretary of State for Environment, Food and Rural Affairs. "Now I miss it but I haven't given up entirely." As a choir regular Spelman sang with her secretary and researcher. "We were a singing office. It's very good for team bonding."

The choir also reveals another, perhaps more endearing, side to its members. Tim Lamming, head of catering in the Lords, often helps his colleagues through tricky passages of music. "Rather than the peers being the authority on everything, they're asking you for guidance," he notes.

This egalitarianism is at the heart of the choir, which bypasses Parliament's hierarchy. "Outside the choir, people feel obliged to call me M'lady," explains Baroness Corston. "But the moment I walk into rehearsal they say, 'Hi Jean'."

Not so David Leakey, the Gentleman

> **"Rather than the peers being the authority, they ask for guidance**

Usher of the Black Rod, a senior officer of the House of Lords, who sings the entire rehearsal in full regalia: white bow tie, black knickerbockers and patent-diamante slippers. "I'm known by everybody from top to bottom of the place as Black Rod," he says forlornly.

Performing in Westminster Hall, the site of 900 years of parliamentary history, cannot fail to inspire. (A little too much at times; Spelman remembers a rehearsal of Parry's anthem *I Was Glad* when the combined vibrations of choir and organ sent a beam tumbling.) Singers also talk about a sense of giving something back to Parliament. The choir and its partner orchestra, the Southbank Sinfonia, perform various in-house duties; they sang for the Pope's visit last year and will perform for the Cultural Olympiad's Arts in Parliament programme next year. "We are a user-friendly face of Parliament," says Baroness McIntosh of Hudnall. "Constituents are interested."

The one thing that the Parliament Choir lacks is competition. Last year it visited Prague to sing with the Czech Parliament Choir — founded after a Czech contact heard about the singing MPs and peers. Over hopes to spark interest from the French Parliament, Germany's Bundestag and the European Union. A Euro-Parliament song contest may yet happen.

What it sings is overwhelmingly high-end, meaty classics (last week it was getting stuck into Mendelssohn's *Hymn of Praise*). There have been diversions into lighter fare, some Gilbert and Sullivan (predictably the Peers' Chorus from *Iolanthe*) and a concert of show-tunes. As far as anyone can recall, Ken "Jazz" Clarke hasn't boo-boo-be-doo-ed with the basses, but Over has plans: "We have thought about doing some jazz and seeing if he would get involved."

Alas, some great characters are missing. You won't see Eric Pickles busting a lung. The Shadow Chancellor Ed Balls, a chorister at university, doesn't have time to sing but is a big choir supporter. Lord Prescott is unlikely to be giving it his pianissimo.

Not that Prezza hasn't been asked. In a choir spin-off, Spelman and Teather performed Delibes' *Flower Duet* from *Lakmé* for a Macmillan Cancer Support concert. At the time they were shadowing John Prescott and asked him to make up a trio. "The answer was no," remembers Teather. "He said, 'I think I get the p*** taken out of me enough'."

***A Westminster Christmas*, presented by John Suchet, is at Central Hall, Westminster, SW1, on Dec 7 (tickets from 0844 8717605; atgtickets.com) and on Classic FM on Dec 24 at 8pm**

Choir Concerts Listed

6 December 2000
St Margaret's Church, Westminster Abbey
Handel *Messiah*
Emma Kirkby soprano
Robin Tyson alto
Timothy Robinson tenor
Neal Davies bass
La Serenissima
Simon Over conductor

21 March 2001
St Margaret's Church,
Westminster Abbey
Schubert *Mass in G*
Poulenc *Organ Concerto*
Fauré *Requiem*
Nicola Jenkin soprano
Hans Voschezang
baritone
Thomas Trotter organ
David Corkhill timpani
London Festival
Orchestra
Simon Over conductor

1 July 2001
Speaker's State
Apartments
BT private event
A programme of solos, duets and ensemble pieces performed by 22 members of the Parliament Choir, interspersed with short interviews with prominent figures in the Choir by James Naughtie.

8 December 2001
Central Hall, Westminster
Bach *Christmas Oratorio*
Lorna Anderson soprano
Richard Wyn Roberts alto
James Gilchrist tenor
Michael George bass
La Serenissima
Simon Over conductor

20 March 2002
Central Hall, Westminster
Handel *Messiah*
Rebecca Outram soprano
Catherine Wyn-Rogers mezzo-soprano
Benjamin Hulett tenor
Neal Davies bass
City of London Sinfonia
Simon Over conductor
284 singers in total, comprising 68 members of Parliament Choir with others drawn from 39 choirs nationwide by invitation to choirs in MPs' constituencies and Peers' local areas.

18 July 2002
Banqueting House, Whitehall
'An Evening of Mozart'
(BT event)
Overture: *The Marriage of Figaro*
Voyagers' Chorus Idomeneo
'Come scoglio' *Cosí fan tutte*
'God is our refuge and strength'
'Ave verum corpus'
Interlude: *Thamos, König in Agypten*
Coronation Mass
Introduced by Natalie Wheen
Flora McIntosh soprano
Nicola Dunne mezzo-soprano
Nathan Vale tenor
Jonathan Pugsley baritone
Southbank Sinfonia
Simon Over conductor

20 October 2002 Trafalgar Day
Old Royal Naval College, Greenwich
(BT event)
Haydn *Te Deum*
Concerto for Trumpet and Orchestra
Nelson Mass
William Smith trumpet
Flora McIntosh soprano
Clare Wilkinson alto
Stephen Douse tenor
Gavin Cranmer-Moralee bass
Trinity College of Music Chamber Orchestra
Trinity College of Music Choir
Simon Over conductor

18 December 2002
Royal Albert Hall
BT Christmas concert

25 February 2003
St John's Smith Square
Vivaldi *Gloria*
Albinoni *Adagio*
Fauré *Requiem*
Lisa Milne soprano
Louise Poole mezzo-soprano
Robert Muuse baritone
Southbank Sinfonia
Simon Over conductor

7 March 2003
Savoy Hotel
(BT event for International Women's Day)

18 June 2003
Westminster Abbey (from Westminster Hall)
Coronation Jubilee concert in presence of
HRH The Prince of Wales
Bliss *The Sovereign's Fanfare*
National Anthem
Handel *Zadok the Priest*
Mozart 'Sanctus' & 'Agnus Dei' from
Coronation Mass
Parry 'I was glad'
Elgar *Coronation Ode*
Walton *Crown Imperial*
Verdi 'Brindisi' from *La Traviata*
Rossini 'Largo al factotum', from *Il Barbiere di Siviglia*
Verdi Triumphal March from *Aida*
Puccini 'Te Deum' from *Tosca*
Mascagni 'Easter Hymn' from *Cavalleria Rusticana*
Dame Felicity Lott soprano
Sir Thomas Allen baritone
Victoria Simmonds mezzo soprano
Wynne Evans tenor
James Rutherford bass-baritone
With singers from the Bach Choir, Saint Michael's Singers
Deansbank Singers, DfES Choir, Treasury Singers, Whitehall Choir
Trumpeters of the Life Guards
Southbank Sinfonia
Simon Over conductor

30 June 2003
St Mary Undercroft
Recording of Sunday Half Hour for broadcast on 17 August and 21 September.

6 November 2003
St John's Smith Square
Rossini *Petite Messe Solennelle*
Malin Christensson soprano
Catherine Wyn-Rogers mezzo-soprano (for Della Jones)
James Gilchrist tenor
Owen Gilhooley bass

Old Royal Naval College, Greenwich

Sir William Walton rehearsing the choristers of Westminster Abbey for the Coronation. William Wallace, then a treble, now a bass in the Parliament Choir, is on Walton's right.

Brahms Requiem,
St John's Smith Square,
15 March 2004

Malcolm Martineau piano
Nicholas O'Neill organ
Simon Over conductor

15 March 2004
St John's Smith Square
Brahms *Hungarian Dances 1,3,5*
Ein Deutsches Requiem
Sally Matthews soprano
William Dazeley baritone
Southbank Sinfonia
Simon Over conductor

24 September 2004
St George's Lutheran Church
Members of choir invited to sing at re-opening of the church
From Brahms' *Requiem*

13 November 2004
Coventry Cathedral
Verdi *Requiem*
Judith Howarth soprano
Wendy Dawn Thompson mezzo-soprano
Rafael Vazquez tenor
Jeremy White bass-baritone
With Saint Michael's Singers
Paul Leddington Wright conductor

30 November 2004
Westminster Cathedral
Verdi *Requiem*
Judith Howarth soprano
Wendy Dawn Thompson mezzo-soprano
Rafael Vazquez tenor
Jeremy White bass-baritone
With guest singers from
The Croydon Philharmonic Choir, Saint Michael's Singers
Bach Choir, BAFCO, Deansbank Singers, DfES Choir, Goldsmiths Choral Union, Treasury Singers, Sussex Chorus
Southbank Sinfonia
Simon Over conductor

13 December 2004
Atrium, Portcullis House
Carol concert

8 March 2005
Cadogan Hall
Haydn *Te Deum*
Trumpet Concerto
Nelson Mass
Ross Brown trumpet
Lucy Crowe soprano
Madeleine Shaw mezzo-soprano
Nathan Vale baritone
Southbank Sinfonia
Simon Over conductor

29 June 2005
BT private event
Locarno Room, Foreign & Commonwealth Office

1 October 2005
Queen's Gallery, House of Lords
Nelson bicentenary concert.
In presence of HRH The Duke of York
Wood *Fantasia on British Sea Songs* arr. O'Neill

30 November 2005
Cadogan Hall
Vivaldi *Gloria*
'Autumn' from *The Four Seasons*
Bach *Magnificat*
Katherine Manley soprano (for Amy Freston)
Louise Mott mezzo-soprano
James Oxley tenor
Roderick Williams baritone
Hye-Won Kim violin
Southbank Sinfonia
Simon Over conductor

13 December 2005
Atrium, Portcullis House
Carol concert
with keyboard accompaniment
O'Neill's 'Sweet Was the Song', first performance

23 January 2006
St Mary Undercroft
Recording of Radio 2's *Sunday Half Hour*

9 May 2006
Cadogan Hall
Handel *Coronation Anthems*
Bach *Concerto for violin and oboe*
Alice Rickards violin
Jennie-Lee Keetley oboe
Southbank Sinfonia
Simon Over conductor

Locarno Room, Foreign and Commonwealth Office

24 October 2006
Royal Hospital, Chelsea
BT event
'Land of Hope and Glory'
Songs and music with a martial theme

18 November 2006
Coventry Cathedral
Mendelssohn *Elijah*
Katherine Manley soprano
Flora McIntosh mezzo-soprano
Paul Charles Clarke tenor
Sir Thomas Allen baritone
Saint Michael's Singers
Southbank Sinfonia
Simon Over conductor

6 December 2006
Westminster Cathedral
Mendelssohn *Elijah*
Katherine Manley soprano
Flora McIntosh mezzo-soprano
Paul Charles Clarke tenor
Sir Thomas Allen baritone
Solo trio
Sarah Teather MP
Elizabeth Honer (Deputy Director of Finance and Administration, House of Commons)
Saratha Rajeswaran (Researcher to Rt Hon Theresa May MP)
Saint Michael's Singers
Southbank Sinfonia
Simon Over conductor

12 December 2006
Atrium, Portcullis House
Carol concert

16 May 2007
Cadogan Hall
Mozart *Requiem*
Piano Concerto No 12 K414
Simona Mihai soprano
Harriet Goodwin mezzo-soprano
Mark Chaundy tenor
Krzysztof Szummanski bass-baritone
Alessio Bax piano
Southbank Sinfonia
Simon Over conductor

25 June 2007
Chapel of St Peter ad Vincula, Tower of London
BT private event
'Pastime with good company'

27 November 2007
Cadogan Hall
Ryba *Czech Christmas Mass*
Handel *Dettingen Te Deum*
Martina Jelínková soprano
Lucie Spičová mezzo-soprano
Jaroslav Brezina tenor
Vojtēch Safarik bass
Henry Wickham baritone
Southbank Sinfonia
Simon Over, conductor

11 December 2007
Atrium, Portcullis House
Carol concert

7 May 2008
Cadogan Hall
Parliamentary Opera Gala
introduced by James Naughtie
Kishani Jayasinghe soprano
Haoyin Xue tenor
Southbank Sinfonia
Simon Over conductor

2 July 2008
Chapel of St Mary Undercroft
BT private event
'Hatched, Matched, and Despatched'
A programme of well-loved classics reflecting the music typically sung in the chapel for baptisms, weddings and memorial services.
Soloists from the Choir of St Margaret's Church
Southbank Sinfonia trumpets
Nicholas O'Neill organ
Simon Over conductor

26 November 2008
Westminster Cathedral
Elgar *The Apostles*
Claire Rutter soprano
Louise Collett mezzo-soprano
James Oxley tenor
Sir Thomas Allen baritone
Stephen Gadd baritone
Robert Rice baritone
With Malcolm Sargent Festival Choir
Saint Michael's Singers
Southbank Sinfonia
Simon Over conductor

16 December 2008
Atrium, Portcullis House
Carol concert

1 April 2009
Cadogan Hall
Haydn *Te Deum*
Trumpet Concerto
Harmoniemesse
Lucy Leleu trumpet
Ana-Maria Rincon soprano
Clare McCaldin mezzo-soprano
Nathan Vale tenor
Thomas Eaglen baritone
Southbank Sinfonia
Simon Over conductor

17 June 2009
Lancaster House
BT private event
'Songs from the shows'

21 November 2009
York Minster
Handel *Messiah*
Rhona McKail soprano
Yaniv D'Or alto
Nicky Spence tenor
Jeremy Huw-Williams bass
Malcolm Sargent Festival Choir
York Teachers' Choir
North Yorkshire County Youth Choir
Southbank Sinfonia
Simon Over conductor
(Concert recorded by Classic FM and broadcast on Christmas Day)

17 March 2010
Westminster Hall
Tenth Anniversary concert
Mozart *Requiem*
Nicholas O'Neill *Of All Persons and Estates*
(first performance)
Eri Nakamura soprano
Kai Rüütel mezzo-soprano
Robert Anthony Gardiner tenor
Lukas Jakobski bass
With Saint Michael's Singers
Southbank Sinfonia
Simon Over conductor

21 July 2010
Sanctuary of the Madonna del Carmine, Anghiari
Fauré *Requiem*
Cantique de Jean Racine
with Anghiari Choir
Southbank Sinfonia
Simon Over conductor

13 November 2010
Coventry Cathedral
Britten *War Requiem*
Performed on the eve of the 70th anniversary of the destruction by bombing of the city of Coventry and its cathedral.
Claire Rutter soprano
Daniel Norman tenor
Stephen Gadd bass
With Saint Michael's Singers
Girl choristers of Coventry Cathedral
Southbank Sinfonia
Paul Leddington Wright conductor

Braving the cold in Prague, 18 December 2010

17 November 2010
Westminster Cathedral
Britten *War Requiem*
Claire Rutter soprano
Daniel Norman tenor
Stephen Gadd bass
With Saint Michael's Singers
Deutscher Chor, London
Girl choristers of Coventry Cathedral
Southbank Sinfonia
Simon Over conductor

18 December 2010
St Vitus Cathedral, Prague
Ryba *Czech Christmas Mass*

6 April 2011
Cadogan Hall
Mozart *Coronation Mass*
Ch'io mi scordi di te
Vivaldi *Magnificat*
Bach *Violin Concerto*
Dame Emma Kirkby soprano
Sigridur Osk mezzo-soprano
David Webb tenor
Laurence Meikle baritone
Charlotte Maclet violin
Southbank Sinfonia
Simon Over conductor

23 July 2011
Piazza del Popolo, Anghiari
Mozart *Coronation Mass*
Members of the Parliament Choir joined the Anghiari Choir

26 October 2011
Gray's Inn
BT private event
'From shore to shore'
Music from around the UK
Cecilia Smiga soprano
Jamie MacDougall tenor
With Gray's Inn Chapel Choir
Southbank Sinfonia
Simon Over conductor

7 December 2011
Central Hall, Westminster
'A Westminster Christmas'
Included 'Silent Night' arr. O'Neill
Choristers of St Margaret's Westminster
London Chamber Brass
Gerard Brooks organ
Southbank Sinfonia
Simon Over conductor
Introduced by John Suchet
(Recorded by Classic FM and broadcast on Christmas Day)

18 April 2012
Cadogan Hall
Nicholas O'Neill *Of All Persons and Estates*
Bruch *Violin Concerto*
Mendelssohn *Lobgesang*
Eugene Lee violin
In-Kyung Cha soprano
Catrin Aur soprano
Sung Eun Seo soprano
Rhys Meirion tenor
With Choir of the National Assembly of Korea
Southbank Sinfonia
Orchestre des Lauréats du Conservatoire de Paris
Simon Over conductor

2 July 2012
Westminster Hall
Commonwealth Carnival of Music
with Choirs from Canada, South Africa and Australia
Dance troupe from India
Commonwealth Youth Orchestra
Ngāti Rānana Maori Choir
Watoto Children's Choir from Uganda
Hosted by Floella Benjamin, Huw Edwards
The Parliament Choir sang a new arrangement by Nicholas O'Neill of 'Ar Hyd y Nos'

Westminster Hall,
July 2012

19 July 2012
Sanctuary of the Madonna del Carmine, Anghiari
Vivaldi *Magnificat*
Gloria
Southbank Sinfonia
Simon Over conductor

10 November 2012
Coventry Cathedral
Brahms *Ein Deutsches Requiem*
Academic Festival Overture
Ilona Domnich soprano
Robert Davies baritone
With Saint Michael's Singers
Southbank Sinfonia
Paul Leddington Wright Conductor

14 November 2012
Westminster Cathedral
Brahms *Ein Deutsches Requiem*
Ilona Domnich soprano
Robert Davies baritone
With Saint Michael's Singers
Southbank Sinfonia
Simon Over conductor

5 December 2012
St John's Smith Square
'A Westminster Christmas'
With London Chamber Brass
percussion and organ
Nicholas O'Neill arrangements of 'awhile awandering' and 'We three kings'

15 May 2013
Queen Elizabeth Hall, Southbank Centre
'Party Favourites'
Choruses, arias and songs from opera and musical theatre; from Tchaikovsky, Puccini and Verdi to Berlin, Loewe and Loesser
Jamie MacDougall tenor
Janis Kelly soprano
Southbank Sinfonia
Simon Over conductor

25 July 2013
Sanctuary of the Madonna del Carmine, Anghiari
Handel *Messiah*
Southbank Sinfonia
Simon Over conductor
24 members of Choir with Anghiari singers

20 November 2013
Cadogan Hall
Haydn *Harmoniemesse*
Poulenc *Gloria*
Mary Bevan soprano
Felicity Turner mezzo-soprano
Bene't Coldstream tenor
Nigel Cliffe bass
Southbank Sinfonia
Simon Over conductor

4 December 2013
St John's Smith Square
'A Westminster Christmas'
With London Chamber Brass
percussion and organ

9 April 2014
Cadogan Hall
Haydn *The Creation*
Katherine Manley soprano
Joseph Timmons tenor
James Gower bass
Southbank Sinfonia
Simon Over conductor

9 July 2014
Westminster Hall
Concert to commemorate the centenary of outbreak of WW1 and tercentenary of

Hanoverian accession
Mendelssohn *Lobgesang*
Handel *Zadok the Priest*
O'Neill *Of All Persons and Estates*
Ilona Domnich soprano
Catherine May soprano
Miloš Bulajić tenor
With the Bundestag Choir
Southbank Sinfonia
Simon Over conductor
(With the support of Bayer, BMW, BT, Simon Blagden MBE, and Commonwealth Carnival of Music)

25 July 2014
Sanctuary of the Madonna del Carmine, Anghiari
Mendelssohn *Hymn of Praise* (*Lobgesang*)
World premiere of Latin translation of German text by Nicholas O'Neill
Members of the Parliament Choir are incorporated into the Anghiari Festival Chorus

November 2014
Coventry Cathedral
Verdi *Requiem*
Claire Rutter soprano
Heather Shipp mezzo-soprano
Alberto Sousa tenor

A view from the basses: centenary concert with the Bundestag, Westminster Hall July 2014

Stephen Gadd baritone
Southbank Sinfonia
Paul Leddington Wright conductor

26 November 2014
Westminster Cathedral
Verdi *Requiem*
Claire Rutter soprano
Heather Shipp mezzo-soprano
Alberto Sousa tenor
Stephen Gadd baritone
With Anghiari Festival Choir (almost 50 Italian singers joined the Parliament Choir)
Bar Choral Society
Malcolm Sargent Festival Choir
Saint Michael's Singers
Southbank Sinfonia
Simon Over conductor

3 December 2014
St John's Smith Square
'A Westminster Christmas'
With solo quartet from the Chapels Royal, HM Tower of London
London Chamber Brass, organ and percussion
O'Neill's special arrangement of 'It came upon a midnight clear' and, to represent the Christmas Truce of 1914 the Tower of London Choir from the gallery interrupted after the line 'O hush the war ye men of strife' and sang 'Silent Night'
The German Ambassador did one of the readings

3 January 2015
Teatro Flavio Vespasiano, Rieti, Lazio, Italy
Handel *Messiah*
20 members of the Parliament Choir
Anghiari Choir
Simon Over conductor

18 March 2015
St John's Smith Square
'Renaissance Rebirth'
Vivaldi *Magnificat*
Monteverdi *Beatus vir*
Vivaldi *Stabat Mater*
Purcell *Come ye sons of art*
O'Neill *O God of earth and altar* (first perfomance)
Kiandra Howarth soprano
James Laing alto
Tom Verney alto
George Humphreys baritone
Southbank Sinfonia
Simon Over conductor

24 July 2015
Piazza Baldaccio, Anghiari
Verdi *Requiem*
Kiandra Howarth soprano
Justina Gringyte mezzo-soprano
Samuel Sakker tenor
Jihoon Kim bass
Southbank Sinfonia
Anghiari Festival Chorus
Simon Over conductor
30 members of the Parliament Choir, 170 singers in total

25 November 2015
Cadogan Hall
'Long to reign over us'
In celebration of HM the Queen becoming Britain's longest-serving monarch, a programme of music written for and

performed at coronations over the centuries, including Handel's *Zadok the Priest*, Parry's 'I was Glad' and Walton's *Crown Imperial*
Te Deum Laudamus a new setting by Nicholas O'Neill
Southbank Sinfonia
Simon Over conductor

9 December 2015
St John's Smith Square
'A Westminster Christmas'
Crispian Steele-Perkins trumpet
Percussion and organ
Nicholas O'Neill's 'Westminster Wassail'

27 April 2016
Cadogan Hall
Poulenc *Gloria*
Nicholas O'Neill *Tu es Petrus* (premiere)
Vaughan Williams *Five Variants of Dives & Lazarus*
Howells *Behold, O God our Defender*
Gounod *St Cecilia Mass*
Ilona Domnich soprano
David Webb tenor
James McOran-Campbell baritone
Southbank Sinfonia
Simon Over conductor

3 May 2016
Cathedral of Notre-Dame de Paris
Poulenc *Gloria*
O'Neill *Tu es Petrus*
Howells *Behold, O God our Defender*
Vaughan Williams *Five Variants of Dives & Lazarus*
Gounod *St Cecilia Mass*
Ilona Domnich soprano
David Webb tenor
James McOran-Campbell baritone
Southbank Sinfonia
Simon Over conductor

Performance in progress

28 July 2016
Sansepolcro Cathedral
Poulenc *Gloria*
Gounod *St Cecilia Mass*
O'Neill *Tu es Petrus*
Anghiari Festival Chorus
Southbank Sinfonia
Simon Over conductor
30 singers from the Parliament Choir, 7 from the Bundestag Choir

8 November 2016
Cadogan Hall
'A concert for all seasons'
Vivaldi *The Four Seasons*
Vivaldi *Gloria*
Durante *Magnificat*
O'Neill *The Human Seasons* setting of a poem by John Keats (premiere)
Rachel Ambrose Evans soprano
Robin Tyson alto
Eugene Lee violin

Waiting in the wings at Notre-Dame, May 2016

Southbank Sinfonia
Simon Over conductor

7 December 2016
St John's Smith Square
'A Westminster Christmas'
Includes first performance of 'This Light of Reason' by Nicholas O'Neill, commissioned by a Choir member to mark the death of Jo Cox MP
Royal Air Force Salon Orchestra
Catherine Ring Percussion
Nicholas O'Neill Organ
Simon Over conductor

12 December 2016
Paul-Löbe-Haus, Bundestag, Berlin
Advent concert
With the Bundestag Choir
Zarko Bulajić and Simon Over conductors

17 May 2017
Royal Festival Hall
Mason Bates *Mothership*
Gershwin *Rhapsody in Blue*
Walton *Belshazzar's Feast*
Benjamin Grosvenor piano
Benedict Nelson baritone
Saint Michael's Singers and singers from Bar Choral Society
The Bach Choir,
London Concert Choir
St Albans Bach Choir
Southbank Sinfonia
Simon Over conductor
(supported by the Walton Foundation)

27 July 2017
Sansepolcro Cathedral
Mozart *Laudate Dominum*
Mozart *Requiem*
Soraya Mafi soprano
Elisabetta Pallucchi mezzo-soprano
Gwilym Bowen tenor
Lawrence White baritone
Anghiari Festival Choir
Southbank Sinfonia
Simon Over conductor

22 November 2017
Cadogan Hall
Orff *Carmina Burana*
O Duo *Bongo Fury*
Philip Glass *Mad Rush*
Monti *Czardas*
Chopin *Minute Waltz*
Frideswides Voices (Will Dawes conductor)
Britten Three songs from *Friday Afternoons*
Cecilia Osmond soprano
Anthony Gregory tenor
Dawid Kimberg baritone
James Longford piano
Nicholas O'Neill piano
O Duo percussion
Simon Over conductor

6 December 2017
St John's Smith Square
'A Westminster Christmas'
Included first performance of 'Carol for Jane' by Nicholas O'Neill with words by Kate Kennedy

25 April 2018
St Clement Danes
'Per Ardua ad Astra' RAF 100
A programme of music associated with the services which take place in St Clement Danes, the Central Church of the RAF, and songs and marches associated with the RAF
Includes O'Neill 'High Flight' setting of a poem by John Gillespie Magee
With Choir of St Clement Danes
Nicholas O'Neill organ and piano
Simon Over conductor
(supported by Airbus)

2 June 2018
Sheldonian Theatre, Oxford
Vaughan Williams *The Lark Ascending*
Augusta Holmès *La Nuit et l'Amour*
Ravel *Le Tombeau de Couperin*
Anthony Ritchie *Gallipoli to the Somme* (Northern hemisphere premiere)
Anna Leese soprano
Jon Stainsby baritone
Annabel Drummond violin
With City Choir Dunedin
Southbank Sinfonia
Simon Over conductor

13 June 2018
Queen Elizabeth Hall, Southbank Centre
Anthony Ritchie *Gallipoli to the Somme*
Vaughan Williams *The Lark Ascending*
Jessie Montgomery *Banner*
Vaughan Williams *Fantasia on a theme by Thomas Tallis*
Anna Leese soprano
Jon Stainsby baritone
Annabel Drummond violin
Allegri Quartet
With City Choir, Dunedin
Southbank Sinfonia
Simon Over conductor

26 July 2018
Piazza Baldaccio, Anghiari
Mozart 'Great' *Mass in C minor*
Soraya Mafi soprano
Rowan Pierce mezzo-soprano
Gwilym Bowen tenor
Gareth Brynmor John baritone
Anghiari Festival Choir
Southbank Sinfonia
Simon Over conductor

31 October 2018
Westminster Hall
A concert to commemorate the centenary of the 1918 Armistice
Mozart 'Great' *Mass in C minor*
Soraya Mafi soprano
Alison Rose mezzo-soprano
Gwilym Bowen tenor
Gareth Brynmor John baritone
With the Bundestag Choir
Southbank Sinfonia
Simon Over conductor

5 December 2018
St John's Smith Square
'A Westminster Christmas'
With Slovenian choir, Gallus Aeternus
Included O'Neill 'Gabriel, that Angel bright' first performance
Imogen Hancock trumpet
percussion and organ
Simon Over conductor

3 April 2019
Guards Chapel, London
Haydn *Missa Sancti Nicolai*
Trumpet Concerto
O'Neill *A Certain Everlasting Polyphony* – text by Johnes Kepler (1571-1630)
Erika Curbelo trumpet
Madison Nonoa soprano

William Purefoy alto
Filipe Manu tenor
Lawrence White bass
Southbank Sinfonia
Simon Over conductor

24 July 2019
Garden of Piero della Francesca, Sansepolcro
Haydn *St Nicholas Mass*
Trumpet Concerto
Erika Curbelo trumpet
Italian soloists
Anghiari Festival Choir
Southbank Sinfonia
Simon Over conductor

9 November 2019
Coventry Cathedral
Elgar *The Dream of Gerontius*
Catherine Wyn-Rogers mezzo-soprano
Robert Murray tenor
Sir Thomas Allen baritone
Coventry Cathedral Chorus
Paul Leddington Wright conductor

13 November 2019
Westminster Cathedral
Elgar *The Dream of Gerontius*
Catherine Wyn-Rogers mezzo-soprano
Robert Murray tenor
Sir Thomas Allen baritone
With Coventry Cathedral Chorus
St Albans Bach Choir
Mosaic Chamber Choir
Southbank Sinfona
Simon Over conductor

4 December 2019
St John's Smith Square
'A Westminster Christmas'
Chloe Morgan soprano
Percussion and organ
Simon Over conductor
First performance of Nicholas O'Neill's setting of Hardy's poem 'The Oxen'

December 2019
Speaker's State Apartments
Members of the Choir joined the Castlegate Singers, a group of disabled singers from Essex

December 2020
St John's Smith Square
'A Westminster Christmas'
A socially-distanced concert performed without an audience, recorded by St John's Smith Square and broadcast over the internet in aid of Shelter

The Castlegate Singers with members of the Choir

Nicholas O'Neill warming up the Choir, Simon Over demanding all

Contributors

Members of the Choir past and present

Alastair Bruce, Lord Aberdare, bass is an elected hereditary Member of the House of Lords who sits as a Crossbencher. He is a passionate devotee of Berlioz's music and chairs the Berlioz Society.

Solomon Abraham, bass is a Civil Servant in the Department for Environment, Food and Rural affairs.

Alison Baverstock, alto is Professor of Publishing at Kingston University.

Rt Hon Alan Beith, Lord Beith, tenor as an MP represented Berwick-upon-Tweed for the Liberals, later Liberal Democrats, for 42 years, and was Deputy Leader of the party from 1992 to 2003. On his retirement as an MP in 2015, he was appointed to the House of Lords.

Katherine Bennett CBE, soprano was until 2021 a Senior Vice President of Airbus. She has recently been appointed CEO of HVM Catapult which helps accelerate new concepts through to commercial reality.

Robin Bridgeman, Viscount Bridgeman, bass is a Conservative elected hereditary Peer who has sat in the House of Lords since 1983. He is Treasurer of the Parliament Choir.

Alixe Buckerfield de la Roche, soprano is a Defence and Security Advisor: she has worked across defence and security strategy and policy with a number of Peers in the House of Lords for over two decades.

Sally Cantello, soprano joined the Choir in 2007. As Chief Executive of the Whitehall and Industry Group, she worked with both Houses of Parliament for eight years.

Philippa Carling, alto is one of the original members of the Choir, and worked in the House of Commons Library for many years.

Janet Cohen, Baroness Cohen, alto sits in the House of Lords as a Labour peer. She is a lawyer and, under the name Janet Neel, the author of seven works of crime fiction. She chaired the Choir from 2006 to 2008.

Rt Hon Jean Corston, Baroness Corston, soprano represented Bristol, East for the Labour Party from 1992 to 2005. On her retirement as an MP in 2015, she was appointed to the House of Lords, and, among many other activities, wrote an influential report on women in prison.

Susan Craig, alto was Director of Personnel Policy, House of Commons, and served as Treasurer to the Choir for many years.

John Dawson, tenor has worked with MPs for over 10 years.

Maggy Dean, alto is Secretary of the Choir's Friends Scheme.

Libby Dewdney-Herbert, soprano is parliamentary assistant to Jeremy Quin MP

Alex Ellis CMG, bass has been High Commissioner to India since 2021, and was HM Ambassador to Brazil between 2013 and 2017.

Graham Evans, tenor represented Weaver Vale for the Conservative Party between 2010 and 2017, and is now a senior counsel in Government Affairs.

Daniella Fetuga-Joensuu, soprano worked as Parliamentary Assistant to The Rt Revd James Langstaff, Bishop of Rochester (who also sang with the Choir), in the House of Lords. She is a volunteer chaplain in Her Majesty's Prisons.

Geoffrey Filkin, Lord Filkin CBE, bass was a Chief Executive in Local Government, before being appointed to the House of Lords in 1999, sitting on the Labour benches. He was a Minister from 2001 to 2005 and later chaired Select Committees. In 2000, he Founded the Choir with Simon Over and was the first Chair, from 2000 to 2002 and Chair again from 2010 to 2011.

Michael German, Lord German OBE, bass is a Liberal Democrat Peer, who has also served on the National Assembly for Wales. He chaired the Choir from 2011 to 2013, and has been Chair again since 2019.

Rt Hon Dame Cheryl Gillan MP, soprano (d.2021) was Conservative MP for Chesham and Amersham from 1992 until her death. She was Secretary of State for Wales from 2010 to 2012. She was also Treasurer of the Choir for a period.

Jane Gordon-Cumming, soprano is the office manager for the Rt Hon Dominic Rabb MP.

Val and Paul Goss, tenori have been members of the Choir for over a decade, always enjoying the chance to make music with friends and colleagues. For many of those years, they have also helped to strengthen the link with Anghiari.

Jean Guise, soprano joined the Choir in 2004, when she was working at the Industry and Parliament Trust.

Dr Elizabeth Hallam Smith, FSA, soprano is Research Consultant, Architecture and Heritage, Houses of Parliament, and Hon Research Professor, University of York.

Virginia Hawkins, alto became the Choir Manager in 2021.

Sue Hayman, Baroness Hayman, alto was Labour MP for Workington 2015-2019 and now sits in the House of Lords where she is Shadow Spokesperson for Environment, Food and Rural Affairs and an Opposition Whip. She chaired the Choir from 2017 to 2019.

Christine Heald, Lady Heald, alto ran the Parliamentary Office of her husband, Sir Oliver Heald MP for many years. She is one of the Choir's most stalwart and valuable volunteers and served as Choir Secretary from 2015-2017.

Patricia Hollis, Baroness Hollis of Heigham (d.2018) helped to found the Choir.

Judith, Lady Horam, soprano has been a journalist and presenter of *Top Gear*, and for many years was a Director of the Dartington Summer School Foundation.

Jane Jacomb-Hood (d. 2021) worked with various arts organisations, including the Royal Shakespeare Company, before becoming the Parliament Choir's first secretary, a post she filled for more than ten years. Living in Aldeburgh she was deeply involved with the cultural life there.

The Hon Sir Bernard Jenkin MP, bass has been Conservative MP since 1992, and now represents Harwich and North Essex. He was Shadow Secretary of State for Defence, 2001-03, and now Chairs the Liaison Committee. He is Vice Chair of the Choir.

Delyth Jewell MS, soprano worked in Parliament as a research assistant to Plaid Cwmru MPs, and since 2019 has been a Member of the Senedd Cwmru.

Judith Jolly, Baroness Jolly, alto is a Liberal Democrat peer who has sat in the House of Lords since 2011. She spoke on health matters for her party until 2020.

Christine, Lady Judd, alto has been a part of parliamentary life for many years as the wife of Lord Judd, an active Labour politician in both Houses of Parliament and a devotee of the Choir.

Jarmila Karas, soprano founded the Emmy Destinn Foundation in 1997, which supports young singers in the early stages of their careers. She first came to the Choir to guide it through the Czech pronunciation of the Ryba Mass, and stayed to sing with the Choir.

Rt Hon David Lammy MP, tenor has been Labour MP for Tottenham since 2000. He is currently Shadow Secretary of State for Justice.

Lt Gen David Leakey CMG, CVO, CBE bass, a former British military commander, was the Gentleman Usher of the Black Rod from 2010 to 2018.

Rt Hon Sir David Lidington, tenor was Conservative MP for Aylesbury from 1992 to 2019. He was Minister of State for Europe in David Cameron's Governments (2010-2016). Under Theresa May, he was successively Leader of the House, Secretary of State for Justice and Lord Chancellor, and from 2018 to 2019 Minister for the Cabinet Office and Chancellor of the Duchy of Lancaster.

Margaret Lykiardopoulos, soprano worked with the House of Lords Library.

Mary Macleod, soprano was Conservative MP for Brentford and Isleworth from 2010 to 2015. She is a Trustee of the Parliament Choir.

Rt Hon Fiona Mactaggart, alto was Labour MP for Slough from 1997 to 2017. From 2003 to 2006 she was Parliamentary Under-Secretary (Home Office).

Susan, Lady Madel, soprano has been part of Parliamentary life for many years and is married to Sir David Madel, bass, a Conservative Member of Parliament for 31 years.

Elizabeth Mann, soprano worked for Southbank Sinfonia in its early years and is very grateful to be allowed to sing with the Parliament Choir. For some years, she has edited the Choir's concert programmes. Along with Vivian Widgery, she was principally responsible for compiling and editing this book.

Sally Martin-Brown, soprano is an all-round musician: singer, teacher, examiner and conductor. She is Director of the University of London Church Choir. During the coronavirus hiatus, she helped to keep the Choir going through weekly Zoom rehearsals.

Genista McIntosh, Baroness McIntosh of Hudnall, alto has been a Member of the House of Lords since 1999. For ten years, she was Executive Director of the Royal National Theatre.

Michael Meur, tenor would never have imagined that he would go from grammar schoolboy to the Parliament

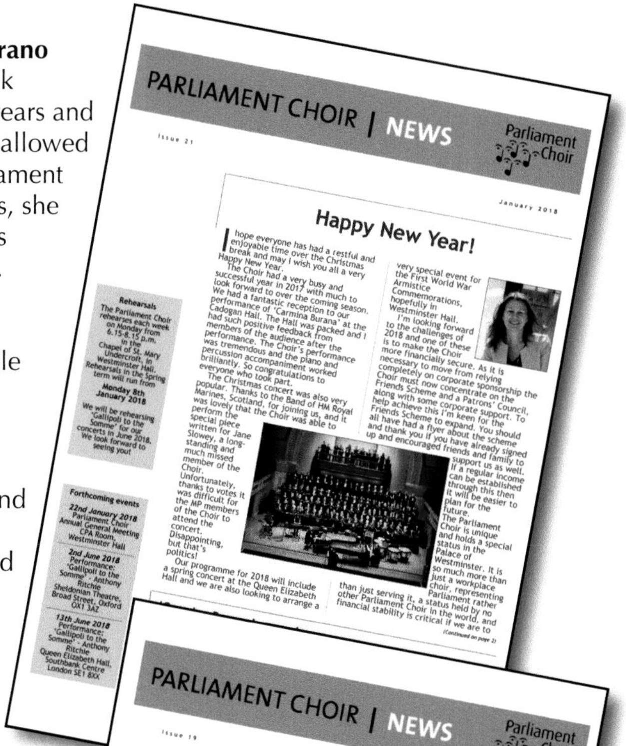

PARLIAMENT CHOIR | NEWS

Parliament Choir

Issue 21

January 2018

Happy New Year!

I hope everyone has had a restful and enjoyable time over the Christmas break and may I wish you all a very Happy New Year.

The Choir had a very busy and successful year in 2017 with much to look forward to over the coming season. We had a fantastic reception to our performance of 'Carmina Burana' at the Cadogan Hall. The Hall was packed and I had such positive feedback from members of the audience after the performance. The Choir's performance was tremendous and the piano and percussion accompaniment worked brilliantly. So congratulations to everyone who took part.

The Christmas concert was also very popular. Thanks to the Band of HM Royal Marines, Scotland, for joining us, and it was lovely that the Choir was able to perform the special piece written for Jane Slowey, a long-standing and much missed member of the Choir. Unfortunately, thanks to votes it was difficult for the MP members of the Choir to attend the concert. Disappointing, but that's politics!

Our programme for 2018 will include a spring concert at the Queen Elizabeth Hall and we are also looking to arrange a very special event for the First World War Armistice Commemorations, hopefully in Westminster Hall.

I'm looking forward to the challenges of 2018 and one of these is to make the Choir more financially secure. As it is necessary to move from relying completely on corporate sponsorship the Choir must now concentrate on the Friends Scheme and a Patrons' Council, along with some corporate support. To help achieve this I'm keen for the Friends Scheme to expand. You should all have had a flyer about the scheme and thank you if you have already signed up and encouraged friends and family to support us as well. If a regular income can be established through this then it will be easier to plan for the future.

The Parliament Choir is unique and holds a special status in the Palace of Westminster. It is so much more than just a workplace choir, representing Parliament rather than just serving it, a status held by no other Parliament Choir in the world, and financial stability is critical if we are to

(Continued on page 2)

Rehearsals
The Parliament Choir rehearses each week on Monday from 6.15-8.15 p.m. in the Chapel of St. Mary Undercroft, in Westminster Hall. Rehearsals in the Spring term will run from
Monday 8th January 2018
We will be rehearsing 'Gallipoli to the Somme' for our concerts in June 2018. We look forward to seeing you!

Forthcoming events
22nd January 2018
Parliament Choir Annual General Meeting
CPA Room, Westminster Hall

2nd June 2018
Performance: 'Gallipoli to the Somme' - Anthony Ritchie
Sheldonian Theatre, Broad Street, Oxford OX1 3AZ

13th June 2018
Performance: 'Gallipoli to the Somme' - Anthony Ritchie
Queen Elizabeth Hall, Southbank Centre, London SE1 8XX

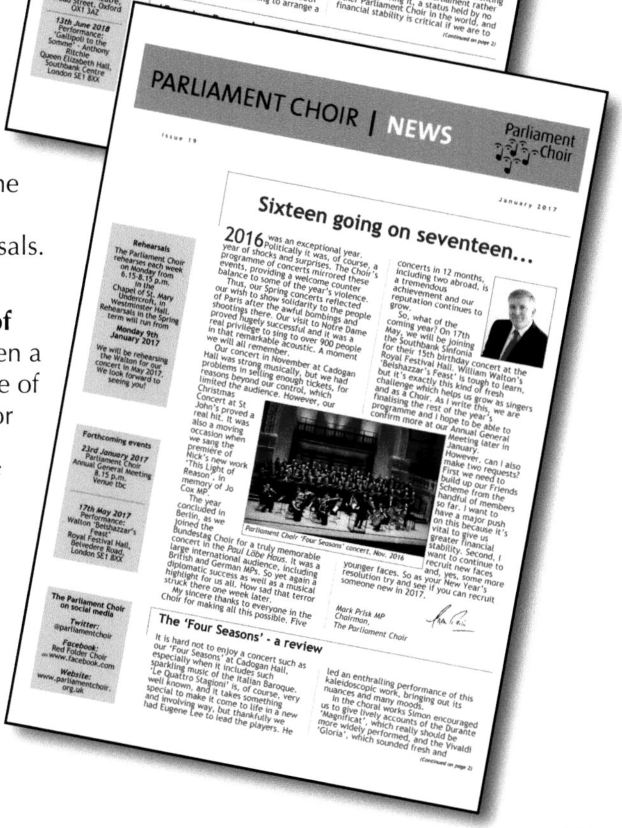

PARLIAMENT CHOIR | NEWS

Parliament Choir

Issue 19

January 2017

Sixteen going on seventeen...

2016 was an exceptional year. Politically it was, of course, a year of shocks and surprises. The Choir's programme of concerts mirrored these events, providing a welcome counter balance to some of the year's violence.

Thus, our Spring concerts reflected our wish to show solidarity to the people of Paris after the awful bombings and shootings there. Our visit to Notre Dame proved hugely successful and it was a real privilege to sing to over 900 people in that remarkable acoustic. A moment we will all remember.

Our concert in November at Cadogan Hall was strong musically, but we had problems in selling enough tickets, for reasons beyond our control, which limited the audience. However, our Christmas Concert at St John's proved a real hit. It was also a moving occasion when we sang the première of Nick's new work 'This Light of Reason', in memory of Jo Cox MP.

The year concluded in Berlin, as we joined the Bundestag Choir for a truly memorable concert in the *Paul Löbe Haus*. It was a large international audience, including British and German MPs. So yet again a diplomatic success as well as a musical highlight for us all. How sad that terror struck there one week later.

My sincere thanks to everyone in the Choir for making all this possible. Five concerts in 12 months, including two abroad, is a tremendous achievement and our reputation continues to grow.

So, what of the coming year? On 17th May, we will be joining the Southbank Sinfonia for their 15th birthday concert at the Royal Festival Hall. William Walton's 'Belshazzar's Feast' is tough to learn, but it's exactly this kind of fresh challenge which helps us grow as singers and as a Choir. As I write this, we are finalising the rest of the year's programme and I hope to be able to confirm more at our Annual General Meeting later in January.

However, can I also make two requests? First we need to build up our Friends Scheme from the handful of members so far. I want to have a major push on this because it's vital to give us greater financial stability. Second, I want to continue to recruit new faces and, yes, some more younger faces. So as your New Year's resolution try and see if you can recruit someone new in 2017.

Mark Prisk MP
Chairman,
The Parliament Choir

Parliament Choir 'Four Seasons' concert, Nov. 2016

The 'Four Seasons' - a review

It is hard not to enjoy a concert such as our 'Four Seasons' at Cadogan Hall, especially when it includes such sparkling music of the Italian Baroque. 'Le Quattro Stagioni' is, of course, very well known, and it takes something special to make it come to life in a new and involving way, but thankfully we had Eugene Lee to lead the players. He led an enthralling performance of this kaleidoscopic work, bringing out its nuances and many moods.

In the choral works Simon encouraged us to give lively accounts of the Durante 'Magnificat', which really should be more widely performed, and the Vivaldi 'Gloria', which sounded fresh and

(Continued on page 2)

Rehearsals
The Parliament Choir rehearses each week on Monday from 6.15-8.15 p.m. in the Chapel of St. Mary Undercroft, in Westminster Hall. Rehearsals in the Spring term will run from
Monday 9th January 2017
We will be rehearsing the Walton for our concert in May 2017. We look forward to seeing you!

Forthcoming events
23rd January 2017
Parliament Choir Annual General Meeting 8.15 p.m.
Venue tbc

17th May 2017
Performance: Walton 'Belshazzar's Feast'
Royal Festival Hall, Belvedere Road, London SE1 8XX

The Parliament Choir on social media
Twitter: @parliamentchoir
Facebook: Red Folder Choir on www.facebook.com
Website: www.parliamentchoir.org.uk

Choir in 40 years, and feels it has been a joy and privilege to sing some great music in many amazing settings.

Rt Hon Alun Michael, tenor was MP for Cardiff, South and Penarth from 1987 to 2012, serving as Shadow Minister and Minister in various Departments, and later as the first First Minister for Wales. He is now South Wales Police and Crime Commissioner. He chaired the Choir from 2008 to 2010.

Tessa Murdoch, soprano is Research Curator, Gilbert Collection, at the V&A Museum.

Annalise Pask, alto

Caroline Pereira, alto

Gillian Perry, alto joined the Choir in 2014 following her husband's death and has welcomed the generosity and kindness of those she did not know before and who have become the best of friends.

Mark Prisk, bass was Conservative MP for Hertford and Stortford from 2001 until 2019 and served as Minister of State for Business and Enterprise, 2010-12 and Minister of State for Housing and Local Government, 2012-13. He chaired the Choir from 2015 to 2017.

Robert Rogers, Lord Lisvane KCB DL, bass was Clerk of the House of Commons from 2011 to 2014. He has been a Member of the House of Lords since 2014.

Maggie Ronald, alto worked across Parliament for two decades and greatly values the joy of singing in the Choir.

Susan Ruckes, soprano worked in the Houses of Parliament telephone switch room from 1997 to 2018.

Jonathan Sayeed, tenor was Conservative MP for Bristol, East from 1983 to 1992 and for Mid-Bedfordshire from 1997 to 2005. He chaired the Choir from 2002 to 2004.

Jane Slowey CBE (d 2017), soprano was Chief Executive of the Foyer Federation from 2004. She viewed her membership of the Choir with great fondness. *Carol for Jane* was commissioned and performed in 2017 as the Choir's memorial to her.

Rt Hon Dame Caroline Spelman, alto was Conservative MP for Meriden from 1997to 2019. She was Secretary of State in the Department for Environment, Food and Rural Affairs, 2010-2012. She chaired the Choir from 2013 to 2015.

Michael Switsur, tenor is a Civil Servant at the Department for Work and Pensions. He has organised Choir members into concert day formations since 2014, and is a Trustee of the Choir.

Mari Takayanagi, soprano is a senior archivist in the House of Lords.

Mike Taylor, bass also sings with the St Albans Bach Choir and is the point of liaison between the two Choirs.

Sarah Teather, soprano was the Liberal Democrat MP for Brent, Central from 2003 to 2015 and served in the Coalition Government as Minister of State for Children and Families.

Lesley Titcomb CBE, alto was Chief Executive of the Pensions Regulator from 2015 to 2019. Her husband is the former MP, Mark Prisk, who also sings in the Choir.

Andrew Tuggey CBE DL, tenor a former soldier, was Chief Executive of the Commonwealth Parliamentary Association from 2004 to 2018. He is now Vice Lord-Lieutenant of Gwent and sings with the Hereford Choral Society.

Aileen Walker OBE, alto worked at the House of Commons for over 30 years. Between 2008 and 2016 she was Director of Public

Engagement. She is now an associate of Global Partners Governance. Until early 2021, she was Secretary of the Parliament Choir.

Alan Walker, tenor joined the choir in 2016 and continues to enjoy and appreciate the varied mix of opportunities to make music in convivial company.

William Wallace, Baron Wallace of Saltaire, bass is an academic, writer and Liberal Democrat politician. He was also a chorister at Westminster Abbey and sang at the Queen's Coronation.

Joan Walmsley, Baroness Walmsley, alto is a Liberal Democrat politician. She chaired the Choir from 2004 to 2006, and is married to Lord Thomas, a stalwart of the basses.

Edward Webb, bass, a photographer responsible for many pictures of the Choir in this book, is also a singer and violinist.

Denise Westbury, soprano has undertaken several roles for BT, and has been involved with the Choir since its earliest days. She works for Openreach and is a Trustee of the Choir.

Vivian Widgery, soprano worked in Hansard, House of Commons for 32 years and has continued to sing in the Choir since leaving the job. She is responsible for the Choir's social media feeds. Along with Elizabeth Mann, she was principally responsible for compiling and editing this book.

Helen Wilkins, alto is the Verger, Chapel of St Mary Undercroft and an Administrative Assistant in Black Rod's Office.

Anna Yallop, alto has served as Chief Executive of the Choir since 2014. She has worked in Parliament since 1997.

Supporters, collaborators

Sir Thomas Allen CBE, one of the world's great operatic baritones, has been a Patron of the Parliament Choir since 2000.

John Anderson was Managing Director, BT Government from 1998 to 2008. His and BT's support made possible the scope of the Choir in ambition and achievement.

Rt Hon Sir Oliver Heald, QC MP, besides being married to a key member of the Choir, is a barrister and has represented Hertfordshire. North-East for the Conservative party since 1992.

Professor Mark Hill QC specialises in Ecclesiastical Law and is an acknowledged authority on religious freedom.

Brian Hughes is a Welsh composer, commissioned by Lord Thomas of Gresford to write *The Bells of Paradise.*

Dame Emma Kirkby is a most distinguished soprano who specialises in the early music repertoire. She has been a Patron of the Choir since 2008.

Eugene Lee is a Korean-born, New Zealand-raised violinist, who took part in the Southbank Sinfonia programme in 2009, and has since continued his connection with the orchestra as Associate Leader. He has played the solo in several concerto performances of Parliament Choir concerts, and in 2018 conducted Mozart's *Gran Partita* which was played as the audience assembled for the Armistice Commemoration concert. He is Assistant Leader of the Philharmonia Orchestra.

Dame Felicity Lott is one of Britain's best-loved sopranos, particularly known for her roles in Mozart and Strauss operas, and as an interpreter of chanson, lieder and English song in the wide-ranging repertoire explored over the years by A Songmaker's Almanac, of which she is a founding member.

Jamie MacDougall, widely acknowledged as 'the voice of classical music in Scotland', through his radio programmes 'Classics Unwrapped' and 'Grace Notes', is also one of Scotland's best-known tenors. He enjoys a busy international career across genres both serious and light, and was due to sing with the Choir in its Spring concert of 2020, a reprise of the very popular 'Party Favourites' of 2013 at the Queen Elizabeth Hall.

Soraya Mafi is one of Britain's most exciting young sopranos, earning rapturous reviews for the beauty of her voice and performances in opera and concert. Of Iranian-Lancastrian heritage she has won several awards, including the Southbank Sinfonia-sponsored Peter Hulsen Prize for Orchestral Song.

James Murphy is Chief Executive of the Royal Philharmonic Society. For six years before that he was Managing Director of Southbank Sinfonia.

James Naughtie, the author, journalist and broadcaster, who presented the 'Today' programme for 21 years and for many years introduced the BBC Proms, has always been very supportive of the Parliament Choir, and has compered Choir concerts in the Speaker's State Apartments and Cadogan Hall.

Phil Noyce is Managing Editor of Classic FM.

Anthony Ritchie is a New Zealand composer and academic, who was commissioned to compose *Gallipoli to the Somme*, a piece to mark the centenary of the end of the First World War, premiered in Dunedin, New Zealand and performed twice in the UK in 2018.

John Rutter CBE is the composer of many of the most popular contemporary anthems and Christmas carols, hymns and larger choral works, and is a renowned choral conductor.

German Parliament Choir (Musikgemeinschaft des deutsches Bundestags)

Zarko Bulajić, Music Director.

Dr Kerstin Bode; Claudia Bülter; Dr Yvonne Gall; Karin Guenther, Dagmar Linnemann-Gaedtke, Dr. Ruth Moeller and **Dr Jutta Struck**, members of the Choir.

Coventry Cathedral Chorus

Paul Leddington Wright was Organist and Director of Music at Coventry Cathedral from 1984-1995, and he continues as Music Director of the cathedral's choral society, the Saint Michael's Singers, now the Coventry Cathedral Chorus.

Barrie Rogers, Professor Gary Watt members of the choir.

The Parliament Choir is a Registered Charity, charity no. 1085042. The Charity's objects ('the objects') are:

1) the study and practice of choral music in order to foster public knowledge and appreciation of such music by means of public performance
2) the promotion of the art of singing and music by means of assistance to young singers and musicians and by the provision of scholarships bursaries and prizes for singers.

Acknowledgements

Sponsors and Supporters

Running a choir is costly, and the many concerts in impressive places and the steady growth in ability and musicianship would not have been possible without the help of the following generous sponsors over the years:

Airbus
Allianz Global Investors
Bouygues
Robert Bosch
BT
The Commonwealth Carnival
Dunedin Symphony Orchestra
Fujitsu
ThyssenKrupp
UK Space
Veolia ES (UK) Ltd
Volkswagen

The Derrill Allatt Foundation
The Swire Foundation
The Walton Foundation

Simon Blagden MBE
The Gosman family
Mrs Lynn Holmes in memory of Brian Holmes
The Jenkin family in memory of Lord Jenkin of Roding
Lord Lea
Lord Lloyd of Berwick
John Magill in memory of Gill Magill
Sir Alan Moses
Gillian Perry
Anna Yallop

The Choir has been very grateful for the bequest of a piano from Caroline Robertson, a much-loved alto, who died at the beginning of 2020. The Choir would also like to acknowledge the generosity of those members who contributed towards the piano's restoration.

Photograph Acknowledgements

With grateful thanks to those who provided photographs for the following pages in this book:

Elizabeth Fenton: 29, 33, 40, 61a, 121
Simon Fernandez: 5, 24, 26, 160, 154, 163
Tony Gray: 167a
Jane Jacomb-Hood: 3, 80, 82, 108, 111, 168, 169
Ralph Larmann: 38, 98, 100c, 104b
David McBride: 30, 31, 32, 67, 84a, 100a, 100b, 102, 103, 125c, 126, 179
Barry Neil: 19, 175
Southbank Sinfonia: 86, 148
Jenny Sturt: 61b, 96
Edward Webb: 9, 12, 52, 57, 69, 70, 84b, 94, 108, 123, 124, 128, 133, 180, 182, 186
Martin Williams: 115

Other picture credits:
17 Hansard
151 Keble: Photo by DAVID ILIFF. License: CC BY-SA 3.0
152 Berthold Werner, public domain.
153 St. Stephen's Chapel Ruins, after the fire in 1834, the west end of the crypt under the chapel, watercolour by G. Moore, © Parliamentary Art Collection, WOA 5195.
155 Reconstruction form http://www.virtualststephens.org.uk
156a WOA 845 Ciuitatis Westmonasteriensis Pars, Monochrome line etching by Wenceslaus Hollar, © Parliamentary Art

Collection, WOA 845

156b extract from a plan of the Palace of Westminster of c. 1760: Soane Museum SM 37/1/24: by courtesy of the Trustees of Sir John Soane's Museum; and © British Library Board: British Library Add MS 29930, f. 101.

157a The Society of Antiquaries of London ref Red Portfolio, Palace of Westminster; and The National Archives, ref. WORK 29/27

157b The National Archives, ref. WORK 29/27

158a View of the Interior of the House of Commons during the Session, 1821-3, monochrome mezzotint by Scott after original by James Stephanoff and Robert Bowyer © Parliamentary Art Collection, WOA 3102

158b Anon, The ruins of the House of Commons following the fire of 1834, Museum of London Prints and Drawings Collection A 12137 © Museum of London

159a Sketch of a ventilator in Ladies Gallery Attic in St Stephens, 1834, Pencil drawing by Frances Rickman, © Parliamentary Art Collection, WOA 26.

159b Illustrated London News 5 Feb 1859

159c St. Stephen's Chapel Ruins, after the fire in 1834, the west end of the crypt under the chapel, watercolour by G. Moore, © Parliamentary Art Collection, WOA 5195

159d Houses of Parliament, St. Stephen's Crypt (restored), watercolour by Edward M. Barry, © Parliamentary Art Collection, WOA 1601

164 The Times

Other images were taken by members of the Choir. All reasonable attempts have been made by the publisher to contact copyright holders.
